T0154728

Footprint Handbook
Ho Chi Minh City &
South Vietnam

DAVID W LLOYD

This is
Ho Chi Minh City &
South Vietnam

The capital of the south and the economic capital of the whole country, forward-looking Ho Chi Minh City feels worlds away from Hanoi. Gleaming skyscrapers rise from the centre, while entire new districts are appearing on former wastelands across the Saigon River. Yet plenty of the old Saigon remains, with the intoxicating Chinatown district serving up incense-filled pagodas among the constant commotion of street-level commerce and the clack of Chinese chess. Ho Chi Minh City is alive with energy from early 'til late, with the city still buzzing long after Hanoi has gone to sleep. Street food stalls and packed-out pavement beer joints rub shoulders with chic cocktail bars and fine international restaurants.

Heading out of the city, two of Vietnam's best islands lie within an hour's flight. Jump on a prop plane bound for the Con Dao archipelago and stay on an isolated, former prison colony island with a dark history that stands in stark contrast with the mellow ambience of today. The wildlife-filled jungle of the interior affords fantastic trekking, while the seas offer the country's best dives.

Alternatively, make for laid-back Phu Quoc with its pristine white-sand beaches and everything from eco-resorts to five-star luxury. Back on the mainland, active travel awaits at the water sports mecca of Mui Ne, which is also famed for its Sahara-like dunes. Or for something more sedate, travel further south to the delta where wetland national parks, relaxing river cruises and floating morning markets provide a glimpse into the water-bound life of the mighty Mekong and its tributaries.

David W Lloyd

Best of
Ho Chi Minh City & South Vietnam

❶ Notre Dame Cathedral

Right in the heart of the downtown, this grand landmark is modelled on its namesake in Paris. Try and visit during early morning or during a service when huge crowds gather on motorbikes out front. Page 12.

❷ War Remnants Museum

Harrowing, but informative, this is the best way to get an understanding of the nation's recent wars from a Vietnamese perspective. Across well curated and engaging exhibitions, the atrocities of combat are relayed in hard-hitting and sometimes graphic detail. Page 16.

❸ Fine Arts Museum

Art fan or not, this cool and peaceful gallery housing many of the country's finest works is a magical place to spend an hour or two. Page 21.

❹ China Town pagodas

Ornate, peaceful and atmospheric, the pagodas of Cholon are not to be missed. Take a walk between the pagodas, down back alleys and discover hidden markets and countless food stalls. Page 23.

❺ Sa Dec

Sa Dec is an infectiously charming riverside town home to diminutive Chinese shophouses, crumbling stuccoed colonial villas and a bustling riverfront market. Watch the river traffic from a waterside café or jump on a boat. Page 59.

❻ Tam Nong Bird Sanctuary

This wonderfully peaceful wetland area is home to 220 bird species. It is a major draw for eager twitchers who come to catch a sighting of the rare red-headed sarus crane. Page 62.

❼ Can Tho floating market

This floating market is a hive of activity every day from 0500 to midday. All manner of fresh produce is sold wholesale from boats and barges, with traders advertising their wares by hanging it from tall polls on deck. Page 65.

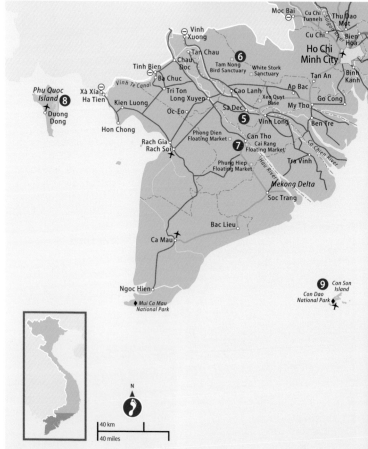

Moc Bai
Cu Chi Tunnels
Thu Dao Mot
Vinh Xuong
Cu Chi
Bien Hoa
Tan Chau
Ho Chi Minh City
Chau Doc
❻
Tam Nong Bird Sanctuary
White Stork Sanctuary
Tinh Bien
Tan An
Binh Kanh
Ba Chuc
Vinh Te Canal
Tri Ton
Cao Lanh
Ap Bac
Phu Quoc Island ❽
Xà Xía
Ha Tien
Long Xuyen
Xeo Quyt Base
Go Cong
Duong Dong
Kien Luong
Oc-Eo
Sa Dec
My Tho
❺
Vinh Long
Ben Tre
Hon Chong
Phong Dien Floating Market
Can Tho
Cai Rang Floating Market
❼
Rach Gia
Rach Soi
Tra Vinh
Co Chien River
Phung Hiep Floating Market
Hau River
Mekong Delta
Soc Trang
Bac Lieu
Ca Mau
Ngoc Hien
❾ Con Son Island
Con Dao National Park
◆ Mui Ca Mau National Park

N

40 km
40 miles

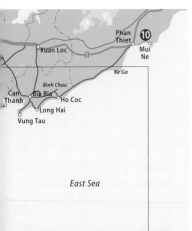

⑧ Phu Quoc

With a forested interior full of waterfalls and cool streams, local restaurants serving excellent seafood and some of Vietnam's most fantastic white-sand beaches, Phu Quoc is a destination not to be missed. Page 83.

⑨ Con Dao

Few international tourists make it here, but those who do will find Vietnam's best diving and a densely jungled national park full of all manner of animals, including monkeys. Take your pick from a host of knock-out beaches, set sail on an island cruise and visit the museum for an insight into Con Dao's fascinating history. Page 89.

⑩ Mui Ne

The water sports capital of Vietnam, with kitesurfers heading here from the world over. Away from the beaches the area is also famed for its Sahara-like red and white dunes. Page 95.

The old iron bridge, Ho Chi Minh City

Sights

palaces, pagodas, paintings aplenty

From the majestic Notre Dame Cathedral, opera house and the old post office to the art deco buildings of Donh Khoi street, there are many sights from the French colonial era. The markets of Ben Thanh and the more local Binh Tay are great places to get a sense of the city. Ho Chi Minh City has a wealth of museums and galleries, while pagoda hunters could lose days in Chinatown alone.

City centre

more elegant, less frenzied

The core of Ho Chi Minh City is, in many respects, the most interesting and historical. Remember, of course, that 'historical' here has a very different meaning from that in Hanoi. In Ho Chi Minh City a 100-year-old building is ancient – and, alas, increasingly rare. Still, a saunter down Dong Khoi Street, in District 1, the old rue Catinat can still give one an impression of life in a more elegant and less frenzied era. Much remains on a small and personal scale and within a 100-m radius of just about anywhere on Dong Khoi or Thai Van Lung streets there are dozens of cafés, restaurants and increasingly upmarket boutiques. However, the character of the street has altered with the opening of luxury chain names and the Times Square development. A little bit of Graham Greene history was lost in 2010 when the Givral Café in the Eden Centre, which featured in *The Quiet American*, was closed as Vincom Towers built another tower block on Lam Son Square.

Lam Son Square and around
Opera House (Nha Hat Thanh Pho) ① *7 Lam Son Sq, T08-3832 2009, nhahat_ ghvk@hcm.fpt.vn.* The impressive, French-era Opera House dominates Lam Son Square. It was built in 1897 to the design of French architect Ferret Eugene and restored in 1998. It once housed the National Assembly; nowadays, when it is open, it provides a varied programme of events, for example, traditional theatre, contemporary dance and gymnastics.

Essential Ho Chi Minh City

Finding your feet

Virtually all of the sights visitors wish to see lie to the west of the Saigon River. To the east there are many large new developments, homes of the city's expat population and the growing Vietnamese middle class.

Most visitors head straight for hotels in Districts 1 (the historic centre) or 3. Cholon or Chinatown (District 5) is a mile west of the centre and is a fascinating place to wander. Port of Saigon is in districts 4 and 8. Few visitors venture.

All the sights of Central Ho Chi Minh City can be reached on foot in no more than 30 minutes from the major hotel areas of Nguyen Hue, Dong Khoi and Ton Duc Thang streets. Visiting all the sights described below will take several days. Quite a good first port of call, however, is the **Panorama 33 Café** on the 33rd floor of Saigon Trade Center, 37 Ton Duc Thang Street, Monday-Friday 1100-2400, Saturday-Sunday 0900-2400.

Best views

Chill Skybar, page 39
OMG bar, page 40
Saigon Saigon bar, page 40

Best pagodas and temples

Xa Loi, page 18
Phung Son Tu, page 22
Thien Hau, page 24
Quan Am, page 25

Getting around

The abundant transport is fortunate, because it is a hot, large and increasingly polluted city. Metered taxis, motorcycle taxis and a handful of cyclos vie for business in a healthy spirit of competition. Many tourists who prefer some level of independence opt to hire a bicycle or motorbike.

Tip...

Take care when carrying handbags and purses. Drive-by snatchings are on the increase.

When to go

Ho Chi Minh City is a great place to visit all year around.

Time required

The major sights can be seen in a weekend, but take a few days longer to soak up the city and explore it further.

Weather Ho Chi Minh City

January	February	March	April	May	June
31°C 21°C 15mm	32°C 22°C 8mm	33°C 23°C 23mm	34°C 24°C 63mm	33°C 25°C 183mm	32°C 24°C 261mm

July	August	September	October	November	December
31°C 24°C 257mm	31°C 24°C 249mm	31°C 24°C 270mm	31°C 23°C 255mm	31°C 23°C 156mm	31°C 22°C 65mm

Continental Hotel North of the Opera House, now repainted, was built in 1880 and is an integral part of the city's history. Graham Greene stayed here and the hotel features in the novel *The Quiet American*. Old journalists' haunt Continental Shelf was, according to war journalist Jon Swain, "a famous verandah where correspondents, spies, speculators, traffickers, intellectuals and soldiers used to meet during the war to glean information and pick up secret reports, half false, half true or half disclosed. All of this is more than enough for it to be known as Radio Catinat. I sometimes went there for a late evening drink among the frangipani and hibiscus blossom ... It was the reverse of the frenzy of the war, and a good place to think".

The Continental lines **Dong Khoi Street** (formerly the bar-lined Tu Do Street, the old Rue Catinat), which stretches down to the river. Many shops specialize in, or sell a mix of, silk clothes and accessories, jewellery, lacquerware and household goods and there are now a number of swanky cafés along the stretch.

Hotel Caravelle Facing the Continental, also adjoining Dong Khoi Street, is the Hotel Caravelle, which houses boutique shops selling luxury goods. The **Caravelle** opened for business in 1959. The 10th floor housed a famous **Saigon** bar, a favourite spot for wartime reporters, and during the 1960s the *Associated Press*, *NBC*, *CBS*, the *New York Times* and *Washington Post* based their offices here. The press escaped casualties when, on 25 August 1964, a bomb exploded in room 514, on a floor mostly used by foreign reporters. The hotel suffered damage and there were injuries but the journalists were all out in the field. It was renamed **Doc Lap** (Independence Hotel) in 1975 but not before a Vietnamese tank trundled down the rue Catinat to Place Garnier (now Lam Son Square) and aimed its turret at the hotel; to this day nobody knows why it did not fire. During the filming of Graham Greene's *The Quiet American*, actors Michael Caine and Brendan Fraser stayed at the hotel.

Nguyen Hue Boulevard At the northwest end of Nguyen Hue Boulevard is the yellow and white **City Hall**, formerly the French **Hôtel de Ville** built in 1897 and now the Ho Chi Minh City People's Committee building, which overlooks a **statue of Bac Ho** (Uncle Ho) offering comfort, or perhaps advice, to a child. This is a favourite spot for Vietnamese to have their photograph taken, especially newly-weds who believe old Ho confers some sort of blessing.

South of City Hall, the **Rex Hotel**, a pre-Liberation favourite with US officers, stands at the intersection of Le Loi and Nguyen Hue boulevards. This was the scene of the daily 'Five O'Clock Follies' where the military briefed an increasingly sceptical press corps during the Vietnam War. Its bar is now somewhat aged, but the view from it is still excellent so it is a worthwhile stop for an afternoon drink.

On weekend evenings thousands of young Saigon men and women and young families cruise up and down Nguyen Hue Boulevard (and Le Loi Boulevard and Dong Khoi Street) on motorbikes. There are now so many motorbikes on the streets of Ho Chi Minh City that intersections seem lethally confused. Miraculously, the riders miss each other (most of the time) while pedestrians safely make their way through waves of machines.

★Notre Dame Cathedral

Visiting times are given as 0500-1100 and 1500-1730. Communion is celebrated here 7 times on Sun (drawing congregations Western churches can only dream of) and 3 times on weekdays.

North up Dong Khoi Street, in the middle of **Cong Xa Paris** (Paris Square), is the imposing, austere red-brick, twin-spired Notre Dame Cathedral, overlooking a grassed square in which a statue of the Virgin Mary stands holding an orb. The statue was the subject of intense scrutiny in 2006 as it was said that it had shed tears. The cathedral was built between 1877 and 1880 and is said to be on the site of an ancient pagoda. A number of the homeless sleep under its walls at night;

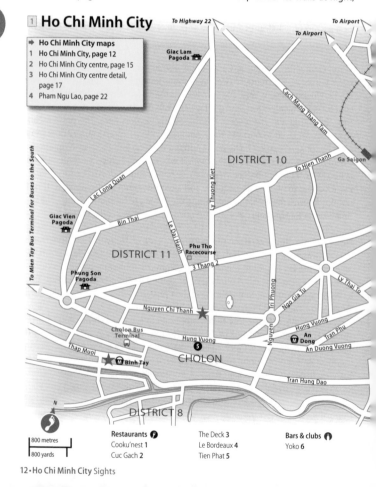

1 Ho Chi Minh City

➡ **Ho Chi Minh City maps**
1 Ho Chi Minh City, page 12
2 Ho Chi Minh City centre, page 15
3 Ho Chi Minh City centre detail, page 17
4 Pham Ngu Lao, page 22

To Highway 22
To Airport
To Airport

Giac Lam Pagoda

Cach Mang Thang Tam

DISTRICT 10

To Hien Thanh

Ga Saigon

Lac Long Quan

Ly Thuong Kiet

To Mien Tay Bus Terminal for Buses to the South

Giac Vien Pagoda

Bin Thai

Le Dai Hanh

DISTRICT 11

Phu Tho Racecourse

3 Thang 2

Phung Son Pagoda

Nguyen Chi Thanh ★

Tri Phuong

Ngo Gia Tu

Ly Thai To

Hung Vuong

Tran Phu

An Dong

Cholon Bus Terminal

Hung Vuong **5**

Nguyen

An Duong Vuong

Thap Muoi

★ Binh Tay

CHOLON

Tran Hung Dao

DISTRICT 8

N

800 metres
800 yards

Restaurants
Cooku'nest **1**
Cuc Gach **2**

The Deck **3**
Le Bordeaux **4**
Tien Phat **5**

Bars & clubs
Yoko **6**

unfortunately the signs asking Vietnamese men not to treat the walls as a public urinal do not deter this unpleasant but widespread practice. Mass times are a spectacle as crowds, unable to squeeze through the doors, listen to the service while perched on their parked motorbikes in rows eight or nine deep.

General Post Office
2 Cong Xa Paris, daily 0730-1930.

Facing onto the Paris Square is the General Post Office, built in the 1880s in French style, it is a particularly distinguished building. The front façade has attractive cornices with French and Khmer motifs and the names of notable French men of

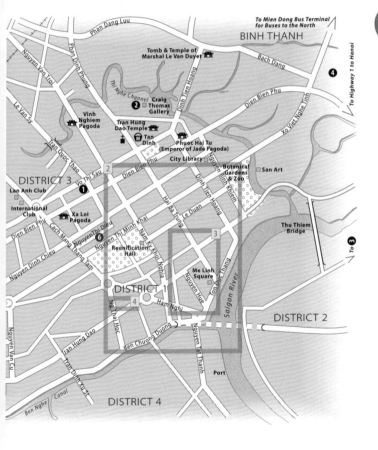

The changing face

Vietnam's economic reforms are most in evidence in Ho Chi Minh City where the average annual income is considerably higher than outside the city. Consequently, ever larger holes are being torn in the heart of central Ho Chi Minh City. Whereas a few years ago it was common to see buildings disappear, now whole blocks fall to the wrecker's ball. From the holes left behind, concrete, steel and glass monuments emerge. There is, of course, a difference from earlier periods of remodelling of the city. Then, it was conducted on a human scale and the largest buildings, though grand, were on a scale that was in keeping with the dimensions of the streets and ordinary shophouses. French buildings in Dong Khoi Street, for example, were consistent with the Vietnamese way of life: street-level trading with a few residential floors above.

The landmark Bitexco tower stands tall in the heart of the city, a graphic symbol of its ambitions for future growth. Other plush modern office and lifestyle spaces such as Kumho Plaza are being joined by developments such as the 25-floor German House across the road and the Vietcombank Tower which stands on the river and ranks as the city's second tallest skyscraper. The Phu My Hung urban area, across the river, offers modern living for the growing Vietnamese middle class and the many expats that call the city home. The latest new urban area, Thu Thiem, has been a long time coming. This vast swathe of land was cleared of its thousands of occupants in the late 1990s, but construction has stalled and it is yet to take shape. Work has also begun on the first underground railway, which is slated to feature grand 3 level station downtown at Ben Thanh market. The much-photographed statue of General Tran Nguyen Han in front of the market was removed in 2014 to make way for this development, providing another signal of the city's intent to look forward, not back.

letters and science. Inside, the high, vaulted ceiling and fans create a deliciously cool atmosphere in which to scribble a postcard. Note the old wall-map of Cochin China that has miraculously survived. The enormous portrait of Ho Chi Minh, hanging at the end of the hall, completes the sense of grandeur.

Independence Palace

135 Nam Ky Khoi Nghia St, T08-3822 3652, www.dinhdoclap.gov.vn, daily 0730-1100, 1300-1600, 15,000d, brochure 10000d, documentary 50,000d. Tours every 10 mins. The hall is sometimes closed for state occasions.

The Independence Palace (also known as the **Reunification Hall**) is in a large park to the southeast of Nguyen Thi Minh Khai Street and southwest of Nam Ky Khoi Nghia Street. The residence of the French governor was built on this site in 1868 and was later renamed the Presidential Palace. In February 1962, a pair of planes took off to attack Viet Cong emplacements – piloted by two of the south's finest

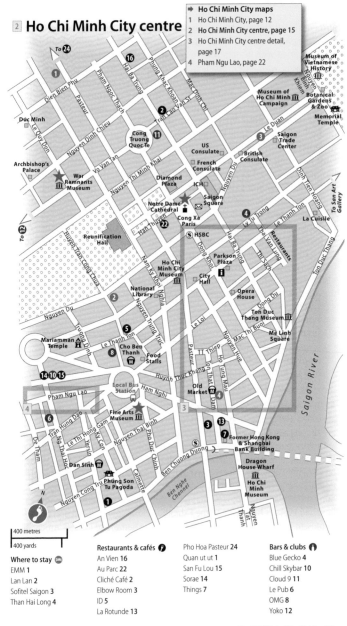

❷ Ho Chi Minh City centre

➡ **Ho Chi Minh City maps**
1 Ho Chi Minh City, page 12
2 Ho Chi Minh City centre, page 15
3 Ho Chi Minh City centre detail, page 17
4 Pham Ngu Lao, page 22

Where to stay 🛏
EMM **1**
Lan Lan **2**
Sofitel Saigon **3**
Than Hai Long **4**

Restaurants & cafés 🍴
An Vien **16**
Au Parc **22**
Cliché Café **2**
Elbow Room **3**
ID **5**
La Rotunde **13**
Pho Hoa Pasteur **24**
Quan ut ut **1**
San Fu Lou **15**
Sorae **14**
Things **7**

Bars & clubs 🍸
Blue Gecko **4**
Chill Skybar **10**
Cloud 9 **11**
Le Pub **6**
OMG **8**
Yoko **12**

airmen – but they turned back to bomb the Presidential Palace in a futile attempt to assassinate President Diem. The president, who held office between 1955-1963, escaped with his family to the cellar, but the palace had to be demolished and replaced with a new building. (Diem was later assassinated after a military coup.) One of the two pilots, Nguyen Thanh Trung is a Vice President of **Vietnam Airlines** and still flies government officials around every couple of months to keep his pilot's licence current. One of the most memorable photographs taken during the war was of a North Vietnamese Army (NVA) tank crashing through the gates of the Palace on 30 April 1975 – symbolizing the end of South Vietnam and its government. The President of South Vietnam, General Duong Van Minh, along with his entire cabinet, was arrested in the Palace shortly afterwards. The hall has been preserved as it was found in 1975 and visitors can take a guided tour. In the **Vice President's Guest Room**, there is a lacquered painting of the Temple of Literature in Hanoi, while the **Presenting of Credentials Room** contains a fine 40-piece lacquer work showing diplomats presenting their credentials during the Le Dynasty (15th century). In the basement there are operations rooms, military maps, radios and other paraphernalia. In essence, it is a 1960s-style building filled with 1960s-style official furnishings that now look very kitsch. Not only was the building designed according to the principles of Chinese geomancy but the colour of the carpets – lurid mustard yellow in one room – was also chosen depending on whether it was to calm or stimulate users of the rooms. Visitors are shown an interesting film about the Revolution and some fascinating photographs and memorabilia from the era. A replica of the tank that bulldozed through the gates of the compound heralding the end of South Vietnam is displayed in the forecourt.

★War Remnants Museum
28 Vo Van Tan St, Q3, T08-3930 5587, www.baotangchungtichchientranh.vn, daily 0730-1200, 1330-1700, 15,000d.

All the horrors of the Vietnam War from the nation's perspective – photographs of atrocities and action, bombs, military tanks and planes and deformed foetuses – are graphically displayed in this well laid-out museum building. In the courtyard are tanks, bombs and helicopters, while the new museum, arranged in five new sections, records man's inhumanity. The display covers the Son My (My Lai) massacre on 16 March 1968, the effects of napalm and phosphorous, and the after-effects of Agent Orange defoliation (this is particularly disturbing, with bottled malformed human foetuses). This museum has gone through some interesting name changes in recent years. It began life as the Exhibition House of American and Chinese War Crimes. In 1990, 'Chinese' was dropped from the name, and in 1994 'American' was too. Since 1996 it has simply been called the War Remnants Museum.

Archbishop's Palace
330 Nguyen Dinh Chieu St and corner of Tran Quoc Thao St.

Around this area is a number of very fine French-era buildings still standing; some have been allowed to fall into decay but others have been well maintained. In particular the Archbishop's Palace and the high schools, **Le Qui Don** ① *2 Le Qui Don St*, and **Marie Curie** ① *Nam Ky Khoi Nghia St*. All have had extensions built in recent years, but at least the schools have attempted to blend the new buildings in with the old. The palace is believed to be the oldest house in Ho Chi Minh City, built

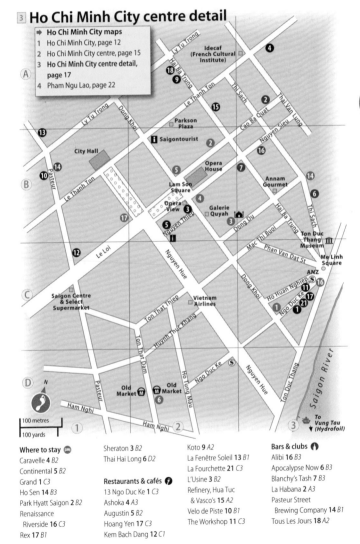

③ **Ho Chi Minh City centre detail**

➡ **Ho Chi Minh City maps**
1   Ho Chi Minh City, page 12
2   Ho Chi Minh City centre, page 15
3   Ho Chi Minh City centre detail, page 17
4   Pham Ngu Lao, page 22

Where to stay 🛏
Caravelle **4** *B2*
Continental **5** *B2*
Grand **1** *C3*
Ho Sen **14** *B3*
Park Hyatt Saigon **2** *B2*
Renaissance
  Riverside **16** *C3*
Rex **17** *B1*

Sheraton **3** *B2*
Thai Hai Long **6** *D2*

Restaurants & cafés 🍴
13 Ngo Duc Ke **1** *C3*
Ashoka **4** *A3*
Augustin **5** *B2*
Hoang Yen **17** *C3*
Kem Bach Dang **12** *C1*

Koto **9** *A2*
La Fenêtre Soleil **13** *B1*
La Fourchette **21** *C3*
L'Usine **3** *B2*
Refinery, Hua Tuc
  & Vasco's **15** *A2*
Velo de Piste **10** *B1*
The Workshop **11** *C3*

Bars & clubs 🎵
Alibi **16** *B3*
Apocalypse Now **6** *B3*
Blanchy's Tash **7** *B3*
La Habana **2** *A3*
Pasteur Street
  Brewing Company **14** *B1*
Tous Les Jours **18** *A2*

in 1790 (although not originally on this spot) for the then French bishop of Adran, Pierre Pigneau de Behaine.

Xa Loi Pagoda
89 Ba Huyen Thanh Quan St, daily 0630-1100, 1430-1700.

Ho Chi Minh City has close to 200 pagodas – far too many for most visitors to see. Many of the finest are in Cholon (see page 23), although there is a selection closer to the main hotel area in central Ho Chi Minh City. The Xa Loi Pagoda is not far from the War Remnants Museum and is surrounded by food stalls. Built in 1956, the pagoda contains a multi-storeyed tower, which is particularly revered, as it houses a relic of the Buddha. The main sanctuary contains a large, bronze-gilded Buddha in an attitude of meditation. Around the walls are a series of silk paintings depicting the previous lives of the Buddha (with an explanation of each life to the right of the entrance into the sanctuary). The pagoda is historically, rather than artistically, important as it became a focus of dissent against the Diem regime (see box, page 21).

Le Duan Street
North of the cathedral is Le Duan Street, the former corridor of power with Ngo Dinh Diem's Palace at one end, the zoo at the other and the former embassies of the three major powers, France, the USA and the UK, in between. Nearest the Reunification Hall is the compound of the **French Consulate**. A block away is the **former US Embassy**. After diplomatic ties were resumed in 1995 the Americans lost little time in demolishing the 1960s building which held so many bad memories. The US Consulate General now stands on this site. A memorial outside, on the corner of Mac Dinh Chi Street, records the attack by Viet Cong special forces during the Tet offensive of 1968 and the final victory in 1975. At 2 Le Duan Street is the **Museum of Ho Chi Minh Campaign (Bao Tang Quan Doi)** ⓘ *T08-3822 9387, Tue-Sun 0730-1100, 1330-1630, 15,000d*, with a tank and warplane in the front compound. It contains an indifferent display of photographs and articles of war.

Botanical Gardens and Zoo
2 Nguyen Binh Khiem St, T08-3829 3728, daily 0700-2000, entrance to gardens and zoo, 12,000d.

At the end of Le Duan Street are the Botanical Gardens which run alongside Nguyen Binh Khiem Street at the point where the Thi Nghe channel flows into the Saigon River. The gardens were established in 1864 by French botanist Jean-Batiste Louis Pierre; by the 1970s they had a collection of nearly 2000 species, and a particularly fine display of orchids. With the dislocations of the immediate postwar years, the gardens went into decline, a situation from which they are still trying to recover. In the south quarter of the gardens is a mediocre zoo with a rather moth-eaten collection of animals that form a backdrop to smartly dressed Vietnamese families posing for photographs.

BACKGROUND
History of the city

Before the 15th century, the area was a small Khmer village surrounded by a wilderness of forest and swamp. By 1623 Ho Chi Minh City had become an important commercial centre, and in the mid-17th century it became the residence of the so-called Vice-King of Cambodia. In 1698, the Viets managed to extend their control this far south and finally Ho Chi Minh City was brought under Vietnamese control.

In the middle of the 19th century, the French began to challenge Vietnamese authority in the south of the country. Between 1859 and 1862, in response to the Nguyen persecution of Catholics in Vietnam, the French attacked and captured the city. They named it Saigon (Soai-gon – 'wood of the kapok tree'), and the Treaty of Saigon in 1862 ratified the conquest and created the new French colony of Cochin China. Saigon was developed in French style: wide, tree-lined boulevards, street-side cafés, elegant French architecture, boutiques and the smell of baking baguettes.

During the 1960s and early 1970s the city boomed and flourished under the American occupation (it was the seat of the South Vietnam government) until the fall or liberation – depending upon your point of view. Officially Ho Chi Minh City (HCMC) since 1975, it remains to most the bi-syllabic, familiar, old 'Saigon'.

Museum of Vietnamese History
2 Nguyen Binh Khiem St, T08-3829 8146, www.baotanglichsuvn.com, Tue-Sun 0800-1130, 1330-1700,15,000d. Labels in English and French. Water puppet shows (see also page 41) are held here daily.

The history museum (Bao Tang Lich Su Viet Nam) is an elegant building constructed in 1928 and is pagodaesque in style. It displays a wide range of artefacts from the prehistoric (300,000 years ago) and the Dongson periods (3500 BC-AD 100), right through to the birth of the Vietnamese Communist Party in 1930. Particularly impressive are the Cham sculptures, of which the standing bronze Buddha, dating from the fourth to sixth century, is probably the finest. There is also a delicately carved Devi (Goddess) dating from the 10th century as well as pieces such as the head of Shiva, Hindu destroyer and creator, from the eighth to ninth century and Ganesh, elephant-headed son of Shiva and Parvati, also dating from the eighth to ninth century.

There are also representative pieces from the Chen-la, Funan, Khmer, Oc-eo and Han Chinese periods, and from the various Vietnamese dynasties together with some hill tribe artefacts. Labelling is in English, French and Vietnamese.

Other highlights include the wooden stakes planted in the Bach Dang riverbed for repelling the war ships of the Mongol Yuan in the 13th century, a beautiful Phoenix head from the Tran dynasty (13th to 14th century) and an Hgor (big drum) from the Jarai people, made from the skin of two elephants. It belonged to the Potauoui (King of Fire) family in Ajunpa district, Gia Lai Province. There are some fine sandstone sculptures too including an incredibly smooth linga from Long An Province (seventh to eighth century) in the Mekong Delta. The linga represents the cult of Siva and signifies gender, energy, fertility and potency.

Near the History Museum is the **Memorial Temple** ① *Tue-Sun 0800-1130, 1300-1600*, constructed in 1928 and dedicated to famous Vietnamese.

Ho Chi Minh City Museum and around

65 Ly Tu Trong St, T08-3829 9741, www.hcmc-museum.edu.vn, daily 0800-1700, 15,000d.

This museum includes a mixed bag of displays concerning the revolution, with a display of photographs, a few pieces of hardware (helicopter, anti-aircraft guns) in the back compound, and some memorabilia. Other exhibits chart the development of the city and its economy. The building itself is historically important. Dominating a prominent intersection, the grey-white classical French-designed building was built as a museum before it became the palace for the governor of Cochin China in 1890. After the 1945 revolution it was used for administrative offices before returning to the French as the High Commissioner's residence in September 1945. During the War, Ngo Dinh Diem resided here under its new name as Southern Governor's Palace; during the reign of Nguyen Van Thieu (1967-1975), it operated as the supreme court.

Southwest from the museum on the corner of Ly Tu Trong Street and Nam Ky Khoi Nghia is the National Library.

Mariamman Hindu Temple

45 Truong Dinh St.

Although clearly Hindu, with a statue of Mariamman flanked by Maduraiveeran and Pechiamman, the temple is largely frequented by Chinese worshippers, providing the strange sight of Chinese Vietnamese clasping incense sticks and prostrating themselves in front of a Hindu deity, as they would to a Buddha image. The Chinese have always been pragmatic when it comes to religions.

Ben Thanh Market (Cho Ben Thanh)

A large, covered central market, Ben Thanh Market sits on a large and chaotic roundabout which, at the time of writing, was undergoing construction as part of the city's first metro line project. Ben Thanh is well stocked with cheap clothes (think souvenir T-shirts), household goods, and a wide choice of souvenirs, lacquerware, embroidery and so on, as well as some terrific lines in food, fresh and dried fruits. Rather touristy, it is still used by locals, but to get a more authentic sense of a busy city market, head to Binh Tay Market (see page 25).

Ben Thanh is also home to a food stall corner offering a huge variety of dishes from around the south of the country.

Outside the north gate (*cua Bac*) on Le Thanh Ton Street are some particularly tempting displays of fresh fruit and beautiful cut flowers.

ON THE ROAD

Buddhist martyrs: self-immolation as protest

In August 1963 there was a demonstration of 15,000 people at the Xa Loi Pagoda, with speakers denouncing the Diem regime and telling jokes about Diem's sister-in-law, Madame Nhu (who was later to call monks "hooligans in robes"). Two nights later, ARVN special forces (from Roman Catholic families) raided the pagoda, battering down the gate, wounding 30 and killing seven people. Soon afterwards Diem declared martial law. The pagoda became a focus of discontent, with several monks committing suicide through self-immolation to protest against the Diem regime.

The first monk to immolate himself was 66-year-old Thich Quang Du, from Hué. On 11 June 1963, his companions poured petrol over him and set him alight as he sat in the lotus position. Pedestrians prostrated themselves at the sight; even a policeman threw himself to the ground in reverence. The next day, the picture of the monk in flames filled the front pages of newspapers around the world. Some 30 monks and nuns followed Thich's example in protesting against the Diem government and US involvement in South Vietnam. Two young US protesters also followed suit, one committing suicide by self-immolation outside the Pentagon and the other next to the UN, both in November 1968.

Madame Nhu, a Catholic, is reported as having said after the monks' death: "Let them burn, and we shall clap our hands." Within five months Diem had been killed in a military coup.

In May 1993, a Vietnamese man immolated himself at the Thien Mu Pagoda in Hué – the pagoda where the first monk-martyr was based (see page 166).

The Ben Thanh Night Market has flourished since 2003. Starting at dusk and open until after midnight the night market is Ho Chi Minh City's attempt to recreate Bangkok's Patpong market. As the sun sinks and the main market closes stalls spring up in the surrounding streets. Clothes and cheap jewellery and an abundance of food stalls are the key attractions.

★ Fine Arts Museum
97A Pho Duc Chinh St, T08-3829 4441, daily 0900-1700.

Housed in an atmospheric colonial building which is slightly dishevelled but rather charming for it, the Fine Arts Museum is a very pleasant place to escape the heat of the city and take a look at some 20s architecture close up. The interior is wonderfully tiled and there is a courtyard to the rear, and an ancient iron lift. The art collection dates spans works from the fourth century right up to the contemporary era. The American War features heavily in the post-1975 work and the theme can become a little tiresome, but there is plenty of other art on offer, including some interesting Cham-era pieces. This is also a good place to pick up prints, with works by Vietnamese artists as well as propaganda posters on offer.

Phung Son Tu Pagoda
338 Nguyen Cong Tru St.

This is a small temple built just after the Second World War by Fukien Chinese; its most notable features are the wonderful painted entrance doors with their fearsome armed warriors. Incense spirals hang in the open well of the pagoda, which is dedicated to Ong Bon, the Guardian of Happiness and Virtue.

The **War Surplus Market (Dan Sinh)** ① *Yersin between Nguyen Thai Binh St and Nguyen Cong Tru St,* is not far from the Phung Son Tu Pagoda. Merchandise on sale includes dog tags and military clothing and equipment (not all of it authentic). The market is popular with Western visitors looking for mementoes of their visit, so bargain particularly hard.

Pham Ngu Lao

an area catering for the backpacker

Most backpackers arriving overland in Ho Chi Minh City are dropped off in this bustling district, a 10- to 15-minute walk from downtown. The countless hotels, guesthouses and rooms to rent open and close and change name or owner with remarkable speed. The area is littered with restaurants, cafés, bars, email services, laundries, tour agencies and money changers, all fiercely competitive; there are mini-supermarkets and shops selling rucksacks, footwear, DVDs, pirated software and ethnic knick-knacks.

➡ **Ho Chi Minh City maps**
1 Ho Chi Minh City, page 12
2 Ho Chi Minh City centre, page 15
3 Ho Chi Minh City centre detail, page 17
4 Pham Ngu Lao, page 22

④ **Pham Ngu Lao**

Pham Ngu Lao

Sapaco Tourist

Train Booking Agency

Do Quang Dau

De Tham

Sinh Tourist ℹ

Nguyen Thai Hoc

Bui Vien

N

Not to scale

Where to stay 🛏
Beautiful Saigon **4**
Chau Long Mini **1**
Long Hostel **2**

Restaurants & cafés 🍴
Café Zoom **9**
Good Morning Vietnam **13**

Kim Café **4**

★This is the heart of Ho Chi Minh City's Chinese community. Cholon is an area of commerce and trade; not global but nevertheless international. In typical Chinese style it is dominated by small and medium-size businesses and this shows in the buildings' shop fronts (look for the Chinese characters on signs over the door). Cholon is home to a great many temples and pagodas – some of which are described below. As one would expect from a Chinese trading district, there is plenty of fabric for sale in the markets.

Cholon or Chinatown is inhabited predominantly by Vietnamese of Chinese origin. Despite a flow of Chinese out of the country post-1975, there is still a large population of Chinese Vietnamese living here. The area encompasses District 5 to the southwest of the city centre, and to the casual visitor appears to be the most populated, noisiest and in general the most vigorous part of Ho Chi Minh City, if not of Vietnam. It is here that entrepreneurial talent and private funds are concentrated; both resources that the government are keen to mobilize in their attempts to reinvigorate the economy.

Cholon is worth visiting not only for the bustle and activity, but also because the temples and assembly halls found here are the finest in Ho Chi Minh City. As with any town in Southeast Asia boasting a sizeable Chinese population, the early settlers established meeting rooms that offered social, cultural and spiritual support to members of a dialect group. These assembly halls (*hoi quan*) are most common in Hoi An and Cholon. There are temples in the buildings, which attract Vietnamese as well as Chinese worshippers, and indeed today serve little of their former purpose. The elderly meet here occasionally for a natter and a cup of tea.

Nghia An Assembly Hall
678 Nguyen Trai St, not far from the Arc en Ciel Hotel.

A magnificent, carved, gold-painted wooden boat hangs over the entrance to the Nghia An Assembly Hall. To the left, on entering the temple, is a larger-than-life representation of Quan Cong's horse and groom. (Quan Cong was a loyal military man who lived in China in the third century.) At the main altar are three figures in glass cases: the central red-faced figure with a green cloak is Quan Cong himself; to the left and right are his trusty companions, General Chau Xuong (very fierce) and the mandarin Quan Binh respectively. On leaving, note the fine gold figures of guardians on the inside of the door panels.

Tam Son Assembly Hall
118 Trieu Quang Phuc St, just off Nguyen Trai St.

The temple, built in the 19th century by Fukien immigrants, is frequented by childless women as it is dedicated to Chua Thai Sanh, the Goddess of Fertility. It is an uncluttered, 'pure' example of a Chinese/Vietnamese pagoda – peaceful and quiet. Like Nghia An Hoi Quan, the temple contains figures of Quan Cong, his horse and two companions.

Thien Hau Temples
710 and 802 Nguyen Trai St.

The Thien Hau Temple at 710 Nguyen Trai Street is one of the largest in the city. Constructed in the early 19th century, it is Chinese in inspiration and is dedicated to the worship of both the Buddha and to the Goddess Thien Hau, the goddess of the sea and the protector of sailors. Thien Hau was born in China and as a girl saved her father from drowning, but not her brother. Thien Hau's festival is marked here on the 23rd day of the third lunar month. One enormous incense urn and an incinerator can be seen through the main doors. Inside, the principal altar supports the gilded form of Thien Hau, with a boat to one side. Silk paintings depicting religious scenes decorate the walls. By far the most interesting part of the pagoda is the roof, which can be best seen from the small open courtyard. It must be one of the finest and most richly ornamented in Vietnam, with the high-relief frieze depicting episodes from the Legends of the Three Kingdoms. In the post-1975 era, many would-be refugees prayed here for safe deliverance before casting themselves adrift on the East Sea. A number of those who survived the perilous voyage sent offerings to the merciful goddess and the temple has been well maintained since. On busy days it is very smoky. Look up on leaving to see over the front door a picture of a boiling sea peppered with sinking boats. A benign Thien An looks down mercifully from a cloud.

A **second temple** dedicated to Thien Hau is a couple of blocks away at 802 Nguyen Trai Street. Chinese migrants from Fukien Province built it in the 1730s, although the building on the site today is not old. The roof can be seen from the road and in addition to the normal dragons are some curious models of what appear to be miniature Chinese landscapes carried by bowed men. Inside it is less busy than the first Thien Hau temple but on good days worshippers hurry from one image of Thien Hau (depicted here with a black face) to another waving burning joss sticks in front of her. Whatever happens in these temples is not religious in the sense of worshipping a god but more a superstition, entreating the spirits for good fortune (hence the lottery ticket sellers outside) or asking them to stave off bad luck. Note that these are not pagodas in the sense that they are not a place for the worship of Buddha and you will see no Buddhist monks here and have no sense of serene or enlightened calm. This temple has some nicely carved stone pillars of entwined dragons and on the wall to the right of the altars is a frieze of a boat being swamped by a tsunami. The walls are festooned with calendars from local Chinese restaurants and gold shops.

Ming Dynasty Assembly Hall
380 Tran Hung Dao St.

The Ming Dynasty Assembly Hall (Dinh Minh Huong Gia Thanh) was built by the Cantonese community which arrived in Saigon via Hoi An in the 18th century.

The assembly hall was built in 1789 to the dedication and worship of the Ming Dynasty although the building we see today dates largely from an extensive renovation carried out in the 1960s. There is some old furniture; a heavy marble-topped table and chairs that arrived in 1850 from China. It appears that the Vietnamese Emperor Gia Long used the Chinese community for cordial relations with the Chinese royal court and one of the community, a man called Trinh Hoai Duc, was appointed Vietnamese ambassador to the Middle Dynasty. In the main hall there are three altars which, following imperial tradition, are: the central altar dedicated to the royal family (Ming Dynasty in this case), the right-hand altar dedicated to two mandarin officers (military) and the left-hand altar dedicated to two mandarin officers (civil).

The hall behind is dedicated to the memory of the Vuong family who built the hall and whose descendants have lived here ever since. There is, in addition, a small side chapel where childless women can seek divine intercession from a local deity, Ba Me Sanh.

Quan Am Pagoda
12 Lao Tu St (just off Luong Nhu Hoc St).

The Quan Am Pagoda is thought to be one of the oldest in the city. Its roof supports four sets of impressive mosaic-encrusted figures, while inside, the main building is fronted with old, gold and lacquer panels of guardian spirits. The main altar supports a seated statue of A-Pho, the Holy Mother. In front of the main altar is a white ceramic statue of Quan Am, the Goddess of Purity and Motherhood (Goddess of Mercy) – see box, page 48. The pagoda complex also contains a series of courtyards and altars dedicated to a range of deities and spirits. Outside, hawkers sell caged birds and vast quantities of incense sticks to pilgrims.

Binh Tay Market
While most tourists visit Ben Thanh Market, it is Binh Tay Market which is the more rewarding. Sandwiched between Thap Muoi and Phan Van Khoe streets, it is one of the most colourful and exciting markets in Ho Chi Minh City, with a wonderful array of noises, smells and colours and stalls that have past from generation to generation creating a rich sense of history and belonging among the stall holders. It sprawls over a large area and is contained in what looks like a rather decayed Forbidden Palace. Every conceivable space is used with stalls festooned with everything from spices to flip flops. This is also a good place to seek out a bowl of noodles or grab a cup of strong iced coffee and watch the madness unfold in front of you. A new high-rise market – the five-storey **An Dong Market** – opened at the end of 1991 in Cholon. It was built with an investment of US$5 million from local ethnic Chinese businessmen.

some atmospheric, impressive pagodas well worth visiting

Outer Ho Chi Minh City includes a clutch of scattered pagodas in several districts, namely Districts 3, 10, 11 and Binh Thanh. All are accessible by cyclo, moto or taxi. There's also a new museum of traditional medicine in District 10.

Phung Son Pagoda
A 40-min walk or 8-min motorbike ride from the Binh Tay Market, set back from the road at 1408 3 Thang 2 Blvd.

The Phung Son Pagoda, also known as **Go Pagoda**, was built at the beginning of the 19th century on the site of an earlier Cambodian structure and has been rebuilt several times. At one time, it was decided to move the pagoda, and all the temple valuables were loaded on to the back of a white elephant. The beast stumbled and the valuables tumbled out into the pond that surrounds the temple. This was taken as a sign from the gods that the pagoda was to stay where it was. In the sanctuary, there is a large, seated, gilded Buddha, surrounded by a variety of other figures from several Asian and Southeast Asian countries. This, being a pagoda, has a very different atmosphere from the temples of Chinatown. There is no frenzied scrum in front of the altars and only a few whisps of smoke. Monks sit in contemplation.

Giac Vien Pagoda
At the end of a narrow and rather seedy 400-m-long alley running off Lac Long Quan St (just after No 247). There is also a temple down here of no interest whatsoever, the pagoda is right at the end.

Giac Vien Pagoda (Buddha's Complete Enlightenment) is similar in layout, content and inspiration to Giac Lam Pagoda (see below). Visiting just one of the two pagodas would be enough for most visitors. The Giac Vien Pagoda was built in 1771 and dedicated to the worship of the Emperor Gia Long. Although restored, Giac Vien remains one of the best-preserved temples in Vietnam. It is lavishly decorated, with more than 100 carvings of various divinities and spirits, dominated by a large gilded image of the Buddha of the Past (Amitabha or *A Di Da Phat* in Vietnamese). It is everything a pagoda should be: demons and gods jump out around every corner, a confusion of fantastic characters. With the smoke and smells, the richness of colour and the darkness, it's an assault on the senses. Among the decorations, note the 'Buddha lamp', funerary tablets and urns with photographs of the deceased. Outside there is a small pavilion in which the ashes of the dead are stored in small urns.

Giac Lam Pagoda
118 Lac Long Quan St, Ward 10, Q Tan Binh, T08-865 3933, about 2 km northeast of Giac Vien Pagoda, through an arch and down a short track about 300 m from the intersection with Le Dai Hanh St. Near the intersection is a modern 7-storey tower and beyond a giant Buddha statue which is also modern. Daily 0500-1200, 1400-2100.

The Giac Lam Pagoda (Forest of Enlightenment) was built in 1744 and is the oldest pagoda in Ho Chi Minh City. There is a sacred Bodhi tree in the temple courtyard and the pagoda is set among fruit trees and vegetable plots. Inside Giac Lam it feels, initially, like a rather cluttered private house. In one section, there are rows of funerary tablets with pictures of the deceased – a rather moving display of man's mortality. The main altar is impressive, with layers of Buddhas, dominated by the gilded form of the Buddha of the Past. Note the 49-Buddha oil lamp with little scraps of paper tucked in. On these scraps are the names of the mourned. The number seven is very important in Buddhism and most towers have seven storeys. Behind the main temple in the section with the funerary tablets is a bust of Ho Chi Minh. At the very back of the pagoda is a hall with murals showing scenes of torture from hell. Each sin is punished in a very specific and appropriate way. The monks are very friendly and will probably offer tea. Some speak good English and French as well as having detailed knowledge of the history of the pagoda. It is a small haven of peace. An unusual feature is the use of blue and white porcelain plates to decorate the roof and some of the small towers in the garden facing the pagoda. These towers are the burial places of former head monks.

Phuoc Hai Tu (Emperor of Jade Pagoda) and around
73 Mai Thi Luu St off Dien Bien Phu St, 0700-1800.

The Phuoc Hai Tu can be found, nestling behind low pink walls, just before the Thi Nghe Channel. Women sell birds that are set free to gain merit, and a pond to the right contains large turtles. The Emperor of Jade is the supreme god of the Taoists, although this temple, built in 1900, contains a wide range of other deities. These include the archangel Michael of the Buddhists, a Sakyamuni (historic) Buddha, statues of the two generals who tamed the Green Dragon (representing the east) and the White Dragon (representing the west), to the left and right of the first altar respectively, and Quan Am (see box, page 48). The Hall of Ten Hells in the left-hand sanctuary has reliefs depicting the 1000 tortures of hell.

Nearby, the architecturally interesting **city library** ① *3 Nguyen Dinh Chieu*, has a cool, modern façade; there is a memorial at the front of the building.

Tran Hung Dao Temple
Near the Emperor of Jade Pagoda at 34 Vo Thi Sau St, daily 0700-1100, 1430-1700.

The small Tran Hung Dao Temple, built in 1932, was dedicated to the worship of the victorious 13th-century General Hung Dao and contains a series of bas-reliefs depicting the general's successes, along with weapons and carved dragons. In the front courtyard is a larger-than-life bronze statue of this hero of Vietnamese nationalism.

Vinh Nghiem Pagoda
To the west, on Nguyen Van Troi St, and just to the south of the Thi Nghe Channel.

Another modern pagoda, the Vinh Nghiem Pagoda, was completed in 1967 and is one of the largest in Vietnam. Built in the Japanese style, it displays a classic seven-storey pagoda in a large and airy sanctuary. On either side of the entrance are two fearsome warriors; inside is a large Japanese-style Buddha in an attitude of meditation, flanked by two goddesses. Along the walls are a series of scrolls depicting the jataka tales, with rather quaint (and difficult to interpret) explanations in English.

Tomb and Temple of Marshal Le Van Duyet
126 Dinh Tien Hoang St, a 10- to 15-min cyclo ride across the Thi Nghe Channel and almost into the suburbs, 0500-1800.

Le Van Duyet was a highly respected Vietnamese soldier who put down the Tay Son Rebellion and who died in 1831. The pagoda was renovated in 1937 – a plaque on the left lists those who made donations to the renovation fund. The main sanctuary contains a weird assortment of objects: a stuffed tiger, a miniature mountain, whale baleen, spears and other weapons of war. Much of the collection is made up of the Marshal's personal possessions. In front of the temple is the tomb itself, surrounded by a low wall and flanked by two guardian lions and two lotus buds. The pagoda's attractive roof is best seen from the tomb.

Museum of Vietnamese Traditional Medicine
41 Hoang Du Khuong St, District 10, T08-386 42430, www.fitomuseum.com.vn, daily 0830-1730.

A fascinating exploration into traditional medicine with 3000 exhibits including instruments, manuscripts, ceramic jars and model of a 19th-century pharmacy.

Around Ho Chi Minh City

there isn't much to see around the city

The Cu Chi Tunnels are the most popular day trip, followed closely by an excursion to the Mekong Delta, especially My Tho (see page 48). It is possible to get to the coast and back in a day by visiting Vung Tau, but this is not a particularly appealing destination for most. Ho Chi Minh City does, on the other hand, have several out-of-town sports facilities with three golf courses and the exhilarating Saigon Water Park all within less than an hour's drive (see page 44).

Cu Chi Tunnels
Most visitors reach Cu Chi on a tour or charter a car and include a visit to Tay Ninh – see below. Regular buses leave for Cu Chi town from the Mien Tay station (Cholon) and the Ham Nghi station; from Cu Chi it is necessary to take a taxi to the tunnels or the infrequent Ben Suc bus, 10 km. It is also possible to take a motorbike from Ho Chi Minh City and back but the road is becoming increasingly dangerous with fast and heavy traffic. Daily 0700-1630, 90,000d.

Cu Chi Tunnels are about 40 km northwest of Ho Chi Minh City. Cu Chi town is on the main road to Tay Ninh and the Cao Dai temple and both the tunnels and the temple can be visited in a single day trip. Dug by the Viet Minh, who began work in 1948, they were later expanded by the People's Liberation Armed Forces (PLAF, or Viet Cong, VC, see page 114) and used for storage and refuge, and contained sleeping quarters, hospitals and schools. Between 1960 and 1970, 200 km of tunnels were built. At the height of their usage, some 300,000 were living underground. The width of the tunnel entry at ground level was 22 cm by 30 cm. The tunnels are too narrow for most Westerners, but a short section of the 250 km of tunnels has been especially widened to allow tourists to share the experience. Tall or large people might still find it a claustrophobic squeeze.

Cu Chi was one of the most fervently communist of the districts around Ho Chi Minh City and the tunnels were used as the base from which the PLAF mounted the operations of the Tet Offensive in 1968. Communist cadres were active in this area of rubber plantations, even before the Second World War. Vann and Ramsey, two American soldiers, were to notice the difference between this area and other parts of the south in the early 1960s: "No children laughed and shouted for gum and candy in these hamlets. Everyone, adult and child, had a cold look" (*A Bright Shining Lie*, Sheehan 1989).

When the Americans first discovered this underground base on their doorstep (Dong Du GI base was nearby) they would simply pump CS gas down the tunnel openings and then set explosives. They also pumped river water in and used German Shepherd dogs to smell out air holes. The VC, however, smothered the holes in garlic to deter the dogs. They also used cotton from the cotton tree – kapok – to stifle the smoke from cooking; 40,000 VC were killed in the tunnels in 10 years. Later, realizing that the tunnels might also yield valuable intelligence, volunteer 'tunnel rats' were sent into the earth to capture prisoners.

Cu Chi district was a free-fire zone and was assaulted using the full battery of ecological warfare. Defoliants were sprayed and 20 tonne Rome Ploughs carved up the area in the search for tunnels. It was said that even a crow flying over Cu Chi district had to carry its own lunch. Later it was also carpet bombed with 50,000 tonnes dropped on the area in 10 years.

At **Cu Chi 1** (Ben Dinh) ① *90,000d*, visitors are shown a somewhat antique but nevertheless interesting film of the tunnels during the war before being taken into the tunnels and seeing some of the rooms and the booby traps the GIs encountered. The VC survived on just cassava for up to three months and at both places you will be invited to taste some dipped in salt, sesame, sugar and peanuts. You will also be invited to a firing range to try your hand with ancient AK47s at a buck a bang.

Cu Chi 2 (Ben Duoc), has a temple, the **Ben Duoc Temple**, in memory of the 50,000 Saigon dead; the exterior is covered in mosaic murals. It stands in front of a rather beautiful sculpture of a tear called *Symbol of the Country's Spiritual Soul*.

Near the tunnels is the Cu Chi graveyard for patriots with 8000 graves. It has a very interesting large and striking bas-relief of war images along the perimeter of the entrance to the cemetery.

Cao Dai Great Temple

Ceremonies are held each day at 0600, 1200, 1800 and 2400, visitors can watch from the cathedral's balcony. Visitors should not enter the central portion of the nave – keep to the side aisles – and also should not wander in and out during services. If you go in at the beginning of the service you should stay until the end (1 hr). Take a tour, or charter a car in Ho Chi Minh City. Regular buses leave for Tay Ninh, via Cu Chi, from Mien Tay station (2½ hrs) or motorbike.

Tay Ninh, the home of the temple, is 96 km northwest of Ho Chi Minh City and 64 km further on from Cu Chi town. It can be visited on a day trip from the city and can easily be combined with a visit to the Cu Chi tunnels. The idiosyncratic Cao Dai Great Temple, the 'cathedral' of the Cao Dai religion, is the main reason to visit the town.

The Cao Dai Great Temple, built in 1880, is set within a very large complex of schools and administrative buildings, all washed in pastel yellow. The twin-towered cathedral is European in inspiration but with distinct oriental features. On the façade are figures of Cao Dai saints in high relief and at the entrance is a painting depicting Victor Hugo flanked by the Vietnamese poet Nguyen Binh Khiem and the Chinese nationalist Sun Yat Sen. The latter holds an inkstone, symbolizing, strangely, the link between Confucianism and Christianity. Novelist Graham Greene in *The Quiet American* called it "The Walt Disney Fantasia of the East". Monsieur Ferry, an acquaintance of Norman Lewis, described the cathedral in even more outlandish terms, saying it "looked like a fantasy from the brain of Disney, and all the faiths of the Orient had been ransacked to create the pompous ritual...". Lewis himself was clearly unimpressed with the structure and the religion, writing in *A Dragon Apparent* that "This cathedral must be the most outrageously vulgar building ever to have been erected with serious intent".

After removing shoes and hats, women enter the cathedral through a door to the left, men to the right, and they then proceed down their respective aisles towards the altar, usually accompanied by a Cao Dai priest dressed in white with a black turban. During services they don red, blue and yellow robes signifying Confucianism, Taoism and Buddhism respectively. The men in coloured robes sporting an embroidered divine eye on their costumes are more senior. During services, on the balcony at the back of the cathedral, a group of men play a stringed instrument called a Dan Co between their feet using a bow; women sing as they play.

Two rows of pink pillars entwined with green dragons line the nave, leading up to the main altar which supports a large globe on which is painted a single staring eye – the divine, all-seeing-eye. The roof is blue and dotted with clouds, representing the heavens, and the walls are pierced by open, lattice-work windows with the divine eye as the centrepiece to the window design. At the back of the cathedral is a sculpture of Pham Com Tac, the last pope and one of the religion's founders who died in 1957. He stands on flowers surrounded by huge brown snakes and is flanked by his two assistants; one is the leader of spirits, the other the leader of materialism.

There are nine columns and nine steps to the cathedral representing the nine steps to heaven. Above the altar is the Cao Dai pantheon: at the top in the centre is Sakyamuni Buddha. Next to him on the left is Lao Tzu, master of Taosim. Left of Lao Tzu, is Quan Am, Goddess of Mercy, sitting on a lotus blossom. On the other side of the Buddha statue is Confucius. Right of the sage is the red-faced Chinese God of War and Soldiers, Quan Cong. Below Sakyamuni Buddha is the poet and leader of the Chinese saints, Li Ti Pei. Below him is Jesus and below Christ is Jiang Zhia, master of Geniism.

About 500 m from the cathedral (turn right when facing the main façade) is the **Doan Ket**, a formal garden.

The town of Tay Ninh also has a good **market** and some **Cham temples** 1 km to the southwest of the town.

Black Lady Mountain (Nui Ba Den)
Buses go from the bus station on Cach Mang Tam Tang St by the western edge of Tan Son Nhat Airport. From Tay Ninh to Nui Ba Den go by taxi. There is now a cable car to the summit.

Also known as *Nui Ba Den*, Black Lady Mountain is 10 km to the northeast of Tay Ninh and 106 km from Ho Chi Minh City. The peak rises dramatically from the plain to a height of almost 1000 m and can be seen in the distance, to the right, on entering Tay Ninh. The Black Lady was a certain Ly Thi Huong who, while her lover was bravely fighting the occupying forces, was ordered to marry the son of a local mandarin. Rather than complying, she threw herself from the mountain. Another version of this story is that she was kidnapped by local scoundrels. A number of shrines to the Black Woman are located on the mountain, and pilgrims still visit the site. Fierce battles were also fought here between the French and Americans, and the Viet Minh. There are excellent views of the surrounding plain from the summit reached by cable car.

Border crossings to Cambodia
The province of Tay Ninh borders Cambodia and, before the 17th century, was part of the Khmer Kingdom. Between 1975 and December 1978, soldiers of Pol Pot's Khmer Rouge periodically attacked villages in this province, killing the men and raping the women. Ostensibly, it was in order to stop these incursions that the Vietnamese army invaded Cambodia on Christmas Day 1978, taking Phnom Penh by January 1979.

Travellers taking the bus to Phnom Penh from Ho Chi Minh City cross at **Moc Bai** (Bavet in Cambodia). Cambodian visas are available at the border; Vietnamese visas are not.

Tourist information

Tourist Information Center
*92-96 Nguyen Hue St, T08-8322 6033,
www.ticvietnam.com. Daily 0800-2100.*
Provides free information,
hotel reservations, an ATM
and currency exchange.

Where to stay

City centre

$$$$ Caravelle
*19 Lam Son Sq, T08-3823 4999,
www.caravellehotel.com.*
Central and one of HCMC's top hotels,
this is a true heritage option having
opened in 1959, although a new tower
was added in 1998. Very comfortable
with 335 rooms, fitted out with all the
mod cons, many with incredible views
and well-trained and friendly staff.
Breakfast is sumptuous and filling and
Restaurant Nineteen, see below, serves
a fantastic buffet lunch and dinner.
Saigon Saigon, see page 40, the roof-
top bar, draws the crowds until the early
hours and offers knockout veiws. A suite
of boutique shops plus a pool and Qi Spa
complete the luxury experience.

$$$$ Continental
*132-134, Dong Khoi St, T08-3829 9201,
www.continentalhotel.com.vn.*
Built in 1880 and renovated in 1989, the
Continental has an air of faded colonial
splendour. There are now smarter
options in town in this price bracket,
but few can match it for history.

$$$$ Grand
*8 Dong Khoi St, T08-3823 0163,
www.grandhotel.vn.*
A 1930s building in the heart of the
shopping district that might look more
comfortable on Brighton's seafront than
in HCMC. It was renovated 10 years ago
but the stained glass and marble staircase
have largely survived the process. Lovely
pool (try to get a pool-side room) and a
very reasonably priced restaurant.

$$$$ Park Hyatt Saigon
*2 Lam Son Sq, T08-3824 1234,
www.saigon.park.hyatt.com.*
This striking hotel is in a class of its own.
It exudes elegance and style and its
location north of the Opera House is
unrivalled. Works of art are hung in the
lobby, rooms are classically furnished in
French colonial style but with modern
touches; the pool area is lovely; the
wonderful lounge area features a baby
grand piano and there are a number of
very good restaurants. **Square One**, is an
excellent restaurant with open kitchens
and displays. There's also a fitness centre
and spa.

$$$$ Renaissance Riverside
*8-15 Ton Duc Thang St, T08-3822 0033,
www.marriott.com.*
Overlooking the water, this upmarket
option offers some of the finest views
in the city in the riverside rooms. It also
has Vietnam's highest atrium. Several
excellent restaurants including Kabin
Chinese restaurant and attractive pool.
Executive floors provide breakfast and
all-day snacks.

$$$$ Rex
*141 Nguyen Hué Blvd, T08-3829 2185,
www.rexhotelvietnam.com.*
A historically important hotel in the heart
of Saigon. During the Vietnam War the
American Information Service made

its base at the hotel and it became a base for daily press briefings to foreign correspondents known as the five o'clock follies. There is now a newer fabulous side extension that has become the principal entrance complete with high-end shopping arcade. The original lobby is decorated entirely in wood and tastefully furnished with wicker chairs. New wing premium rooms are very smart, if a little business-like; cheaper 'Superior' rooms in the old wing have small bathtub and are interior facing.

$$$$ Sheraton
88 Dong Khoi St, T08-3827 2828, www.sheraton.com/saigon.
This tall glass-clad hotel has certainly proved popular since it opened in late 2003. There is very good lunch and dinner on offer at the **Saigon Café**, and Level 23, with its brilliant views across HCMC, is recommended for a night-time drink. The hotel, with modern, stylish rooms is sandwiched into a downtown street and boasts boutique shops, a gorgeous pool, a spa and tennis courts.

$$$$ Sofitel Plaza Saigon
17 Le Duan St, T08-3824 1555, www.sofitel.com.
A smart, fashionable and comfortable hotel with a fantastic roof-top pool surrounded by frangipani plants. Gets rave reviews for its excellent service.

$$$ EMM Hotel Saigon
157 Pasteur, T08-3936 2100, www.emmhotels.com.
This is the first of what promises to be a new chain of funky modern hotels in Vietnam. Set over 2 floors, the rooms are very well furnished with modern touches and prints of the city. A good buffet breakfast is served in a cool restaurant space with an outdoor area offering

great views. A reasonable gym and a travel desk for tour bookings.

$$$ Lan Lan Hotel 2
46 Thu Khoa Huan, T08-3822 7926, www.lanlanhotel.com.vn.
Excellent value rooms. Those on the upper floors have expansive views of the city. Helpful staff, buffet breakfast and in-room wifi. Has a 2nd location on the same road.

$$ Ho Sen
4B-4C Thi Sach St, T08-3823 2281, www.hosenhotel.com.vn.
This rather bland-looking hotel is nonetheless very clean and in a great location, so it's a good find. Rooms are very quiet and fairly spacious. Staff are friendly and helpful.

$$ Tan Hai Long 3
65 Ho Tung Mau St, T08-3915 1888, www.thlhotelgroup.com.
A well-positioned hotel with small rooms, good-sized bathrooms and good service. Great value.

Pham Ngu Lao

$$ Beautiful Saigon
62 Bui Vien St, T08-3836 4852, www.beautifulsaigonhotel.com.
A good addition to the backpacker zone replacing an old hotel, this is more for the flashpackers and welcome it is too. Very nice smart and tidy rooms all with mod cons, Wi-Fi and breakfast at fair prices and recommended by happy guests.

$ Chau Long Mini Hotel
185/8 Pham Ngu La, T08-3836 9667.
Simple, clean rooms, some with balconies. Family-run and welcoming. Great budget option.

$ Long Hostel
373/10 Pham Ngu Lao, T08-3836 0184,
longhomestay@yahoo.com.
Run by the supremely friendly and
charming Ms Long, a retired teacher
who serves tea and fruit to guests on
arrival, this hotel has spotless rooms, all
with TV and a/c. Highly recommended.
Book ahead.

Outer Ho Chi Minh City

$$$$ Thao Dien Village
195 Nguyen Van Huong St, Thao Dien
Ward, Q2, T08-3744 6458,
www.thaodienvillage.com.
A stylish boutique hotel and spa resort in
the expat enclave. Lovely to escape the
hustle of downtown. Popular restaurant.
Also a great spa and pool.

Restaurants

HCMC has a rich culinary tradition
and, as home to people from most
of the world's imagined corners, its
cooking is diverse. You could quite
easily eat a different national cuisine
every night for several weeks. French
food is well represented and there are
many restaurants from neighbouring
Asian countries especially Japan, Korea,
China and Thailand. The area between
Le Thanh Ton and Hai Ba Trung streets
has become a 'Little Tokyo' and 'Little
Seoul' on account of the number of
Japanese and Korean restaurants.

Pham Ngu Lao, the backpacker area, is
chock-a-block with low-cost restaurants
many of which are just as good as the
more expensive places elsewhere. Do
not overlook street-side stalls where
staples include of *pho* (noodle soup),
bánh xeo (savoury pancakes), *cha
giò* (spring rolls) and *banh mi pate*
(baguettes stuffed with pâté and salad),
all usually fresh and very cheap. The
major hotels all have gourmet shops
selling bread and pastries. Eating out
is an informal business; suits are not
necessary anywhere, and in Pham Ngu
Lao expect shorts and sandals.

The Ben Thanh night market
(see page 20) is a major draw for
Vietnamese and overseas visitors.
Stalls are set up at dusk and traffic
suppressed. There is a good range of
inexpensive foodstall dishes and lots of
noodles; it stays open until around 2300.

City centre

$$$ An Vien
178A Hai Ba Trung St, T08-3824 3877.
Daily 1200-2300.
Excellent and intimate restaurant
that serves the most fragrant rice in
Vietnam. Attentive service and rich
decor. The *banh xeo* and crispy fried
squid are recommended.

$$$ Hoa Tuc
74 Hai Ba Trung St, T08-3825 1676.
Open 1000-2230.
Set in the buzzing Hai Ba Trung
courtyard space. Dine amid the art deco
accents on soft shell crab or a salad of
pink pomelo, squid and crab with herbs.
The desserts are tantalizing.

$$$ La Fourchette
9 Ngo Duc Ke St, T08-3829 8143.
Daily 1200-1430, 1830-2230.
Truly excellent and authentic French
bistro offering a warm welcome, well-
prepared dishes and generous portions

> **Tip...**
> If Japanese food is your thing, eat
> up. HCMC, it is said, has some of the
> cheapest Japanese food in the world.

of tender local steak. Booking advised. Recommended.

$$$ San Fu Lou
76A le Lai St, T08-3823 9513, www.sanfulou.com.
Opened in 2014, this is an uber-cool venue with sharp service offering excellent dim sum with some classic dumplings and some unique creations. A buzzing joint. Best to dine with a group and try as much as possible.

$$$ Sorae Sushi
AB Tower, 76A Le Lai St, T08-3827 2372, www.soraesushi.com.
Outrageously slick space on the upper floors of the AB Tower affording awesome views through massive floor-to-ceiling windows, although the sleek interior means there is plenty for the eyes inside. The food is first-rate, as is the service. Truly high-end dining that would slot right in among London's finest. Expect to do some serious damage to your wallet if you arrive hungry or in the mood for a fine sake.

$$$-$$ The Refinery
74 Hai Ba Trung St, T08-3823 0509. Open 1100-2300.
This former opium factory (through the arch and on the left) is a little understated in its reincarnation. It could equally be slotted into this guide's 'bar' section thanks to the great cocktails, but it also does some quality dishes such as the herb-encrusted steak and grilled barramundi. Always busy with a good atmosphere.

$$ Augustin
10D Nguyen Thiep St, T0890-382966, 294 8081. Mon-Sat 1100, 1130-1400 and 1800-2230.
Fairly priced and some of the best, unstuffy French cooking in HCMC;

tables pretty closely packed, congenial atmosphere. Excellent onion soup, baked clams and rack of lamb.

$$ Elbow Room
52 Pasteur St, T08-3821 4327, www.elbowroom.com.vn.
Cosy, bare-brick American diner serving the best burgers in town and awesome shakes – don't miss the vanilla version.

$$ Guc Cach
10 Dang Tat, T08-4801 4410.
The 2nd restaurant run by a local architect, **Guc Cach** is known for its great atmosphere, old school Saigon decor and excellent Vietnamese fare. The soft shell crab is superb. Recommended.

$$ KOTO Saigon
151A Hai Ba Trung St, T08-3934 9151, www.koto.com.au.
KOTO stands for Know One, Teach One. It is a training restaurant for disadvantaged young people, plus it serves good food, so a visit here is a no brainer. Serves a selection of Vietnamese classics alongside other Southeast Asian options and a handful of Belgian dishes.

$$ Quan Ut Ut
168 Vo Van Kiet, T9-3914 4500, www.quanutut.com.
Set over 3 floors with canal views, this ever-buzzing joint is a temple for grilled meat lovers. Tender ribs cooked to pefection, first-rate mac and cheese and a burger that's a solid contender for the best in town. Also serves a very tasty pale ale. A top spot.

$$-$ Ashoka
17A/10 Le Thanh Ton St, T08-3823 1372. Daily 1100-1400, 1700-2230.
Indian restaurant popular with expats. Highlights are the mutton shami kebab, prawn vindaloo and kadhai fish –

barbecued chunks of fresh fish cooked in *kadhai* (a traditional Indian-style wok with Peshwari ground spices and sautéd with onion and tomatoes).

$ 13 Ngo Duc Ke
15 Ngo Duc Ke St, T08-3823 9314.
Daily 0600-2230.
Fresh, well cooked, honest Vietnamese fare. Chicken in lemongrass is a great favourite and *bo luc lac* melts in the mouth. Popular with locals.

$ Au Parc
23 Han Thuyen St, T08-3829 2772.
Mon-Sat 0730-2230, Sun 0800-1700.
Facing on to the park in front of the old Presidential Palace, this stylish café serves a some delicious Greek and Turkish options, sandwiches, salads, juices and drinks. Also does a good Sunday brunch that's popular with the city's expats.

$ Hoang Yen
5-7 Ngo Duc Ke St, T08-3823 1101.
Daily 1000-2200.
Plain setting and decor but absolutely fabulous Vietnamese dishes, as the throngs of local lunchtime customers testify. Soups and chicken dishes are ravishing.

$ Pho Hoa Pasteur
260C Pasteur St. Daily 0600-2400.
Probably the best known *pho* restaurant and packed with customers. The *pho* costs more than average, but it is good quality and there are around 10 varieties on the English menu.

Cafés

Cooku'nest Café
13 Tu Xuong St, Q3, T08-2241 2043.
This kooky venue looks like it has been hoiked off an Alpine slope.

It's a pine cabin equipped with cuckoo clock. Sit upstairs on the floor next to tiny tables and mingle with the local student gang. There's live music every night. Wi-Fi available.

Kem Bach Dang
26-28 Le Loi Blvd.
On opposite corners of Pasteur St. A very popular café serving fruit juice, shakes and ice cream. Try the coconut ice cream (*kem dua*) served in a coconut.

La Fenêtre Soleil
2nd floor, 135 Le Thanh Ton St (entrance at 125 Nam Ky Khoi Nghia St), T08-3822 5209. Mon-Sat, café 0900-1900, bar 1900-2400.
Don't be put off by the slightly grimy side entrance; clamber up into the boho-Indochine world of this gorgeous café/bar, artfully cluttered with antiques, lamps, comfy sofas and home-made cakes, muffins, smoothies and other delights. The high-energy drinks of mint, passionfruit and ginger juice are lovely. Highly recommended.

Tous les Jours
180 Hai Ba Trung St, Q3, and also in several other locations including Diamond Plaza, T08-3823 8302. Open 0600-2300.
A smorgasbord of cakes and pastries awaits the hungry visitor.

Pham Ngu Lao
Nearly all these restaurants are open all day every day from early or mid-morning until 2230 or later – when the last customer leaves, as they like to say. All are geared to Westerners and their habits and tastes and in just about all of them there will be at least one person who speaks English and French. Most tend to be cheap but prices have risen in recent times; do check.

Betel nut

Betel nut has been a stimulant for the Vietnamese for hundreds of years. The ingredients combine the egg-shaped betel palm (*Areca catechu*) nut (*cau*) with Piper betel vine leaves (*trau*) and lime. When chewed (known as *An trau*) the ingredients stain the mouth and lips and red juice can often be seen dribbling down the chins of users. It often stains teeth black due to the polyphenol in the nut and leaf, which is considered attractive. The origin of the substance lies in Vietnamese legend and its use is found at weddings where a betel quid (a combination of powdered betel nut, betel leaves, lime and other flavourings) is laid out for guests. The areca nut is also a customary wedding gift given to the bride's family by the bridegroom's family. Betel and areca nuts are also presented at Tet (Lunar New Year).

$$ Good Morning Vietnam
197 De Tham St, T08-3837 1894.
Open 0900-2400.
One of the popular chain of Italian restaurants in southern Vietnam. Italian owned and run and serving up Italian flavours. Their pizzas are delicious and salads are good.

$ Cafe Zoom
169A De Tham St, T1222 993585,
www.vietnamvespaadventure.com.
Laid-back vibe and venue serving top burgers and fries – look for the classic Vespas lined up out front.

$ Kim Café
268 De Tham St, T08-3836 8122.
Open from early till late.
Wide range of food, popular with travellers.

Cholon

In Cholon you'll find a few cavernous Chinese restaurants and also lots of tiny streetside noodle stands.

$$ Tien Phat
18 Ky Hoa St, Q9, T08-3853 6217.

Conveniently located near the temples of Cholon. Open for breakfast and lunch. Specializes in dim sum. There is a good selection all freshly prepared, nice with hot tea.

Outer Ho Chi Minh City

$$$ The Deck
38 Nguyen U Di, An Phu, Q2, T08-3744 6322, www.thedecksaigon.com.
A very popular expat spot with tables on a deck right on the Saigon River. The food is, in the main, delicious and creative.

$$$-$$ Le Bordeaux
72 D2 St, Cu Xa Van Thanh Bac, Q Binh Thanh, T08-3899 9831, www.restaurant-lebordeaux.com.vn. Mon 1830-2130, Tue-Sat 1130-1330, 1830-2130.
Rather a tragedy that it is in such an awkward location. If you can find it you are in for a treat. Lovely decor and warm atmosphere, receives high accolades for its French cuisine but it is not cheap.

Food stalls

For those staying centrally, a wander along Nguyen Thai Binh is recommended. At number 75 you'll find **Pho Phuong Bac** which sells good *pho* in the morning and a variety of great dished throughout the day and evening. All along this road there are small eateries selling everything from spring rolls to rice buffets (*com bing dan*), most of which are packed out with office workers during lunch time. Nearby at 40 Ton That Dam St, **Hu Tieu Nam Loi** is a long-running chicken and fish *hu tieu* joint that is worth seeking out. Just north of the centre on the south side of Tan Dinh is another good area to seek out food, including excellent *banh xeo*. The stalls in Benh Thanh shouldn't be overlooked; the *banh canh cua* (40,000d) and *nuoc mia* (sugarcane juice, 10,000d) at stall 1028 are delectable. Over in District 4, Vinh Kanh St is the place to head for roadside seafood. The great scallops and crab claws at **Can An Hien** (number 12) are mouth watering. **Anh Thu**, 49 Dinh Cong Trang St, and other stalls nearby on the south side of Tan Dinh market serve *cha gio*, *banh xeo* and *bi cuon*.

Cafés

A swathe of new thoughtfully designed, original, one-off cafés have opened, invigorating the city's caffeine scene. Alongside this, Starbucks has entered the fray alongside chains including **Gloria Jean's**, **Coffee Bean** and **Tea Leaf**.

A Cafe
15 Huynh Khuong Ninh.
Run by artist, Nguyen Thanh Truc, this is real find. The intimate café offers a peaceful place to enjoy a good book, quiet conversation and superb coffee. Beans are roasted on-site and the coffee can be brewed in every way imaginable. Well worth going out of your way for.

Cliché Café
20 Tran Cav Van, T08-3822 0412.
Open 0800-1030.
Head straight upstairs to take a seat among all manner of knick knacks in this popular café. Serves excellent, strong iced coffee and good value set lunches.

ID
34D Thu Khoa Huan. Open 0800-2230.
Plenty of comfortable seating, low lighting, vinyl nailed to the walls, and, like most cafés in this vein, a collection of retro audio equipment. A good place to relax.

La Fenêtre Soleil
44 Ly Tu Trong St, T08-3824 5994.
This place has moved and reinvented itself with a cool café vibe by day but regular DJ and salsa moves by night.

La Rotunde
77B Ham Nghi, T0983-889935.
More like somebody's Indochina apartment than a public café, this is a wonderfully unique café space that also serves an excellent Vietnamese buffet lunch.

L'Usine
151 Dong Khoi, District 1, T08-6674,
www.lusinespace.com.
Part café, part lifestyle store, **L'Usine** is an uber cool venue. Legendary cupcakes, delicious freshly cut sandwiches and perfect shakes. A hipster hangout. There is also now a 2nd branch on Le Loi.

Things
14 Ton That Dam. Open 0900-2200.
Shabby chic, with such oddities as a cupboard full of Converse and a bed in the corner. Friendly owner Linh (also a TV presenter) is a good source of what's new in town. Very quirky.

Velo de Piste
10 Pasteur.

By day this café is referred to as Heritage, but later in the afternoon tables made from suitcases perched on stools appear on the pavement and the place takes on a decidedly Shoreditch-esque hipster vibe. Single speed bikes hang from the walls and a collection of old typewriters sit on shelves.

The Workshop
27 Ngo Duc Ke St.

An extremely sleek coffee shop that makes the very best of the period building that houses it, with exposed brick, huge windows and chunky wooden tables. Run by self-professed coffee nerds Dung and Duy with consultation from one of Asia's leading coffee minds, Will Frith. The first-rate coffee is roasted on the premises. Highly recommended.

Bars and clubs

Along with the influx of foreigners and the freeing up of Vietnamese society has come a rapid increase in the number of bars in HCMC and they cater to just about all tastes. Everything is on offer, from roadside plastic chair drinking to uber-chic sky bar cocktails with killer views.

Alibi
5A Nguyen Sieu St, T08-3825 6257, www.alibi.vn.

Goes on after hours and is a magnet for tourists and expats. Consistently popular and in a new location. Very smooth 2-floor venue decorated with deep reds and pictures of old Saigon. Remains under the tourist radar. Weekend DJs, a long wine list and a well-rounded menu to boot.

Apocalypse Now
2BCD Thi Sach St, T08-3825 6124.

Cover charges at weekends. Open until 0300/0400. This legendary venue remains one of the most popular and successful bars and clubs in HCMC. Draws a very wide cross section of punters of all ages and nationalities. DJs often spin a fun/cheesey selection of floor fillers. Can take on a slight meat market feel in the wee hours.

Blanchy's Tash
95 Hai Ba Trung, T09-0902 8293, www. blanchystash.com. Open 1100-late.

Upscale bar. Weekends are rammed downstairs where music blasts, while the rooftop terrace is more relaxed. Regular DJ nights, excellent cocktails, and an expensive, well-regarded restaurant.

Blue Gecko
31 Ly Tu Trong St, T08-3824 3483, www.bluegeckosaigon.com.

This bar has been adopted by HCMC's Australian community so expect cold beer and Australian flags above the pool table.

Chill Skybar
76A Le Lai, District 1, T09-3272 0730, www.chillsaigon.com. Open 1600-late.

With a view that has to be seen to be believed, a mixologist of international acclaim and the kind of crowd that means you'll want to dress your best (flip flops and shorts are not permitted), **Chill Skybar** is a rather pretentious, but worth a look to see Saigon's more lavish side. The cocktails are wallet-busting.

Cloud 9
2 Cong Truong Quoc Te, District 3, T08-0948-343399.

Another of the city's roof-top bars, **Cloud 9** is a chic nightspot with contemporary design and excellent drinks. Dress sharp.

La Habana
6 Cao Ba Quat, T08-3829 5180, www.lahabana-saigon.com.
Latin beats and mojitos make for a great night out, particularly on salsa nights when the dance floor fills with local talent keen to show off their skills. Serves the finest paella in town.

Le Pub
175/22 Pham Ngu Lao, T08-3837 7679. Open 0900-2400.
The no-nonsense pub formula here makes a good place for a cold beer although an awful music policy can sometimes make it impossible to bear. Western and Vietnamese food.

OMG bar
15 Nguyen An Ninh, T09-3720 0222.
While it will be a little heavy on the neon for some tastes, the reason to drink here isn't to enjoy the decor, but to enjoy the excellent view of downtown HCMC, looking right out across Ben Thanh market and the Bitexco Tower. Also serves food and holds regular party nights.

Pasteur Street Brewing Company
144 Paster St, T9-0551 4782.
The first craft beer establishment in town, this is a very cool operation run by beer geeks who have scoured Vietnam to come up with interesting locally brewed beers with bite. Sleek decor, a small menu of food designed to complement the beer and knowledgable staff make this a must for any beer connoisseur.

Rex Hotel Bar
See Where to stay, above.
An open-air rooftop bar which has a kitsch revolving crown. There are good views, cooling breeze, snacks and meals – and a link with history (page 11).

Saigon Saigon
10th floor, Caravelle Hotel, 19 Lam Son Sq, T08-3824 3999.
Breezy and cool, with large comfortable chairs and superb views by day and night. Excellent cocktails but not cheap.

Vasco's
74/7D Hai Ba Trung St, T08-3824 2888. Open 1600-2400.
A hugely popular spot in a great courtyard setting. A great place to kick off an evening out. Good happy hour offers.

Yoko
22A Nguyen Thi Dieu, T08-3933 0577. Open 1800-2400.
Ever busy live music venue. Slightly more rock and underground than the **Acoustic Cafe** over on Ngo Thoi Nhiem. An excellent night out. Arrive early to bag a seat.

Entertainment

Cinemas
French Cultural Institute (Idecaf), *31 Thai Van Lung, T08-3829 5451, www. idecaf.gov.vn.* Shows French films. **Lotte Cinema,** *Diamond Plaza, 34 Le Duan St, www.lottecinemavn.com.* The cinema on the 13th floor of this shopping centre screens English-language films.

Traditional music and opera
Conservatory of Music (Nhac Vien Thanh Pho Ho Chi Minh), *112 Nguyen Du St, T08-3824 3774, www.hcmcons.vn.* Traditional Vietnamese music and classical music concerts are performed by the young students who study music here and sometimes by local and visiting musicians.

Opera House, *Lam Son Sq, T08-3832 2009, www.hbso.org.vn.* Regular classical concerts, opera and ballet. Check the website for upcoming shows.

Water puppetry
Golden Dragon Water Puppet Theatre, *55B Nguyen Thi Minh Khai St, T08-3930 2196, www.thaiduongtheatre.com.* A 50-min performance daily at 1700, 1830 and 1945.
Museum of Vietnamese History, *2 Nguyen Binh Khiem St, T08-3829 8146, www.baotanglichsuvn.com.* There are daily 15-min water puppetry performances in the tiny theatre in an outdoor, covered part of the museum, see page 19. The advantage of this performance over the Hanoi theatre is that the audience can get closer to the puppetry and there is better light.

Shopping

Antiques
Most shops are on **Dong Khoi**, **Mac Thi Buoi** and **Ngo Duc Ke** streets. For the knowledgeable, there are bargains to be found, especially Chinese and Vietnamese ceramics – however you will need an export permit to get them out of the country (see page 156). Also available are old watches, colonial bric-a-brac, lacquerware and carvings, etc. For the less touristy stuff, visitors would be advised to spend an hour or so browsing the treasure trove shops in **Le Cong Trieu St** (aka **Antique St**). It runs between Nam Ky Khoi Nghia and Pho Duc Chinh streets just south of Ben Thanh Market. Among the bric-a-brac and tat are some interesting items of furniture, statuary, stamps, candlesticks, fans, badges and ceramics. Bargaining is the order of the day and some pretty good deals can be struck.

Art galleries
Craig Thomas Gallery, *27i Tran Nhat Duat, T09-0388 8431, www.cthomasgallery.com. Tue-Sat 1200-1800, Sun 1200-1700.* Exhibitions of young, emerging and mid-career Vietnamese contemporary artists.
Galerie Quynh, *Dong Khoi, T08-3836 8019, www.galeriequynh.com. Tue-Sat 1000-1800.* Promotes a select group of Vietnamese artists and plays host to travelling international exhibitions.
San Art, *ground floor, 48/7 Pham Viet Chanh, T08-3840 0898, www.san-art.org. Tue-Sat 1030-1830.* Artist-run exhibition space and reading room. Regular programme of events, including lectures.

Bicycles
As well as the cheap shops along Le Thanh Ton St, close to the Ben Thanh Market there are now a handful of shops selling high quality international brands including **Saigon Cycles** which stocks Surly and Trek – **Skygarden**, Phu My Hung, www.xedapcaocap.com.

Books, magazines and maps
Books and magazines All foreigners around Pham Ngu Lao and De Tham streets are game to the numerous booksellers who hawk mountains of pirate books under their arms. The latest bestsellers together with enduring classics (ie *The Quiet American*) can be picked up for a couple of dollars.
Artbook, *43 Dong Khoi St, T08-3910 3518, www.artbookvn.com.* For art, architecture and coffee table books.
Fahasa, *40 Nguyen Hue Blvd, T08-3912 5358, www.fahasasg.com.* A very large store with dozens of English titles and magazines.

Maps HCMC has the best selection of maps in Vietnam, at stalls on Le Loi Blvd between Dong Khoi St and Nguyen Hue Blvd. Bargain hard – the bookshops are probably cheaper.

Western newspapers and magazines
Sold in the main hotels. Same day *Bangkok Post* and *The Nation* newspapers (English-language Thai papers), and up-to-date *Financial Times*, *Straits Times*, *South China Morning Post*, *Newsweek* and *The Economist*, available from larger bookshops.

Ceramics
Vietnam has a ceramics tradition going back hundreds of years. There has been a renaissance of this art in the past decade. Shops selling new and antique (or antique-looking ceramics) abound on the main shopping streets of **Dong Khoi** and **Le Thanh Ton**. There is a lot of traditional Chinese-looking blue and white and also very attractive celadon green, often with a crackled glaze. There are many other styles and finishes as local craftsmen brush the dust off old ideas and come up with new ones. **Nga Shop**, see Lacquerware, below, has a good range.

Clothing, silk and *ao dai*
Dong Khoi is home to many excellent boutiques. Vietnamese silk and traditional dresses (*ao dai*) are to be found in the shops on here. A number of shops in De Tham St sell woven and embroidered goods including bags and clothes.
Devon London, *151 Dong Khoi, www. devonlondon.com.* Modern clothing from one of Vietnam's most promising young designers.
Ipa Nima, *77-79 Dong Khoi St and in the New World Hotel, T08-3822 3277,*
www.ipa-nima.com. Sister branch of the Hanoi store with sparkling bags and accessories.
Khaisilk, *107 Dong Khoi, T08-3829 1146.* **Khaisilk** belongs to Mr Khai's growing empire. He has a dozen shops around Vietnam. Beautifully made, quality silk products from dresses to scarves to ties can be found in this luxury outlet.

Department stores
Diamond Department Store, *Diamond Plaza 1st-4th floor, 34 Le Duan St, T08-3822 5500. Open 1000-1000.* HCMC's central a/c department store set over a couple of floors. It sells luxury goods, clothes with some Western brands, watches, bags and perfumes. There is also a small supermarket inside. A bowling alley complex and cinema dominate the top floor.
Parkson Plaza, *35 Bis-45 Le Thanh Ton St.* A high-end department store.

Foodstores
Shops specializing in Western staples, such as cornflakes, peanut butter and Marmite, abound on Ham Nghi St around Nos 62 and 64 (**Kim Thanh**). There are also now mini-marts, such as **Circle K**, on many of the streets downtown.
Annam Gourmet Hai Ba Trung, *16-18 Hai Ba Trung St, T08-3822 9332, www.annam-gourmet.com. Mon-Sat 0800-2100, Sun 1000-2000.* Local organic vegetables and other international delicacies at this new culinary emporium.

Gifts and handicrafts
Dogma, *43 Ton That Thiep, www.dogma. vietnam.com.* Sells propaganda posters, funky T-shirts and postcards.
Gaya, *1 Nguyen Van Trang St, corner of Le Lai St, T08-3925 2495, www. gayavietnam.com. Open 0900-2100.*

A 3-storey shop with heavenly items: exquisitely embroidered tablecloths, bamboo bowls, ceramics and large home items such as screens; also gorgeous and unusual silk designer clothes by, among others, Romyda Keth, based in Cambodia. If you like an item but it does not fit they will take your measurements but it could take a fortnight to make.

Mai Handicrafts, *298 Nguyen Trong Tuyen St, Q Tan Binh, T08-3844 0988.* A little way out of town but sells an interesting selection of goods, fabrics and handmade paper all made by disadvantaged people in small income-generating schemes.

Nagu, *132-134 Dong Khoi St (next to the Park Hyatt), www.zantoc.com.* Delicate embroidered silk products among other fashion, home and giftware.

Nguyen Freres, *2 Dong Khoi St, T08-3823 9459, www.nguyenfreres.com.* An absolute Aladdin's cave. Don't miss this – even if it's just to potter among the collectable items.

Saigon Kitsch, *43 Ton That Tiep St. Open 0900-2000.* This is the place to come for communist kitsch ranging from propaganda art posters to placemats and mugs. Also retro bags and funky jewellery on sale.

Jewellery

Jewellery is another industry that has flourished in recent years and there is something to suit most tastes. At the cheaper end there is a cluster of gold and jewellery shops around **Ben Thanh Market** and and also in the **International Trade Centre** on Nam Ky Khoi Nghia St. In these stalls because skilled labour is so cheap one rarely pays more than the weight of the item in silver or gold. At the higher end **Therese**, with a shop in the **Caravelle Hotel**, has established an international reputation.

Lacquerware

Vietnamese lacquerware has a long history, and a reputation of sorts (see page 139). Visitors to the workshop can witness the production process and, of course, buy the products if they wish. Lacquerware is available from many of the handicraft shops on Nguyen Hue Blvd and Dong Khoi St. Also from the **Lamson Lacquerware Factory**, 106 Nguyen Van Troi St (opposite **Omni Hotel**). Accepts Visa and MasterCard.

Duy Tan, *41 Ton That Thiep St, T08-382 3614. Open 1100-2000.* Pretty ceramics and lacquerware.

Nga Shop, *49-57 Dong Du St, T08-3823 8356, www.huongngafinearts.vn.* **Nga** has become one of the best-known lacquer stores as a result of her high-quality designs. Other top-quality rosewood and ceramic handicrafts suitable for souvenirs are available.

Linen

Good-quality linen tablecloths and sheets are avaliable from shops on Dong Khoi and Le Thanh Ton streets.

Outdoor gear

Vietnam produces a range of equipment for camping, such as walking boots, fleeces and rucksacks. Real and fake goods can be bought, especially from around Pham Ngu Lao and De Tham streets.

War surplus

From **Dan Sinh Market**, Yersin St, between Nguyen Thai Binh St and Nguyen Cong Tru St.

What to do

Bowling

Diamond Superbowl, *4th floor of Diamond Plaza, 34 Le Duan St, right behind the cathedral, T08-3825 7778, ext 12.* 24 lanes on the top floor, which also has a fast-food outlet, video games and plenty of pool tables.

Cookery classes

Saigon Cooking Class, *held at the new Hoa Tuc (see Restaurants), 74 Hai Ba Trung St, T08-3825 8485, www.saigoncookingclass.com.*
Vietnam Cookery Center, *362/8 Ung Van Khiem St, Q Binh Thanh, T08-3512 2764, www.vietnamese-cooking-class-saigon.com.* Offers short and in-depth courses for adults and children.

Golf

Bochang Dong Nai Golf Resort, *Dong Nai Province, 50 km north of HCMC up Highway 1, T61-386 6288, http://dongnaigolf.com.vn.* A very attractive 27-hole golf course with restaurant and bar and accommodation.
Golf Vietnam and Country Club, *Long Thanh My Ward, Q9, T08-6280 0124, http://vietnamgolfcc.com.* An internationally owned 36-hole course with an east and west course, just north of the city. The complex also has tennis and badminton courts, a boating lake and children's playground. On-site accommodation is available.
Song Be Golf Resort, *77 Binh Duong Blvd, Lai Thieu, Q Thuan An, Binh Duong Province, 22 km from HCMC on Highway 13, T650-375 6660, http://songbegolf.com.* An attractive golf resort set in 100 ha of land with lakes and tree-lined fairways. For non-golfers there are tennis courts, a gym, sauna and children's playground.

Swimming

Some hotels allow non-residents to use their pool for a fee. Decent pools are at the **Sofitel Plaza**, **Grand** and **Caravelle**.
International Club, *285B Cach Mang Thang Tam St, Q10, T08-3865 7695.*
Lan Anh Club, *almost next door to the International Club at 291 Cach Mang Thang Tam St, T08-3862 7144.* Pleasant with a nice pool and tennis courts.
Saigon Water Park, *Go Dua Bridge, Kha Van Can St, Q Thu Duc, T08-3897 0456. Mon-Fri 0900-1700, Sat and Sun 0900-2000.* Admission is charged according to height. A little way out but is enormous fun. It has a variety of water slides of varying degrees of excitement and a child's pool on a 5-ha site. It is hugely popular with the Vietnamese.

Tennis

Tennis is possible at the **Rex Hotel** and **New World Hotel** and also **Lan Anh Club**, 291 Cach Mang Thang Tam St.

Therapies

L'Apothiquaire, *61-63 Le Thanh Ton St, T08-3822 1218, www.lapothiquaire. com.* Massages, chocolate therapy, spa packages and slimming treatments in this lovely spa.
Qi Salon and Spa, *Caravelle Hotel, www.qispa.com.vn.* You can indulge in everything from a 20-min Indian head massage to a blow-out 5-hr Qi Special.

Tours

Buffalo Tours, *81 Mac Thui Buoi St, T08-3827 9170, www.buffalotours.com.* Organizes trips to the Mekong Delta, city tours, the Cu Chi tunnels and Cao Dai Temple. Staff are helpful. Good countrywide operator with longstanding reputation. Also has an office in the **EMM Hotel** (see Where to stay).

Exotissimo, *64 Dong Du St, T08-3827 2911, www.exotissimo.com*. An efficient agency that can handle all travel needs of visitors to Vietnam. Its local excursions are very well guided.

Handspan Adventure Travel, *F7, TitanCentral Park Building, 10th floor, 18A Nam Quoc Cang, 208 Nguyen Trai, Q1, T08-3925 7605, www.handspan. com*. Reputable and well-organized. Specializes in adventure tours.

Kim Café, *189 De Tham St, District 1, T08-3920 5552, www.kimtravel.com*. Organizes minibuses to Nha Trang, Dalat, etc, and tours of the Mekong. A good source of information. Backpacker friendly prices.

Sinh Tourist (formerly **Sinh Café**), *246-248 De Tham St, T08-3838 9597, www.thesinhtourist.vn*. **Sinh Tourist** now has branches and agents all over main towns in Vietnam. Its tours are generally good value and its open ticket is excellent value. For many people, especially budget travellers, **Sinh** is the first port of call. The company also deals with visa extensions, flight, train and hotel bookings and car rentals. This one is the HQ.

Sophie's Tour, *T0121-830 3742, www. sophiesarttour.com*. Run by Sophie, a long-term Saigon expat with a passion for the city and its art. Engaging 4-hr tour looking at the works of artists who studied, fought and witnessed major events in Vietnam's recent history from colonialism to the present. Highly recommended.

XO Tours, *T09-3308 3727, www.xotours.vn*. **XO** tours take clients around the city on the back of motorbikes ridden by women wearing traditional ao dai. The foodie tour introduces dishes and districts tourists don't normally see. Shopping and sightseeing tours also offered. Fun, different and highly rated.

Vietnam Vespa Adventures, *Cafe Zoom, 169A De Tham St, T08-3920 3897, www.vietnamvespaadventure.com*. Half-day tours of the city, 3-day tours to Mui Ne and 8-day tours to Dalat and Nha Trang. The city tours are fun, insightful and recommended.

Transport

Air
Airport information
HCMC may not be Vietnam's capital, but it is the economic powerhouse of the country and the largest city and thus well connected with the wider world – indeed, more airlines fly into here than into Hanoi.

Tan Son Nhat Airport, 49 Troung Son, Tan Binh, T08-3844 8358, www. saigonairport.com, is 30-40 mins northwest of the city, depending on the traffic. Airport facilities include banks and ATMs and locker rooms, desks for airlines including **Vietnam Airlines** and VietJetAir, and an information desk. Lost and found, T08-3844 6665 ext 7461.

Airline offices
AirAsia, 254 De Tham St, T08-3838 9810, www.airasia.com. **Air France**, 130 Dong Khoi St, T08-3829 0981, www.airfrance. com. **Bangkok Airways**, Unit 103, Saigon Trade Center, 37 Ton Duc Thang St, T08-3910 4490, www.bangkokair.com. **Cathay Pacific**, 72-74 Nguyen Thi Minh Khai St, T08-3822 3203, www.cathaypacific.com. **Emirate Airlines**, 170-172 Nam Ky Khoi Nghia, Q3, T08-3930 2939, www.emirates. com. **Eva Air**, 2A-4A, Ton Duc Thang St, T08-3844 5211, www.evaair.com. **Gulf Air**, 18 Dang Thi Nhu St, Q1, T08-3915 7614, www.gulfair.com. **JAL**, www.jal. co.jp. **Jetstar**, 112 Hong Ha, Q Tan Binh, T08-3845 0092, www.jetstar.com.

Lao Airlines, www.laoairlines.com.
Lufthansa, 19-25 Nguyen Hue Blvd,
T08-3829 8529, www.lufthansa.com.
Malaysia, Saigon Trade Center, 37 Ton
Duc Thang St, T08-3829 2529, www.
malaysiaairlines.com. **Qantas**, HT&T
Vietnam, Level 2, Ben Thanh TSC Building,
186-188 Le Thanh Ton St, T08-3910 5373,
www.quantas.com.au. **Qatar**, Suite 8,
Petro Vietnam Tower, 1-5 Le Duan St,
T08-3827 3777, www.qatarairways.
com. **Singapore Airlines**, 29 Le Duan St,
T08-3823 1588, www.singaporeair.com.
Thai Airways, 29 Le Duan St, T08-3822
3365, www.thaiairways.com.vn. **Tiger
Airways**, T1206 0114, www.tigerairways.
com. **Vietnam Airlines**, 6th floor, Sun
Wah Tower, 115 Nguyen Hue St, T08-3832
0320, www.vietnamairlines.com. Mon-Fri
0800-1830, Sat 0800-1200, 1330-1700.

Bicycle and motorbike
If staying in HCMC for any length of
time it might be a good idea to buy
a bicycle (see Shopping, above, and
page 41). Alternatively, bikes and
motorcycles can be hired for cheaply
around Pham Ngu Lao.

Bikes should always be parked in
designated compounds (*gui xe*) for
a small fee (don't lose your ticket!) or
with a guard in front of businesses.

Bus
Local
The bus service in HCMC has now
become more reliable and frequent.
They run at intervals of 10-20 mins –
depending on the time of day. In rush
hours they are jammed with passengers
and can run late. There are bus stops
every 500 m or so. Most buses start from
or stop by the Ben Thanh bus station
opposite Ben Thanh Market, T08-3821
4444. A free map of all bus routes can

also be obtained here in the chaotic
waiting room.

Long distance
With the completion of a new ring road
around HCMC, long-distance public
buses, unless specifically signed HCMC or
'Ben Xe Ben Thanh' do not come into the
city. Passengers are dropped off on the
ring road at Binh Phuoc bridge. However,
companies such as **Sinh Tourist** and
Phuong Trang (futabuslines.com.vn)
run services from Pham Ngu Lao.

From **Mien Dong Terminal**, north
of the city, buses north to **Dalat**, **Hué**,
Danang and all significant points on
the road to Hanoi. The **Hoang Long**
bus company runs deluxe buses daily to
Hanoi. Has an office at 47 Pham Ngu Lao,
T08-915 1818 and it is possible to book
online at www.hoanglongasia.com.

From **Mien Tay Terminal**, some
distance southwest of town, buses south
to the **Mekong Delta** towns. There
is also a bus station in Cholon which
serves destinations such as **Long An**,
My Thuan, **Ben Luc** and **My Tho**.

International bus
Many tour operators run tours and
transport to Cambodia (see Tour
operators) crossing the border at
Moc Bai. Visas for Cambodia can be
bought at the border. **Sapaco Tourist**,
309-327 Pham Ngu Lao St, T08-3920
3623, www.sapacotourist.com, runs
buses from Pham Ngu Lao to **Phnom
Penh** from 0600-1400, 8 daily 6 hrs;
to **Siem Reap**, US, 12 hrs.

Cyclos
Cyclos are a peaceful way to get around
the city. They can be hired by the hour
or to reach a specific destination. Some
drivers speak English. Each tends to

have his own patch, which is jealously guarded. Expect to pay more outside the major hotels.

Cyclos are much rarer these days but can be found waiting in tourist spots. Some visitors complain of cyclo drivers in HCMC 'forgetting' the agreed price (though Hanoi is worse). Cyclos are being banned from more and more streets in the centre of HCMC, which may involve a longer and more expensive journey. This excuse is trotted out every time (particularly if extra money is demanded) and it is invariably true. If taking a tour agree a time and price and point to watches and agree on the start time.

Taxi

HCMC has quite a large fleet of meter taxis. There are many taxi companies fighting bitterly for trade. Competition has brought down prices so they are now reasonably inexpensive and for 2 or more are cheaper than cyclos or *xe om* (motorcycle taxi).

Not all taxis are trustworthy, but it is easy to avoid scams. Simply use one of these companies, which are all over town: **Mai Linh** (T08-3822 2666, www.mailinh.vn) or **Vinasun** (T08-3827 2727).

Xe om are the quickest way to get around town and cheaper than cyclos; agree a price and hop on the back. *Xe om* drivers hang around on most street corners. Short journeys run from around 15,000d but you may end up paying more.

Train

The station is 2 km from the centre of the city at 1 Nguyen Thong St, Q3, T08-3931 2795. Facilities for the traveller are much improved and include a/c waiting room, post office and bank (no TCs). Regular daily connections with **Hanoi** and all points north. Trains take between 29½ and 42½ hrs to reach Hanoi; hard and soft berths are available. Sleepers should be booked in advance.

There is now a **Train Booking Agency** at 275c Pham Ngu Lao St, T08-3836 7640, 0730-1830, which saves an unnecessary journey out to the station. Alternatively, for a small fee, most travel agents will obtain tickets. The railway timetable can be seen online at www.vr.com.vn.

My Tho
& around

My Tho is an important riverside market town, 71 km southwest of Ho Chi Minh City and 5 km off the main highway to Vinh Long. It is the stepping-off point for boat trips to islands in the Tien River. Visitors enjoy the chance to wander among abundant fruit orchards and witness local industries at first hand. Around My Tho are the northern delta towns of Ben Tre, Vinh Long, Tra Vinh, Sa Dec and Cao Lanh.

Vinh Long at the end of the 19th century
Source: *The French in Indochina*, first published in 1884

The town has had a turbulent history: it was Khmer until the 17th century, when the advancing Vietnamese took control of the surrounding area. In the 18th century Thai forces annexed the territory, before being driven out in 1784. Finally, the French gained control in 1862. Today, it is much more peaceful destination.

Sights

On the corner of Nguyen Trai Street and Hung Vuong Street, and five minutes' walk from the central market, is My Tho church painted with a yellow wash with a newer, white campanile. The central market covers a large area from Le Loi Street down to the river. The river is the most enjoyable spot to watch My Tho life go by.

It is a long walk to **Vinh Trang Pagoda** ① *60 Nguyen Trung Trac St, daily 0900-1200, 1400-1700 (best to go by bicycle or xe om).* The entrance to the temple is through an ornate porcelain-encrusted gate. The pagoda was built in 1849 and displays a mixture of architectural styles: Chinese, Vietnamese and colonial. The façade is almost fairytale in inspiration. Two huge new statues of the Buddha now dominate the area.

Not far from My Tho is the hamlet of **Ap Bac**, the site of the communists' first major military victory against the ARVN. The battle demonstrated that without direct US involvement the communists could never be defeated. John Paul Vann was harsh in his criticism of the tactics and motivation of the South Vietnamese Army who failed to dislodge a weak VC position. As he observed from the air, almost speechless with rage, he realized how feeble his Vietnamese ally was; an opinion that few senior US officers heeded – to their cost (see *Bright Shining Lie* by Neil Sheehan).

Essential My Tho and around

Getting around

The much-improved Highway 1 is the main route from Ho Chi Minh City to My Tho, and there are regular connections with other main towns in the area. There is an efficient public bus service, taxis aplenty, a few river taxis and boats and *xe om*.

When to go

December to May is when the Mekong Delta is at its best. During the monsoon from June to November the weather is poor with constant background drizzle interrupted by bursts of torrential rain.

Time required

Ideal for a weekend.

Best sleeping and eating

A bowl of hu tieu my tho, page 51
Banh Xeo 46, page 51
A homestay on Cai Mon island, page 51

Tourist information

Tien Giang Tourist
8 30 Thang 4 St on the river, Ward 1,
T730-387 3184, www.tiengiangtourist.vn.
Boat trips, fishing tours and even nigh
firefly watching tours. Also has a ticket
office for transport. The staff are friendly
and helpful and have a good command
of several languages.

Where to stay

$$-$ Song Tien Annex
33 Trung Trac St, T0730-397 7883,
www.tiengiangtourist.com.
This is a large 20-room hotel boasting
big beds and bathtubs on legs. The large,
renovated Song Tien around the corner
is another good option if this is full.

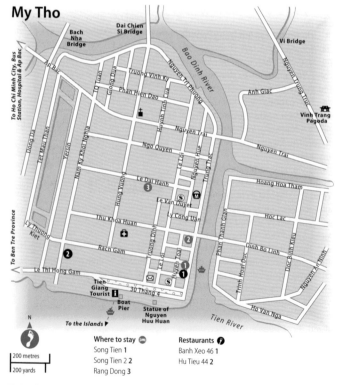

My Tho

Where to stay
Song Tien **1**
Song Tien 2 **2**
Rang Dong **3**

Restaurants
Banh Xeo 46 **1**
Hu Tieu 44 **2**

200 metres
200 yards

$ Rang Dong
No 25, 30 Thang 4 St, T730-3874400,
www.rangdonghotel.net.
Private mini hotel, near river with a/c,
TV and hot water. Friendly staff are
very helpful.

Restaurants

A speciality of the area is *hu tieu my
tho* – a spicy soup of vermicelli, sliced
pork, dried shrimps and fresh herbs.
At night, noodle stalls spring up on
the pavement on Le Loi St at the
junction with Le Dai Han St.

$ Banh Xeo 46
11 Trung Trac St.
Serves *bánh xèo*, savoury pancakes filled
with beansprouts, mushrooms and
prawns; delicious.

$ Bo De Quan
69A Nguyen Trung Truc.
Just across the street from a pretty
temple, this is a great veggie Vietnamese
restaurant set in a verdant garden.

$ Hu Tien 44
44 Nam Ky Khoi Nghia St. Daily 0500-1200.
Specializes in *hu tien my tho*.

What to do

Ben Tre Tourist, *8, 30 Thang 4 St,
T730-387 5070, www.bentretourist.vn.*
Although this company operates island
tours from My Tho, it would be best to
use its specialist knowledge of Ben Tre
province. Escape the My Tho crowds
with homestays at Cai Mon and take a
tour to the gardens and canals of this
neigbouring province.
Tien Giang Tourist, *Dockside location
is at No 8, 30 Thang 4 St, T730-387 3184,
www.tiengiangtourist.com.* Dinner with
traditional music on the Mekong, canoe
and boat hire.

Transport

Boat
As in all Mekong Delta towns, local travel
is often by boat to visit the orchards,
islands and remoter places.

Bus
The bus station (Ben Xe My Tho) is
3-4 km from town on Ap Bac St towards
HCMC with regular connections every
30 mins from 0430 to **HCMC**'s Mien Tay
station (2 hrs); **Vinh Long** (2½ hrs); and
Cao Lanh (2½ hrs). There are also buses
to **Can Tho** and **Chau Doc**.

The islands

go in the afternoon when they are quieter

There are four islands in the Tien River between My Tho and Ben Tre: Dragon,
Tortoise, Phoenix and Unicorn. The best way of getting to them is to take a tour.
A vast pier and boat service centre has been built on 30 Thang 4 Street where
all the tour operators are now concentrated. To avoid the hundreds of visitors
now descending on these islands, go in the afternoon after the tour buses have
gone. Hiring a private boat is not recommended due to the lack of insurance, the
communication difficulties and lack of explanations. Prices vary according to the
number of people and which islands you choose to visit.

Dragon Island

Immediately opposite My Tho is Dragon Island, Tan Long Island. It is pleasant to wander along its narrow paths. Tan Long is noted for its longan production but there are many other fruits to sample, as well as honey and rice whisky.

Phoenix Island

The Island of the **Coconut Monk**, also known as Con Phung (Phoenix Island), is about 3 km from My Tho. The 'Coconut Monk' established a retreat on this island shortly after the end of the Second World War where he developed a new 'religion', a fusion of Buddhism and Christianity. He is said to have meditated for three years on a stone slab, eating nothing but coconuts – hence the name. Persecuted by both the South Vietnamese government and after reunification, the monastery has fallen into disuse.

Unicorn Island

Unicorn Island is a garden of Eden – stuffed with longan, durian, roses, pomelo and a host of other fruit trees. Honey is made on this island too.

Ben Tre

appealing backwater delta town

Ben Tre is a typical Vietnamese delta town with a charming riverfront feel. The small bridge over the river is wooden slatted but with iron supports. Bountiful fruit stalls are laid out on the waterfront and locals sell potted plants on barges by the river. Small cargo ships pass dilapidated shacks falling into the muddy waters. It doesn't attract a lot of visitors. Its main claim to fame is that it is the birthplace of Nguyen Dinh Chieu, a blind and patriotic poet. In recent years, though, it has improved its tourism facilities.

Ben Tre is no longer an island province; a bridge links it from just outside My Tho. The province is essentially a huge island of mud at one of the nine mouths of the Mekong. It depends heavily on farming, fishing and coconuts although there are some light industries engaged in processing the local farm output and refining sugar. During the wars of resistance against the French and Americans, Ben Tre earned itself a reputation as a staunch Viet Minh/Viet Cong stronghold.

Sights

Vien Minh Pagoda is located on Nguyen Dinh Chieu Street and is the centre for the association of Buddhists in Ben Tre Province. It was originally made of wood but was rebuilt using concrete in 1958.

In **Binh Phu village**, 2 km from downtown, you can see rice wine being made. **Phu Le village** also makes rice wine.

Nguyen Dinh Chieu Temple is 36 km from the town centre in An Duc village. The temple is dedicated to the poet Nguyen Dinh Chieu who is Ben Tre's most famous son. It is well kept and photogenic and worth a visit. The monks are friendly and helpful.

Tourist information

Ben Tre Tourist
16 Hai Ba Trung St, T75-382 2392,
www.bentretourist.vn.
Friendly and helpful.

Where to stay

$ Hung Vuong
148-166 Hung Vuong St, T75-382 2408.
Spacious a/c rooms (39 in total) with
huge bathtubs feature in this waterfront
hotel that is in a great location. Each
room has 2 beds plus TV, fridge and
balcony. Restaurant; breakfast is
included. Some English is spoken.

Restaurants

Most of the hotels have restaurants;
there is a floating restaurant on the
river but it has moved from its town
centre location to 1 km upstream. The
best option is local noodle and rice
stands. The hotel restaurants are open
all day.

$ Nha Hang Noi Ben Tre
Hung Vuong, T75-382 2492.
Open 0700-2200.
A large space popular with big groups.
Serves a variety of dishes plus karaoke.

Shopping

The main items to buy are coconuts
and related coconut-made products.
They might not be too versatile but
they are very pretty and make ideal
novelty presents for friends and family
at home.

What to do

Tours of the islands in the Tien River
from Ben Tre cost half the price of
those leaving from My Tho and include
taking a horse and cart. The 4-hr Ben
Tre ecological tour will take you to see
local agricultural industries.

Ben Tre Tourist, *16 Hai Ba Trung St,*
T75-382 2392, www.bentretourist.vn.
Daily 0700-1100, 1300-1700. Island tours,
bicycle rental and a motorboat for hire.

Transport

Car or bus
Hourly buses connect Ben Tre with
HCMC (150 km) via the My Thuan toll
bridge. Regular services connect Ben Tre
with **My Tho**, 16 km, 30 mins and **Can
Tho** (100 km, 2½ hrs).

Vinh Long

a base for boat trips

Vinh Long is a rather ramshackle, but nonetheless clean, riverside town on the
banks of the Co Chien River and is the capital of Vinh Long Province. It is the
launch pad for lovely boat trips through An Binh Island via the small floating
market at Cai Be. An Binh is the centre of the Mekong homestay industry (see
box, opposite). Vinh Long makes a reasonable stopping-off point on the road to
Long Xuyen, Rach Gia and Ha Tien.

Mekong homestays

Facing Vinh Long town in the Co Chien River, a tributary of the Mekong, is a large island known as An Binh that is further sliced into smaller islands by ribbons of canals. **Cuu Long Tourist** runs several homestays on the island – a wonderful way to immerse yourself in local life.

The accommodation is basic with camp beds, shared bathrooms and mosquito nets and a home-cooked dinner of the fruits of the delta (elephant ear fish with abundant greens including mint and spring rolls and beef cooked in coconut).

Sunset and drinks in patios or terraces or riverfront lookouts chatting with the owner completes the night. A dawn paddle in the Mekong, surrounded by floating water hyacinth and watching the sun rise is the reward for early risers.

These tranquil islands are stuffed with fruit-bearing trees and flowers. Travel is by sampan or you can walk down the winding paths that link the communities.

During your stay you will take tea and fruit at a traditional house, see rice cakes and popcorn being made, and visit a brick factory and watch terracotta pots being created close to the unusually shaped kilns that dot this area of the delta.

Sights

Vinh Long was one of the focal points in the spread of Christianity in the Mekong Delta and there is a cathedral and Roman Catholic seminary in town. The richly stocked and well-ordered **Cho Vinh Long** (central market) is on 1 Thang 5 Street down from the Cuu Long hotel and stretches back to near the local bus station. A new market building has also been built opposite the existing market. There is a **Cao Dai church** not far from the second bridge leading into town from Ho Chi Minh City and My Tho, visible on the right-hand side.

At sunset families cluster along the **river promenade** to fly colourful kites in animal shapes. In the mornings, fruits are for sale along **Hung Dao Vuong Street** and teenagers play ball and throw home-made shuttlecocks in the afternoons along **Hung Vuong Street**.

Vinh Long Museum ① *T70-382 3181, daily 0800-1100 and 1330-1630, Fri-Sun 1800-2100, free*, displays photographs of the war including the devastation of the town in 1968, some weaponry and a room dedicated to Ho Chi Minh.

Van Thieu Mieu Temple ① *0500-1100, 1300-1900*, a charming mustard yellow cluster of buildings is 2 km from town along Tran Phu Street. In the first building to the right on entering the complex is an altar dedicated to Confucius.

The **Khmer Temples** at Tra Vinh (see below) can be visited on a day trip from Vinh Long.

ON THE ROAD

Hydrology of the Mekong Delta

The Mekong River enters Vietnam in two branches known traditionally as the Mekong and the Bassac but now called the Tien and the Hau. Over the 200-km journey to the sea they divide to form nine mouths, the so-called Nine Dragons or *Cuu Long*.

In response to the rains of the Southwest monsoon, river levels begin to rise in June, usually reaching a peak in October and falling to normal in December. This seasonal pattern is ideal for rice growing, around which the whole way of life of the delta has evolved.

The Mekong has a unique natural flood regulator in the form of Cambodia's great lake, the Tonlé Sap. As river levels rise the water backs up into the vast lake which more than doubles in size, preventing more serious flooding in the Mekong Delta. Nevertheless, the Tien and Hau still burst their banks and water inundates the huge Plain of Reeds (*Dong Thap Muoi*) and the Rach Gia Depression, home to thousands of waterbirds.

The annual flood has always been regarded as a blessing bringing, as it does, fertile silt and flushing out salinity and acidity from the soil. Since the 1990s, however, frequent serious flooding has made this annual event less benign and an increasingly serious problem.

From 1705 onwards Vietnamese emperors began building canals to improve navigation in the delta. This task was taken up enthusiastically by the French in order to open up new areas of the delta to rice cultivation and export. Interestingly it is thought the canals built prior to 1975 had little effect on flooding.

Since 1975 a number of new canals have been built in Cambodia and Vietnam and old ones deepened. The purpose of some of these predominantly west–east canals is to carry irrigation water to drier parts. Their effect has been to speed up the flow of water across the delta from about 17 days to five. Peak flows across the border from Cambodia have tripled in 30 years, partly as a result of deforestation and urbanization upriver.

In addition, the road network of the delta has been developed and roads raised above the normal high-water levels. This has the effect of trapping floodwater, preventing it from reaching the Gulf of Thailand or East Sea and prolonging floods. Many canals have gates to prevent the inundation of sea water; the gates also hinder the outflow of floodwaters.

(Information taken from a paper by Quang M Nguyen)

River trips

The river trips taking in the islands and orchards around Vinh Long are as charming as any in the delta, but getting there can be expensive. See What to do, below.

There is a floating market at **Cai Be**, about 10 km from Vinh Long. This is not quite so spectacular as the floating markets around Can Tho (see page 65) but nevertheless make for a diverting morning's trip.

An Binh Island, just a 10-minute ferry ride from Phan Boi Chau Street, represents a great example of delta landscape. The island can be explored either by boat, paddling down narrow canals, or by following the dirt tracks and crossing monkey bridges on foot. Monkey bridges are those single bamboo poles with, if you are lucky, a flimsy handrail that is there for psychological reassurance rather than to stop you from falling off. But don't worry, the water is warm and usually shallow and the mud soft. On the island is the ancient **Tien Chau Pagoda** and a *nuoc mam* (fish sauce factory).

Listings Vinh Long

Tourist information

Cuu Long Tourist
No 1, 1 Thang 5 St, T70-382 3616, www.cuulongtourist.com. Daily 0700-1700.
This is one of the friendlier and more helpful of the state-run companies and runs tours and homestays.

Where to stay

For homestays, see box, page 54.

$ Cuu Long (B)
No 1, 1 Thang 5 St (ie No 1 May St), T70-382 3616, www.cuulongtourist.com.
Set back from the river, in the centre of action. 34 comfortable a/c rooms; price includes breakfast.

$ Nam Phuong
11 Le Loi St, T70-382 2226, khachsannamphuongvl@yahoo.com.
These are extremely basic and cheap rooms – one for those on a serious budget.

Restaurants

There are a few restaurants along 1 Thang 5 St, just beyond Cuu Long Hotel.

$ Nem Nuong
12 1 Thang 5 St. Open all day.
Sells grilled meat with noodles.

$ Phuong Thuy Restaurant
No 1, 1 Thang 5 St, T70-382 4786. Open 0600-2100.
A restaurant on the river with Vietnamese and Western dishes and welcoming service. Cuttlefish and shrimp feature strongly.

What to do

Cuu Long Tourist, *No 1, 1 Thang 5 St, T70-382 3616, www.cuulongtourist.com.*
Trips to An Binh Island include a visit to the floating market of Cai Be. A tour of the area including homestay, dinner and breakfast can be arranged (see box, page 54). A day trip to Cai Be passing the floating market is possible, as is the arrangement from HCMC.
Mekong Travel, *No 8, 30 Thang 5 St, T70-383 6252, www.mekongtravel.com.vn.*
Offers the same homestay and floating market options.

Transport

The road runs direct from Ho Chi Minh City via the My Thuan bridge. There are good connections to all other Mekong towns.

Bus
The local bus station is on 3 Thang 2 St, between Hung Dao Vuong and

Hung Vuong in the centre of town with services to Sa Dec and Can Tho. The long-distance bus station is at Dinh Tien Hoang St, Ward 8 for connections with **HCMC**'s Mien Tay station. Links with **My Tho**, **Long Xuyen**, **Tra Vinh**, **Rach Gia**, and other **Mekong Delta** destinations.

Tra Vinh

religious edifices and Khmer culture

Tra Vinh is the capital of the province of the same name and has a large Khmer population – 300,000 people (30% of the province's population) are Khmer, and at the last count there were 140 Khmer temples. The large Khmer population is a bit of an enigma, for while Khmer people can be found across the Mekong Delta the concentration is highest in this, the most distant Mekong province from Cambodia. For whatever reason, Tra Vinh established itself as a centre of population some 500 years ago; then, as Vietnamese settlers began fanning across the delta displacing the Khmer, the population of this area remained firmly rooted creating a little pocket of Cambodian ethnicity and culture far from home. The modern market building, adorned with a huge picture of Ho Chi Minh, is the pivot of the city.

Sights
For those interested in religious edifices, Tra Vinh is the place to visit. In one of the more obscure surveys undertaken to calculate the number of religious buildings per head of population it was found that with more than 140 Khmer temples, 50 Vietnamese pagodas, five Chinese pagodas, seven mosques and 14 churches serving a town of only 70,000 souls, Tra Vinh was the outright winner by miles.

So many attractive buildings coupled with the tree-lined boulevards – some trees are well over 30-m tall – make this one of the more attractive cities in the delta. It is well worth an overnight stay here to recharge the batteries.

The market is on the central square between Dien Bien Phu Street – the town's main thoroughfare – and the Tra Vinh River, which is a relatively small branch of the Mekong compared with most delta towns. A walk through the market and along the riverbank makes a pleasant late afternoon or early evening stroll.

The **Ong Met Pagoda** on Dien Bien Phu Street north of the town centre dates back to the mid-16th century. It is a gilded Chinese-style temple where the monks will be only too happy to ply you with tea and practice their English, although the building itself is fairly unremarkable.

The two best reasons to come to Tra Vinh are to see the **storks** and the **Khmer temples**. Fortunately, these can be combined at the nearby **Hang Pagoda**, also known as **Ao Ban Om**, about 5 km south of town and 300 m off the main road. It is not particularly special architecturally, but the sight of the hundreds of storks that rest in the grounds and wheel around the pointed roofs at dawn and dusk (1600-1800) is truly spectacular.

There's also the **Bao Tang Van Hoa Dan Toc Khmer** ⓘ *0700-1100, 1300-1700*, a small collection of artefacts next to the square-shaped lotus filled pond of Ba

Om just south of town (there are plans for a hotel here). Labels are in Vietnamese and Khmer only; naga heads, Hanuman masks and musical instruments feature. Opposite is the **Chua Angkorajaborey (Ang)** or Chua Van Minh in Vietnamese dating from AD 990, which is rather peaceful.

Listings Tra Vinh

Tourist information

Tra Vinh Tourist
64-66 Le Loi St, T74-385 8556,
travinhtourist@yahoo.com.
Owner of the **Cuu Long Hotel**, friendly and helpful. City tours offered.

Where to stay

$ Cuu Long
999 Nguyen Thi Minh Khai St,
T74-386 2615.
The rooms are equipped with a/c, satellite TV, and en suite facilities. The restaurant provides a good selection of food but the service can be very slack with a lack of English.

$ Tra Vinh Palace
3 Le Thanh To St, T74-386 4999.
A comfortable but rather gaudy hotel with very large rooms 10 mins' walk from the central market. The sister hotel, Tra

Vinh Palace 2 has cheaper rooms and is a few streets away.

Restaurants

$ Cuu Long
See Where to stay.
Restaurant has a good selection of food.

$ Tuy Huong
8 Dien Bien Phu St.
Opposite the market; good, simple Vietnamese dishes.

$ Viet Hoa
80 Tran Phu St.
Walk through the garage to sample the squid, shrimp and crab dishes. English menu.

Transport

The bus station is on Nguyen Dang St, about 500 m south of town. Regular connections with **Vinh Long**.

★Sa Dec's biggest claim to fame is that it was the birthplace of French novelist Marguerite Duras, and the town's three main avenues – Nguyen Hue, Tran Hung Dao and Hung Vuong garlanded with fragrant frangipani – together with some attractive colonial villas betray the French influence on this relatively young town. Sa Dec, a small and friendly town about 20 km west of Vinh Long, is also renowned for its flowers and bonsai trees.

The town was formerly the capital of Dong Thap Province, a privilege that was snatched by Cao Lanh in 1984 but a responsibility that Sa Dec is better off without. The delightful journey between the two towns passes brick kilns, and bikers transporting their wares (namely tropical fish in bottles and dogs).

Sights

Sa Dec's bustling riverside market on Nguyen Hue Street is worth a visit. Many of the scenes from the film adaptation of Duras' novel *The Lover* were filmed in front of the shop terraces and merchants' houses here. Sit in one of the many riverside cafés to watch the world float by – which presumably, as a young woman, is what Duras did.

Duras' lover **Huynh Thuy Le's house** ⓘ *Nha Co Huynh Thuy Le, 255A Nguyen Hue St, Ward 2, T67-377 3937, Mon-Sat 0730-1700, Sun 0830-1700, 10,000d*, is a lovely Sino-influenced building on the main street. There are stunning gold-leaf carved animal figures framing arches and the centrepiece is a golden shrine to Chinese warrior Quan Cong. The Ancient House was built in 1895 and restored in 1917. There are photographs of the Huynh family (he later married and had five daughters and three sons; he died in 1972), Duras and the Sa Dec school. Duras' childhood home is not across the river as some guidebooks say; it no longer exists. She lived in a house near the Ecole de Sa Dec (now Truong Vuong primary school on the corner of Hung Vuong and Ho Xuan Huong St), which is pictured inside the Nha Co Huynh Thuy Le.

Phuoc Hung Pagoda ⓘ *75/5 Hung Vuong St*, is a splendid Chinese-style pagoda constructed in 1838 when Sa Dec was a humble one-road village. Surrounded by ornamental gardens, lotus ponds and cypress trees, the main temple to the right is decorated with fabulous animals assembled from pieces of porcelain rice bowls. Inside are some marvellous wooden statues of Buddhist figures made in 1838 by the venerable sculptor Cam. There are also some superbly preserved gilded wooden beams and two antique prayer tocsins. The smaller one was made in 1888 and its resounding mellow tone changes with the weather. The West Hall contains a valuable copy of the 101 volume Great Buddhist Canon. There are also some very interesting and ancient photos of dead devotees and of pagoda life in the past.

A few kilometres west of Sa Dec is the **Tu Ton Rose Garden (Vuon Hong Tu Ton)** ⓘ *28 Vuon Hong St, Khom 3, Ward 3, T67-376 1685, 0600-2000, free*. The garden is next to a lemon yellow building with yellow gates. This 6000-ha nursery borders the river and is home to more than 40 varieties of rose and 540 other types of plant,

BACKGROUND

Mekong Delta

The region has had a restless history. Conflict between Cambodians and Vietnamese for ownership of the wide plains resulted in ultimate Viet supremacy although important Khmer relics remain. But it was during the French and American wars that the Mekong Delta produced many of the most fervent fighters for independence.

The Mekong Delta or Cuu Long (Nine Dragons) is Vietnam's rice bowl and, before the partition of the country in 1954, rice was traded from the south where there was a rice surplus, to the north where there was a rice deficit, as well as internationally. Even prior to the creation of French Cochin China in the 19th century, rice was being transported from here to Hué, the imperial capital. The delta covers 67,000 sq km, of which about half is cultivated. Rice yields are in fact generally lower than in the north, but the huge area under cultivation and the larger size of farms means that both individual households and the region produce a surplus for export. In the Mekong Delta there is nearly three times as much rice land per person as there is in the north. It is this that accounts for the relative wealth of the region.

The Mekong Delta was not opened up to agriculture on an extensive scale until the late 19th and early 20th centuries. Initially it seems that this was a spontaneous process: peasants, responding to the market incentives introduced by the French, slowly began to push the frontier

from medicinal herbs to exotic orchids. Wander amid the potted hibiscus, beds of roses and bougainvillea and enjoy the visiting butterflies.

Listings Sa Dec

Tourist information

Dong Thap Tourist Company
Based at the Huynh Thuy Le Old House, T67-377 3937, www.dongthaptourist.com, is a contact here; its main office is in Cao Lanh. Trips to Xeo Quit and Cao Lanh organized.

Where to stay

$ Bong Hong
251A Nguyen Sinh Sac St, T67-386 8287, bonghonghotel@yahoo.com.vn.

Massive hotel a short distance before the bus station on Highway 80 leading into town. Some good-value a/c rooms with TV and fridge. Cheaper rooms have fan and cold water only. Breakfast not included. Tennis court on site.

$ Nha Co Huynh Thuy Le
255A Nguyen Hue St, Ward 2, T67-377 3937. Run by **Dong Thap Tourist**, this lovely home has 4 fan rooms with 2 single beds in each and would be the most enjoyable way to spend time in Sa Dec. The 2 front rooms are much more

of cultivation southwards into this wilderness area. The process gathered pace when the French colonial government began to construct canals and drainage projects to open more land to wet rice agriculture. By the 1930s the population of the delta had reached 4.5 million with 2,200,000 ha of land under rice cultivation. The Mekong Delta, along with the Irrawaddy (Burma) and Chao Phraya (Thailand) became one of the great rice exporting areas of Southeast Asia, shipping over 1.2 million tonnes annually.

Given their proximity to prosperous Ho Chi Minh City the inhabitants of the Mekong Delta might have expected some of the benefits of development to trickle their way: in this they have largely been disappointed. Most of the Mekong Delta provinces are trying and to a degree securing investment into their respective provinces. Be it hotels, cafés, karaoke in Ha Tien to canning and storage plants in Can Tho, they are trying to improve their collective lot. The main problem that they face is that everyone knows that each year during the monsoon season wide areas of the Mekong flood. The government is slowly but surely building up river defences against the annual floods but it is a laborious process.

Tourist services are improving year on year. A series of bridges have opened over the years drastically cutting road travel time to the delta region, but it still takes the best part of a day to get down to Chau Doc. Ho Chi Minh City tour operators run tours to Can Tho, My Tho and Chau Doc and agents within these towns run tours to surrounding sights and organize onward transport. Many local and Ho Chi Minh City operators also arrange boat and bus transport to Phnom Penh, Cambodia.

attractive than the plain 2 back rooms with stained-glass windows and carved wooden doors. The shared bathroom is at the back with cold water. The price includes breakfast and dinner. See also Restaurants, below.

Restaurants

$ Cay Sung
2/4 Hung Vuong St. Open all day.
It serves a good selection of rice dishes. There is a menu in English available.

$ Nha Co Huynh Thuy Le
255A Nguyen Hue St, Ward 2, T67-377 3937.
Run by **Dong Thap Tourist**, reserve a day in advance for the chance to dine in the home of Marguerite Duras' lover.

Transport

The bus station is about 500 m southeast of town on the main road just before the bridge. Buses to **Vinh Long** and **Long Xuyen** leave from here. The town is 143 km from HCMC and 102 km from Chau Doc, and 20 km from Vinh Long along Highway 80.

Cao Lanh for many years was a small, underdeveloped Mekong town. However, since becoming the capital of Dong Thap Province, an honour previously bestowed on Sa Dec, it has changed and has become a thriving market town. It also benefits from being the closest main city to Xeo Quyt base (Rung Cham forest), and Tram Chim National Park and its bird sanctuary, which are main tourist attractions. In fact, the excursions are the only real reason to visit Cao Lanh.

Sights

To the northeast along Nguyen Hue Street is the war memorial, containing the graves of Vietnamese who fell in the war with the USA. The **tomb of Ho Chi Minh's father** ⓘ *Nguyen Sinh Sac (Tham Quan Khu Di Tich Nguyen Sinh Sac), next to Quan Nam restaurant at 137 Pham Huu Lau St, open 0700-1130, 1330-1700, small fee*, is set under a shell structure and sits in front of a lotus pond. A small stilt-house museum sits in the tranquil grounds.

The vast **Plain of Reeds (Dong Thap Muoi)** is a swamp that extends for miles north towards Cambodia, particularly in the late monsoon season (September to November). It is an important wildlife habitat (see below) but in the wet season, when the water levels rise, getting about on dry land can be a real problem. Extraordinarily, the Vietnamese have not adapted the stilt house solution used by the Khmer and every year become flooded. In the rural districts houses are built on the highest land available and in a good year the floor will be just inches above the lapping water. At these times all transport is by boat. When the sky is grey the scene is desolate and the isolation of the plain can truly feel like the end of the Earth has been reached. Tower Mound (Go Thap) is the best place from which to get a view of the immensity and beauty of the surrounding Plain of Reeds. There was a watchtower here although no one seems sure if it was 10-storeys high or the last in a chain of 10 towers. There are earthworks from which General Duong and Admiral Kieu conducted their resistance against the French between 1861 and 1866.

★**Tram Chim National Park (Tam Nong Bird Sanctuary)** ⓘ *T67-382 7436*, is an 8000-ha reserve 45 km northwest of Cao Lanh. It contains around 220 species of bird at various times of year, but most spectacular is the red-headed crane (sarus), rarest of the world's 15 crane species. Between August and November these spectacular creatures migrate across the nearby Cambodian border to avoid the floods (cranes feed on land), but at any other time, and particularly at dawn and dusk, they are a magnificent sight. Floating rice is grown in the area around the bird sanctuary and although the acreage planted diminishes each year this is another of nature's truly prodigious feats. The leaves float on the surface while the roots are anchored in mud as much as 4-5 m below; but as so much energy goes into growing the stalk little is left over for the ears of rice, so yields are low.

Tourist information

Dong Thap Tourist Co
2 Doc Binh Kieu St, T67-385 5637,
www.dongthaptourist.com.
Mon-Sat 0700-1130, 1330-1700.
Some staff have a reasonable command
of English and are helpful.

Where to stay

$$$-$ Song Tra
178 Nguyen Hue St, T67-385 2624,
www.dongthaptourist.com.
A rather basic hotel, but Cao Lanh is
short on better options. The rooms
come equipped with a/c, satellite TV
and en suite facilities.

$ Binh Minh Hotel
157 Hung Vuong St, T67-385 3423.
A good little hotel but note that it's
actual entrance is not on Hung Vuong,
it is just around the corner on Do
Cong Tuong St. The owner, a local
schoolteacher, is friendly and helpful.
If you are travelling solo or on a budget
then this would be a good choice. Fan
and a/c rooms.

Restaurants

The restaurants in Song Tra, Xuan Mai
and Hoa Binh hotels are all open for
breakfast, lunch and dinner. There is
not much difference in their quality,
presentation choice and value.

$ A Chau
Ly Thuong Kiet St. Open 0800-2100.
Specializes in fried pancakes.

$ Hong Nhien
143 Hung Vuong St, behind the Song
Tra Hotel.
Serves *com tam* and *hu tieu* in a simple
set up.

What to do

Birdwatching at the nearby sanctuaries
is the most common activity. It is also
possible to hire boats from **Dong Thap**
Tourist Company, 2 Doc Binh Kieu St,
T67-385 5637. Dong Thap also organizes
trips to the mausoleum of Nguyen Sinh
Sac, Xeo Quyt, Sa Dec and the Gao Giong
Eco-tourism Zone.

Transport

The bus station is located at the corner
of Ton That Tung and Doc Binh Kieu St.
Connections with all delta towns. To
HCMC from the bus station on Vo Thi
Sau St and Nguyen Van Troi St, 3 hrs.

Can Tho
& around

floating markets and river trips

Can Tho is a large and rapidly growing commercial city lying chiefly on the west bank of the Can Tho River. Capital of Can Tho Province and the region's principal transport hub, it is also one of the most welcoming of the delta towns and launch pad for trips to see some of the region's floating markets. South of Can Tho are the towns of Soc Trang, Bac Lieu and Ca Mau.

Can Tho

the largest city in the heart of the delta

A small settlement was established at Can Tho at the end of the 18th century, although the town did not prosper until the French took control of the delta a century later and rice production for export began to take off. Despite the city's rapid recent growth there are still strong vestiges of French influence apparent in the broad boulevards flanked by flame trees, as well as many elegant buildings. Can Tho was also an important US base.

Sights
Hai Ba Trung Street, alongside the river, is the heart of the town; at dusk families stroll in the park here in their Sunday best. Opposite the park is **Chua Ong Pagoda** ⓘ *34 Hai Ba Trung St*, dating from 1894 and built by Chinese from Guangzhou. Unusually for a Chinese temple it is not free-standing but part of a terrace of buildings. The right-hand side of the pagoda is dedicated to the Goddess of Fortune, while the left-hand side belongs to General Ma Tien, who, to judge from his unsmiling statue, is fierce and warlike and not to be trifled with. The layout is a combination of typical pagoda – with a small open courtyard for the incense smoke to escape – and typical meeting house, complete with its language school, of the overseas Chinese in Southeast Asia.

The bustling market that used to operate on Hai Ba Trung Street along the bank of the river, and gave the town a bit of character, has been moved 1 km downriver. A new riverside promenade has been created. There's also a new crafts market building with a riverside restaurant, see Restaurants, page 67.

Munirang-syaram Pagoda ⓘ *36 Hoa Binh Blvd (southwest of post office)*, was built just after the Vietnam War and is a Khmer Hinayana Buddhist sanctuary. **Bao Tang Can Tho** ⓘ *Hoa Binh St, Tue-Thu 0800-1100, 1400-1700, Sat-Sun 0800-1100, 1830-2100*, in an impressive building, is the local history museum.

Binh Thuy Temple ⓘ *7 km north along the road to Long Xuyen*, dates from the mid-19th century; festivals are held here in the middle of the fourth and 12th lunar months. Nearby, 500 m down Bui Huu Nghia Road, opposite Binh Thuy temple, visit **Nha Co Binh Thuy aka the ancient house** ⓘ *10,000d to go inside the house* (also known as Vuon Lan if you get a moto to take you there), which was used as a setting in the film The Lover.

Essential Can Tho and around

Getting around

Some of the sites, the floating markets for instance, are best visited by boat. There are also river taxis and an efficient public bus service.

When to go

As in all the other Mekong cities the best time is from December to April when the temperatures are warm and there is no rain. May to November is the monsoon season and as such it is prone to flooding (although it does fare better than other cities).

Time required

Two days is enough.

★Floating markets

The daily markets are busiest at around 0600-0900. Women with sampans to rent will approach travellers in Hai Ba Trung St near the market waving a book of testimonials from previous satisfied customers. A trip of at least 5 hrs is recommended to see the landscape at a leisurely pace. If you take a larger boat you will not be able to manoeuvre in and out of the market.

There are boat trips to the floating markets at Phung Hiep, 33 km away (an eight-hour round trip by sampan or take a bus to Phung Hiep and rent a boat there) and Phong Dien, 15 km down the Can Tho River (a five-hour trip). Cai Rang is 7 km away and is easy to visit for those with only a couple of hours to spare.

Bustling affairs, the vendors attach a sample of their wares to a bamboo pole to attract customers. Up to seven vegetables can be seen dangling from staffs – wintermelon, pumpkin, spring onions, giant parsnips, grapefruit, garlic, mango, onions and Vietnamese plums. Housewives paddle their sampans from boat to boat and barter, haggle and gossip in the usual way. At the back of the boats, the domesticity of life on the water is in full glare – washing is hung out and motors are stranded high above the water. Orchards and gardens abound; small sampans are best as they can negotiate the narrowest canals to take the visitor into the heart of the area, a veritable Garden of Eden. Phung Hiep also features yards making traditional fishing boats and rice barges.

Where to stay

$$$$ Victoria Can Tho Resort
Cai Khe ward, T710-381 0111,
www.victoriahotels.asia.
A 92-room riverside hotel set in lovely,
well-tended garden on its own little
peninsula. It is Victoria Hotel 'French
colonial' style at its best with a breezy
open reception area and emphasis on
comfort and plenty of genuine period
features. It has a pool, spa pavilion,

tennis court and restaurant. The staff are
multilingual and helpful. The a/c rooms
are well decorated and have satellite TV,
Wi-Fi, en suite facilities, decent-sized
bathtub, well-stocked minibar and
electronic safe in the room. Even if you
decide to stay in a more centrally and
somewhat cheaper hotel then a visit to
the grounds and one of the restaurants
would be a pleasant experience. The
hotel offers a complimentary boat
shuttle to the town centre.

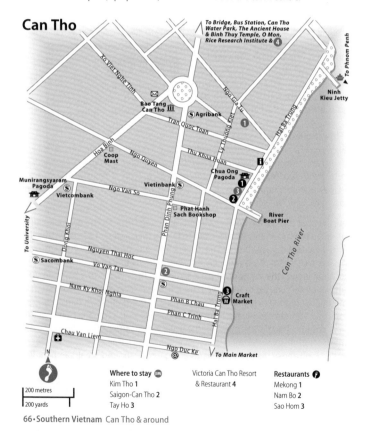

Can Tho

Where to stay 🛏
Kim Tho **1**
Saigon-Can Tho **2**
Tay Ho **3**

Victoria Can Tho Resort
& Restaurant **4**

Restaurants 🍴
Mekong **1**
Nam Bo **2**
Sao Hom **3**

$$ Kim Tho
14 Ngo Gia Tu St, T710-322 2228,
www.kimtho.com.
A lovely if a little dated hotel with some
rooms offering great river views. Very
welcoming and plenty of character. The
standout attraction is the roof-top café
with fabulous views. Includes breakfast.

$ Saigon-Can Tho
55 Phan Dinh Phung St, T710-382 5831,
www.saigoncantho.com.vn.
A/c, comfortable, central business hotel
in the competent hands of Saigontourist.
The staff are friendly and helpful. The
rooms are well equipped with a/c, satellite
TV, en suite facilities and minibar. There's a
currency exchange, free internet and Wi-Fi
for guests, sauna and breakfast included.

$ Tay Ho
42 Hai Ba Trung St, T710-382 3392,
tay_ho@hotmail.com.
This lovely place has a variety of rooms
and a great public balcony that can be
enjoyed by those paying for back rooms.
All rooms now have private bathrooms.
River view rooms cost more. The staff
are friendly.

Restaurants

Hai Ba Trung St by the river offers
a good range of excellent and very
well-priced little restaurants, and the
riverside setting is an attractive one.

$$$-$$ Victoria Can Tho Spices
See Where to stay.
Excellent location on the riverbank
where it's possible to dine alfresco or
inside its elegant restaurant. The food is
delicious and the service is excellent.

$$-$ Sao Hom
Nha Long Cho Co, T710-381 5616,
http://saohom.transmekong.com.

This new and very busy restaurant on
the riverfront serves plentiful food and
provides very good service. Watching
the river life and the floating pleasure
palaces at night is a good way to spend
an evening meal here. Shame about the
illuminated billboards on the opposite
bank. This place is popular with large
tour groups that alter the character of
the restaurant when they swarm in.

$ Mekong
38 Hai Ba Trung St.
Perfectly good little place near the
river in this popular restaurant strip.
Serves decent Vietnamese fare at
reasonable prices.

$ Nam Bo
50 Hai Ba Trung St, T710-382 3908.
Excellent little place serving tasty
Vietnamese and French dishes in an
attractive French house on the corner
of the street; try to get a table on the
balcony. Small café downstairs.

Bars and clubs

The **Golf Can Tho Hotel** and **Victoria
Can Tho Hotel** have well-stocked bars
(see Where to stay, above).

What to do

Boat trips
Trans Mekong, *97/10 Ngo Quyen, P An
Cu, T710-382 9540, www.transmekong.
com.* Operates the *Bassac*, a converted
24-m wooden rice barge that can sleep
12 passengers in 6 a/c cabins with
private bathrooms. Prices include dinner
and breakfast, entry tickets to visited
sites, a French- or English-speaking
guide on board and access to a small
boat, *Bassac II*, catering for 24 guests.
The Victoria Can Tho operates the

Rice research

Can Tho has its own university, founded in 1966 and also a famous rice research institute, located at O Mon, 25 km away on Highway 91. Like the International Rice Research Institute (IRRI), its more famous counterpart at Los Baños in the Philippines (and to which it is attached), one of the Can Tho institute's key functions is developing rice hybrids that will flourish in the varied conditions of the delta. Near the coast, rice has to be tolerant of salt and tidal flooding. In Dong Thap Province, near Cambodia, floating rice grows stalks of 4-5 m in order to keep its head above the annual flood. The task of the agronomists is to produce varieties that flourish in these diverse environments and at the same time produce decent yields.

Lady Hau, an upmarket converted rice barge for trips to the floating markets.

Cookery classes
The Victoria Can Tho, *see Where to stay*. Offers a Vietnamese cooking class in the hotel, in a rice field, at the 'Ancient House' or on its boat the *Lady Hau* with a trip to the local market.

Swimming
The Victoria Can Tho (see Where to stay, above) has a pool open to the public for a fee.

Tennis
Tennis courts are available at the **Golf Hotel** and **Victoria Can Tho** (see Where to stay).

Therapies
The Victoria Can Tho boasts several massage cabins on the riverfront offering a host of treatments. Open to non-guests.

Tour operators
Can Tho Tourist, *20 Hai Ba Trung St, T710-382 1852, http://canthotourist.vn*. Organizes tours in small and larger boats – the latter not the best way to see the delta. The staff are helpful and knowledgeable. Tours include trips to Cai Rang, Phong Dien and Phung Hiep floating markets, to Soc Trang, city tours, canal tours, bicycle tours, trekking tours, stork sanctuary tour and homestays that involve working with farmers in the fields. General boat tours also arranged. **Victoria Can Tho**, *T710-381 0111, www.victoriahotels.asia*. Expensive tours to see delta sights; city tour; floating markets and Soc Trang offered. The *Lady Hau* cruises to Cai Rang floating market (breakfast on board). Sunset cruises also possible.

Transport

Air
Vietnam Airlines, 66 Chau Van Liem St. The airport is situated about 7 km from the city centre. Flights to **Hanoi**.

Bicycle
Bikes can be hired for from **Can Tho Tourist**, see Tour operators, above.

Boat
A bridge has been built to Can Tho but ferries will still operate for direct routing as the bridge is 10 km from Can Tho. There are no public boats leaving Can Tho.

Bus
The bus station is about 2 km northwest of town along Nguyen Trai St, at the intersection with Hung Vuong St. Hourly connections to **HCMC**'s Mien Tay terminal, 4-5 hrs (**Phuong Trang** bus company, T710-376 9768, provides a good service), and other towns in the Mekong Delta: **Rach Gia**, 0400-1800, 5 hrs; **Chau Doc**, 8 daily, 4 hrs; **Long Xuyen**, 6 daily; **My Tho**, hourly; **Vinh Long**, hourly, 55,000d; **Ca Mau**, hourly Soc Trang. **Can Tho Tourist**, see Tour operators, above, will book a ticket for you for a small fee and include transfer from your hotel to the bus station.

Car
Cars with drivers can be hired from larger hotels.

Taxi
Mai Linh Taxi, T710-382 8282.

Bac Lieu

Bac Lieu is a small and pretty riverside city and the provincial capital of Bac Lieu Province. New hotels and buildings are being erected and they are trying to capture some of the lucrative Tra Vinh market (there are many Khmer living here and several temples). Bac Lieu has a bird sanctuary that has large numbers of white herons.

It is not as rich in rice production as other Mekong provinces on account of its proximity to the sea, so the enterprising locals have salt farms instead. They also make a living out of oysters and fishing. Life has always been hard in the province due to saltwater intrusion.

Sights
The **bird sanctuary**, 3 km southwest of town, is home to a large white heron population. The best times to visit are December and January. The birds nest in January and then migrate and do not return until late May. Do apply plenty of mosquito repellent as the place is inundated with biting insects.

Xiem Can Temple (Komphir Sakor Prekchru) ① *12 km west of Bac Lieu, free to enter but alms would be appreciated*, is a pretty Khmer temple complex. It was built in 1887 and a small group of monks still resides here.

Hoi Binh Moi Temple (Resay Vongsaphuth lethmay) is one of the newer temples, constructed in 1952. A recent addition (1990) is the ossuary tower. There is a small monastic school attached to the temple.

Tourist information

Bac Lieu Tourist Company
*2 Hoang Van Thu St, T781-382 4272,
www.baclieutourist.com.*
Has a reasonable selection of quite
moderately priced tours.

Where to stay

$$ Cong Tu Bac Lieu
*13 Dien Bien Phu St, T781-395 3304,
http://congtubaclieu.vn/.*
A stunning French colonial home that
has undergone a rather over the top
sprucing up. Its ochre front with duck
egg blue shutters looks out over the
river. There's fanciful stucco work and
elaborate tiling throughout.

$ Bac Lieu Hotel
*4-6 Hoang Van Thu St, T781-382 2437,
baclieuhotel@yahoo.com.*
Very basic, but very cheap lodgings.

Restaurants

Bac Lieu hotel has reasonable restaurants
for breakfast, lunch and dinner.

$ Cong Tu Bac Lieu
This compound is popular all day. Serves
up Vietnamese food in the surrounds of
a colonial mansion.

Festivals

Late Nov/early Dec The main festival in
the area is the **Ngo boat racing**, which
is held in Soc Trang, 70 km north of Bac
Lieu, at the same time as the **Soc Trang
Oc Om Boc festival**.

Tip…
If you wish to see the boat races in
a more relaxed atmosphere then
base yourself in Bac Lieu, just over
an hour's drive away.

Transport

Bac Lieu is 70 km from Soc Trang,
113 km from Can Tho, 287 km from
Ho Chi Minh City and 67 km from
Ca Mau. The roads have improved
but it is a long drive.
 Buses go to **Soc Trang**, **Can Tho**,
HCMC, **Ca Mau** and **Long Xuyen**
from the station on Hai Ba Trung St.

Ca Mau Province

an area of interest to botanists and ornithologists

Ca Mau is the provincial capital of Ca Mau Province, Vietnam's most southerly
province, and is a huge, ugly, cluttered urban sprawl. The province consists
primarily of the U Minh cajeput forest and swamp, both of which are the largest
in Vietnam. Right at the tip of the country is the new Mui Ca Mau National Park.
Apart from a reasonable selection of churches and pagodas Ca Mau's main
attractions interest botanists and ornithologists.

Cao Mau

A **Cao Dai Temple** is located on Phan Ngoc Hien Street. Although not as large as the main one in Tay Ninh it is still an impressive structure. It houses quite a few monks and is thriving. The monks will be happy to explain Cao Daism.

U Minh Forest

U Minh Forest is the main reason most people visit Ca Mau. It was a favoured hiding place for the Viet Cong troops during the war. Despite the chemical damage and the huge postwar deforestation to make way for shrimp farms there are still trees and large numbers of birds to be seen and it is a favourite destination for ornithologists. It is also of interest to botanists. **Minh Hai Tourist** operates an all-day tour of the forest and mangrove swamps for US$52 per person including tour guide, car and ticket. Note that tours may be off limits from May to October due to forest fires. In the monsoon season flooding occurs on a regular basis. December to February should be the best months to visit.

Mui Ca Mau National Park

Mui Ca Mau National Park, at the southern edge of the country, has been named a UNESCO World Biosphere Reserve. The 41,862-ha park of mangrove and mudflats is home to hundreds of animals and birds. Some of the birds include the Far Eastern curlew, Chinese egret and black-headed ibis.

Listings Ca Mau

Tourist information

Du Lick Ca Mau
91 Phan Ngoc Hien St, T780-383 1828, www.dulichcamau.com. Mon-Fri 0730-1100, 1330-1700, Sat 0730-1100.
A well-run and professional travel agency offering the full spectrum of services.

Where to stay

$ Dong Anh
25 Tran Hung Dao.
Probably the best option in town with very clean rooms and decent beds.

$ Quoc Te
179 Phan Ngoc Hien St, T780-366 6666, www.hotelquocte.com.

Ca Mau is short on good options which makes this rather average budget hotel a reasonable option, but don't expect great things.

Restaurants

There are plenty of very cheap restaurants close to the market on Ly Bon St.

$ Hu Tieu Nam Vang
2C Tran Hung Dao St, diagonally opposite Hoang Gia hotel.
Cheap and friendly and serving *hu tieu*.

$ Trieu Phat
26 Phan Ngoc Hien St.
Serves *com* and hu *tieu*.

Transport

There are direct flights from Ho Chi Minh City, bus connections and a boat from Rach Gia. The city has plenty of taxis and river taxis and a public bus service.

Air
The airport is located at 93 Ly Thuong Kiet St heading out of town. Flights to **HCMC**.

Boat
It is possible to take a daily ferry from Ca Mau to **Rach Gia**, from Ferry Pier B (located off Cao Thang St near the floating market).

Bus
Ca Mau is almost at the end of Highway 1A. Bac Lieu, Soc Trang and onwards connection to Can Tho are along Highway 1A. Rach Gia is reached by Highway 63. Good bus connections to **Can Tho**, **Bac Lieu**, **Soc Trang** and **Rach Gia**. The bus service to **HCMC** takes 11 hrs by regular bus and 8 hrs by express, daily 0530-1030.

Chau Doc
& around

Chau Doc was once an extremely attractive riverside town on the west bank of the Hau. It still has a pretty riverfront, but the bustling market town is no longer as appealing as it once was. One of its biggest attractions is the nearby Nui Sam, which is dotted with pagodas and tombs. Across the river you can boat over to Cham villages and see the floating fish farms. South of Chau Doc the road passes the sorrowful Ba Chuc ossuary. There are also three international border crossings to Cambodia.

Chau Doc

an important trading centre for the surrounding agricultural communities

The large market sprawls from the riverfront down and along Le Cong Thanh Doc, Phu Thu, Bach Dang and Chi Lang streets. It sells fresh produce and black-market goods smuggled across from Cambodia.

Near the market and the river, at the intersection of Tran Hung Dao Street and Nguyen Van Thoai Street, is the **Chau Phu Pagoda**. Built in 1926, it is dedicated to Thai Ngoc Hau, a former local mandarin. The pagoda is rather dilapidated, but has some fine carved pillars, which miraculously are still standing. A **Cao Dai temple**, which welcomes visitors, stands on Louise Street.

The **Vinh Te Canal**, north of town, is 90 km long and is a considerable feat of engineering, begun in 1819 and finished in 1824 using 80,000 workers. Its purpose was twofold: navigation and defence from the Cambodians. So impressed was Emperor Minh Mang in the achievement of its builder, Nguyen Van Thoai (or Thoai Ngoc Hau), that he named the canal after Thoai's wife, Chau Thi Vinh Te.

Where to stay

$$$$-$$$ Victoria Chau Doc
32 1 Le Loi St, T076-386 5010,
www.victoriahotels-asia.com.
This old, cream building with its
beautiful riverfront deck and pool
complete with loungers and view of
the river confluence is the perfect place
location in which to relax. All rooms
are attractively decorated. The hotel
group runs a daily speedboat to and
from Phnom Penh. A refined place with
superb service.

$$$$-$$$ Victoria Nui Sam Lodge
Sam Mountain, www.victoriahotels.asia.
A fantastic addition to the area, this
beautiful resort offers 36 bungalows
dotted across the mountain offering
knock-out views. The service is excellent
and the kitchen is first rate. A fantastic
hideaway in the Mekong. Also has
a wonderful swimming pool with
unobstructed views of the paddy fields
stretching as far as the eye can see.

$ Hai Chau hotel
63 Thuong Dang Le St.
A good budget option. The garish
exterior doesn't bode well, but the
rooms are clean and the a/c works well.

Essential Chau Doc

Getting around

Chau Doc itself is easily small enough
to explore on foot. By means of a
bridge or sampan crossing, some
nearby Cham villages can be reached
and explored on foot too. Nui Sam,
the nearby sacred mountain, can be
reached by motorbike or bus.

When to go

Chau Doc suffers not only from
the universal Mekong problem of
the monsoon floods, but also from
the fact that Nui Sam is one of the
holiest sites in southern Vietnam
and, as such, attracts vast numbers of
pilgrims on auspicious days. From a
climatic viewpoint then the best time
to visit is December to April.

Time required

Ideal for two days of exploring.

Restaurants

$$$ La Bassac
In Victoria Chau Doc.
The French and Vietnamese menus at this
suave riverside restaurant with stunning
terrace include buffalo paillard with
shallot confit, basa in banana leaf with
saffron, rack of lamb coated in Mekong
herbs, sweet potato puree and pork wine
reduction or spaghetti with flambéed
shrimps in vodka paprika sauce. The bar is
a lovely spot for a pre-dinner drink.

$$ Thanh Thao
74 Trung Nu Vuong T073-869095.
Serves a huge selection of fresh seafood,
including crab, squid and lobster. A
no-nonsense eatery that's very popular
with locals.

$ Bay Bong
22 Thung Dang Le St, T076-386 7271.
Specializes in hot pots and soups and
also offers a good choice of fresh fish.
The staff are friendly.

A gift for Phuc Khoat

Until the mid-18th century Chau Doc was part of Cambodia: it was given to the Nguyen lord, Nguyen Phuc Khoat, after he had helped to put down a local insurrection. The area still supports a large Khmer population, as well as the largest Cham settlement in the delta. Cambodia's influence can be seen in the tendency for women to wear the *kramar*, Cambodia's famous chequered scarf, instead of the *non la* conical hat, and in the people's darker skin, indicating Khmer blood.

$ Mekong
41 Le Loi St, T076-386 7381, opposite Victoria Chau Doc. Open for lunch and dinner.
It is located right beside a in a lovingly restored French villa. Good selection of food including grilled prawns and fried rice dishes. and the staff are friendly.

$ Sunrise Palace
Next to the tourist pier. Open 1100-2230.
The beef in Chau Doc is probably the best in Vietnam and here the *bo nuong* (grilled beef), served with herbs, is excellent. Good *de nuong* (goat) too. Serves delicious Russian live beer that goes perfectly with the food. The outdoor seating is best – inside is a wedding venue space.

Bars and clubs

Victoria Chau Doc
See Where to stay, above.
Has a bar and a pool table.

Festivals

On all almost every weekend there is one festival or another. The busiest festivals are centred on Tet, 4 months after Tet and the mid-autumn moon festival.

What to do

Swimming
There is a swimming pool at the **Victoria Chau Doc**.

Therapies
A massage and fitness centre can be found at the **Victoria Chau Doc**. All the services are available to the general public.

Tour operators
Mekong Tours, *Vinh Phuoc Hotel, and 14 Nguyen Huu Canh St, T076-386 8222, and at Thanh Nam 2 hotel.* Local trips include the fish farms, floating markets and Cham village. Trips to Phu Quoc and boat trips to Phnom Penh (8-10 hrs or express boat 5 hrs; Cambodian visas can be bought at the border). A/c and public buses also booked to Ha Tien. Open Tour Bus ticketing and visa applications. Private boats can be arranged, but this is now rare so prices are not set.
Victoria Chau Doc, *32 Le Loi St, T76-386 5010, www.victoriahotels-asia.com.* Tours to Nui Sam, the city and a very interesting tour to the floating market, fish farms and Muslim village, cooking class, Tra Su forest tour, farming tour and Le Jarai cruise tour. Minimum 2 people for all tours.

Transport

It is possible (but expensive) to get to Chau Doc by boat from Can Tho (private charter only or by the Victoria Hotel group boat for guests only). Road connections with Can Tho, Vinh Long and Ho Chi Minh City are good.

Boat

There are daily departures to **Phnom Penh**. A couple of tour operators in town organize boat tickets, see Tour operators, above. **Victoria Hotel** speedboats go to Phnom Penh. Make sure you have a valid Vietnamese visa if you are entering the country as these cannot be issued at the border crossing; Cambodian visas can be bought at all the nearby crossings.

Bus

The station is 3 km south from the town centre T76-386 7171. Minibuses stop in town on Quang Trung St. Connections with **HCMC** (6 hrs), hourly, 0600-2400; **Tra Vinh**; **Ca Mau**; **Long Xuyen**; **Can Tho**, every 30 mins; **Rach Gia**; and **Ha Tien**. There is an uncomfortable 10-hr bus ride from Chau Doc to Phnom Penh via Moc Bai, see page 31.

Mekong Tours, see Tour operators, runs a bus to **Phnom Penh** via Tinh Bien (see border crossings to Cambodia, page 31).

Around Chau Doc

a mountain, mosques and fish farms

Nui Sam (Sam Mountain)
Take a bus (there is a stop at the foot of the mountain) or xe om.

This mountain, about 5 km southwest of town, was designated a 'Famed Beauty Spot' in 1980 by the Ministry of Culture and is one of the holiest sites in southern Vietnam. Rising from the flood plain, Nui Sam is a favourite spot for Vietnamese tourists who throng here, especially at festival time.

The mountain, really a barren, rock-strewn hill, can be seen at the end of the continuation of Nguyen Van Thoai Street. It is honeycombed with tombs, sanctuaries and temples. Most visitors come only to see Tay An Pagoda, Lady Xu Temple, and the tomb of Thoai Ngoc Hau (see below). But it is possible to walk or drive right up the hill for good views of the surrounding countryside: from the summit it is easy to appreciate that this is some of the most fertile land in Vietnam. At the top is a military base, formerly occupied by American soldiers and now by Vietnamese watching their Cambodian flank. Near the top the **Victoria Hotel** group has built a hotel used for conferences only.

Tay An Pagoda is at the foot of the hill, facing the road. Built originally in 1847, it has been extended twice and now represents an eclectic mixture of styles – Chinese, Islamic, perhaps even Italian. The pagoda contains a bewildering display of more than 200 statues.

A short distance on from the pagoda, to the right, past shops and stalls, is the **Chua Xu**. This temple was originally constructed in the late 19th century, and then rebuilt in 1972. It is rather a featureless building, though highly revered by the Vietnamese and honours the holy Lady Xu whose statue is enshrined in the new multi-roofed pagoda. The 23rd to the 25th of the fourth lunar month is the period when the holy Lady is commemorated, during which time, hundreds of Vietnamese flock to see her being washed and reclothed. Lady Xu is a major pilgrimage for traders and business from Ho Chi Minh City and the south, all hoping that sales will thereby soar and profits leap.

On the other side of the road is the **tomb of Thoai Ngoc Hau** (1761-1829); an enormous head of the man graces the entranceway. Thoai is a local hero having played a role in the resistance against the French but more for his engineering feats in canal building and draining swamps. He is also known as Nguyen Van Thoai and this name is given to one of Chau Doc's streets. The real reason to come here is to watch the pilgrims and to climb the hill.

Hang Pagoda, a 200-year-old temple situated halfway up Nui Sam, is worth visiting for several reasons. In the first level of the temple are some vivid cartoon drawings of the tortures of hell. The second level is built at the mouth of a cave which last century was home to a woman named Thich Gieu Thien. Her likeness and tomb can be seen in the first pagoda. Fed up with her lazy and abusive husband she left her home in Cholon and came to live in this cave, as an ascetic supposedly waited on by two snakes.

Nui Sam is the most expensive burial site in southern Vietnam. Wealthy Vietnamese and Chinese believe it is a most propitious last resting place. This is why the lower flanks are given over almost entirely to tombs.

Cham villages
There are a number of Cham villages around Chau Doc. **Phu Hiep**, **Con Tien** and **Chau Giang** are on the opposite bank of the Hau River. There are several mosques in the villages as the Cham in this part of Vietnam are Muslim. At Chau Phong visitors can enjoy homestays. To reach the villages, take a sampan from the ferry terminal near the Victoria Chau Doc Hotel.

A visit to the floating fish farm villages (some 3000 floating houses), such as **Con Tien**, is a worthwhile and informative experience. A floating farm will have some 150,000 carp contained in a 6-m-deep iron cage beneath the house. Fish are worth around 600d for a baby and up to 25,000d for 500 g for a five-month-old fish. Catfish and mullet are also raised. (Chau Doc has a catfish monument on the riverfront promenade.) When the fish are ready for sale, boats with nets under them are used to transport the fish to Long Xuyen.

Border crossings to Cambodia
It is possible to cross the border to Cambodia north of Chau Doc at the **Vinh Xuong** (Omsano in Cambodia) boat crossing; just south of Chau Doc at **Tinh Bien** near Nha Ban (Phnom Den, Takeo, on the Cambodian side), and at **Xà Xía**, near Ha Tien (Prek Chak in Cambodia). It is possible to exit at Vinh Xuong and get a Cambodian visa but it's not possible to get a Vietnamese visa to enter Vietnam. At Tinh Bien you can buy a Cambodian visa but not a Vietnamese visa on entering. At Xà Xía, you can get a Cambodian visa but not a Vietnamese visa. There is a Vietnam consulate in Sihanoukville.

Chau Doc to Ha Tien

Ha Tien can be reached either by boat or by road. The scenery as the road skirts the Cambodian border is beautiful and the local way of life little changed in hundreds of years. The road passes Ba **Chuc ossuary** where the bones of 1000 Vietnamese killed in 1978 by the Khmer Rouge are displayed in a glass-sided memorial. Skulls are also stacked up in a glass-sided memorial, and each section is categorized by gender and by age – from children to grandparents. Nearby, there is a house in a small row of shops where photographs of the massacre are displayed; they are grisly and abhorrent.

An alternative route to Ha Tien is to follow Highway 91 to **Nha Ban town**. Turn right and follow the signs to Tri Ton town, along the way you drive through the Plain of Reeds, pass Cam Mountain and also various Khmer temples that are beautiful and thankfully tourist free. Upon arrival in **Tri Ton town** (some of the shops have signs in Khmer script) turn right and head for the Vam Ray ferry. Once across the **Ha Tien-Rach Gia canal** you are on Highway 80. Turn left to **Rach Gia** and right to **Ha Tien**.

Rach Gia

thriving port with little touristic appeal

Despite Rach Gia having undergone somewhat of a transformation in recent years, from being a rather unpleasant little town to a thriving port with a new urban development on reclaimed land, there isn't much reason for the tourist to linger. Rach Gia is the capital of Kien Giang Province. The wealth of the province is based on rice, seafood and trade. *Nuoc mam*, the renowned Vietnamese fish sauce, is produced here.

Sights

There are a number of pagodas to visit, the wharf area is interesting and the bustling fish market displays the wealth of the seas here. Some attractive colonial architecture survives. The centre of the town is in fact an island at the mouth of the Cai Lon River.

Rach Gia's pagodas include the **Phat Lon Pagoda**, which is on the mainland north of town just off Quang Trung Street, and the **Nguyen Trung Truc Temple**, which is not far away at 18 Nguyen Cong Tru Street, close to the port. The latter is dedicated to the 19th-century Vietnamese resistance leader of the same name. Nguyen Trung Truc was active in Cochin China during the 1860s, and led the raid that resulted in the attack on the French warship *Esperance*. As the French closed in, he retreated to the island of Phu Quoc. From here, the French only managed to dislodge him after threatening to kill his mother. He gave himself up and was executed at the market place in Rach Gia on 27 October 1868. His statue also dominates the main small city park at the top of Le Loi street and the riverbank.

Tam Bao Temple dates from the 18th century but was rebuilt in 1917. During the First Indochina War it was used to conceal Viet Minh nationalists who published a newspaper from here. There is the small **Rach Gia Museum** ⓘ *27 Nguyen Van Troi St, T77-386 3727, Mon-Fri 0700-1100, free*, which houses a good selection of pottery and artefacts from Oc-Eo in a lovely old building.

Listings Rach Gia

Tourist information

Du Lich Kien Giang
392 Lâm Quang Ky, T0939-759 888, www. dulichkiengiang.vn.

Where to stay

$ Hoang Gia 2
32 Le Thanh Ton St, T77-392 0980, www. hoanggiahotels.com.vn.
Located near the bus station, this is a basic budget option.

$ Kim Co
141 Nguyen Hung Son St, T77-387 9610, www.kimcohotel.com.
Good, clean rooms and well located. Wi-Fi available.

Restaurants

There is a good selection of cafés on Nguyen Trung Truc, Nguyen Thai Hoc and Tran Hung Dao. At the centre of the coastal strip is the Lac Hong Park where you'll find food stalls, cafés and the Lagoon Seafood Center as well as dozens of folk flying colourful kites.

$ Hai Au
2 Nguyen Trung Truc St, T77-386 3740.
Good choice of food, well presented in a smart building with a lovely outdoor terraced area covered in creepers overlooking the river.

Festivals

Apart from the main festival they have occasional processions to thank Ca Ong, the God of the Sea, for protecting them.

Transport

There are daily flights from Ho Chi Minh City and Phu Quoc. In the peak season it is advisable to book well in advance as the flights tend to fill up fast. There are good road connections with Ha Tien, Long Xuyen, Can Tho. There are also boats to Phu Quoc.

Air
Daily connections with **Phu Quoc Island**, 40 mins, and **HCMC**, 50 mins. The airport is at Rach Soi about 10 km south of Rach Gia. **Airline offices Vietnam Airlines**, 16 Nguyen Trung Truc St, T77-392 4320.

Boat
Daily connections to **Phu Quoc**, departing from the ferry terminal on Nguyen Cong Tru St. A variety of ferry companies including **Superdong** ferries, T77-387 7742, **Duong Dong Express**, T77-387 9765, www.duongdongexpress. com.vn, and **Savanna** leave daily at 0745-0800 arriving 1030 and 1300. From the Rach Meo ferry terminal, 2 km south of town on Ngo Quyen St close to the junction with Nguyen Van Cu St, boats go to **Vinh Thuan** and **Ca Mau**.

Bus

There are 2 stations; the city centre terminal at Nguyen Binh Kiem St and a terminal at Rach Soi, 7 km south of town near the airport. From the 1st bus station, connections to **HCMC**, 8 hrs, **Can Tho**, **Vinh Long**, **Ha Tien** and **Long Xuyen**. **Mai Linh** and **Phung Trang** companies operate express buses to **HCMC**, 5 hrs. From the 2nd bus station, services to **Chau Doc** and **HCMC**.

Taxi

Mai Linh wait at the Nguyen Truc Trac city park. **Taxi Phuong Trinh**, 26 Nguyen Van Troi St, T77-387 8787.

Oc-Eo

piles of stones is all that is left of this ancient city

The site is near the village of Tan Hoi and is only accessible by boat. Hire a small boat (the approach canal is very shallow and narrow) from the river front beyond the Vinh Tan Van Market, northeast along Bach Dang St. The trip takes several hours.

Oc-Eo is an ancient city about 10 km inland from Rach Gia. It is of great interest and significance to archaeologists, but there is not a great deal for the visitor to see bar a pile of stones on which sits a small bamboo shrine. The site is overseen by an elderly custodian who lives adjacent to it.

This port city of the ancient kingdom of Funan (see page 106) was at its height between the first and sixth centuries AD. Excavations have shown that buildings were constructed on piles and the city was interlinked by a complex network of irrigation and transport canals. Like many of the ancient empires of the region, Oc-Eo built its wealth on controlling trade between the East (China) and the West (India and the Mediterranean). Vessels from Malaya, Indonesia and Persia docked here. No sculpture has yet been found, but a gold medallion with the profile of the Roman emperor Antonius Pius (AD 152) has been unearthed.

Ha Tien

one-time attractive town now spoiled by development

Ha Tien used to be a quaint small town with a tranquil pace of life and an attractive US-built pontoon bridge that carried bikers and pedestrians across to the opposite bank of the river. However, today hotels clutter the riverbank and there is lots of construction. The boom has no doubt been helped by the opening of the border with Cambodia at Xa Xia. Step back off the main thoroughfare and you will find vestiges of its quaint appeal.

Sights

Despite its colourful history, modern Ha Tien does not contain a great deal of interest to the visitor and apart from a handful of buildings there is little of architectural merit.

ON THE ROAD
Military might

Ha Tien's history is strongly coloured by its proximity to Cambodia, to which the area belonged until the 18th century. The numerical and agricultural superiority of the Vietnamese allowed them to gradually displace the Khmer occupants and eventually military might, under Mac Cuu, prevailed. But it is not an argument the Khmer are prepared to walk away from, as their incursions into the area in the late 1970s showed, and bitter resentments remain on both sides of the border.

There are a number of pagodas in town. The **Tam Bao Temple**, at 328 Phuong Thanh Street, was founded in the 18th century, as too was **Chua Phu Dung** (Phu Dung Pagoda), which can be found a short distance along a path to the northwest just off Phuong Thanh Street. A lengthy story is attached to this temple, the 'Cotton Rose Hibiscus Pagoda'. In 1730, newly widowed Nguyen Nghi fled invaders from Laos and landed in Ha Tien with his son and 10-year-old daughter, Phu Cu (the ancient form of Phu Dung with the same floral meaning). Nguyen Nghi was soon appointed Professor of Literature and Poetry to Duke Mac Cuu's son, Mac Tu (see Den Mac Cuu below) and privately tutored his own little daughter, who had taken to dressing as a boy in order to be able to attend school. After Duke Mac Cuu's untimely death in 1735 his son was granted the name Mac Thien Tich and the title Great Admiral Commander-in-Chief, Plenipotentiary Minister of Ha Tien Province. Later he inaugurated a poetry club at which young Phu Cu, still in the guise of a boy, declaimed exquisitely, setting passions ablaze. Surreptitious investigations put the Great Admiral's mind at rest: 'he' was in fact a girl. A long poetic romance and royal wedding followed. After years of happy marriage the angelic Phu Cu one day begged her husband to let her break with their poetic love of the past and become a nun. The Great Admiral realized he could not but comply. He built the Phu Cu, Cotton Rose Hibiscus Pagoda, wherein his beloved wife spent the rest of her life in prayer and contemplation. The towering pagoda was built so high that it served as a constant reminder and could, in due course, be seen from his own tomb.

Den Mac Cuu, the temple dedicated to the worship of the Mac Cuu and his clan, was built in 1898-1902. Mac Cuu was provincial governor under the waning Khmer rule and in 1708 established a Vietnamese protectorate. The temple lies a short way from the town and sits at the foot of Nui Lang (Tomb Mountain). To the left of the altar house is a map showing the location of the tombs of members of the clan. Mac Cuu's own tomb lies a short distance up the hill along a path leading from the right of the temple, from where there are good views of the sea.

Around the back of Nui Lang (a short drive, or longish trek) is **Lang Mo Ba Co Nam** (tomb of Great Aunt Number Five), an honorary title given to the three-year-old daughter of Mac Cuu who was buried alive. It has become an important shrine to Vietnamese seeking her divine intercession in time of family crisis and is more visited than Mac Cuu's tomb.

Tourist information

Ha Tien Tourism Coop Ltd
1 Phuong Thanh St, T77-395 9598,
hatientourism@gmail.com.
Organizes boat tickets to Phu Quoc and
buses to Cambodia and destinations in
the south of Vietnam including Ho Chi
Minh City.

Where to stay

$$$ River Hotel Ha Tien
Tran Hau Business Centre, T077-3955 888,
www.riverhotelvn.com.
Very smart, new riverfront hotels with
high quality rooms, many of which have
excellent views. The best place in town.

$ Du Hung
27A Tran Hau St, T77-395 1555.
A recommended budget hotel with
spacious rooms and all facilities close
to the ferry port.

$ Kim Co 1
141 Nguyen Hun Son.
A good central option with clean rooms
and pleasant staff.

Restaurants

There are numerous food stalls along
the river and Ben Tran Hau and Dong
Ho streets.

$ Ha Tien Floating Restaurant
T77-395 9939.
Quite a nice surprise for Ha Tien
with Australian beef on the menu.

There's a huge menu of chicken, frog
and eel as well as fish. Popular with
local businesspeople.

Cafés

Thuy Tien Café
Nguyen Van Hai St.
This is the pick of the bunch. A small,
stilted affair overlooking the river and
the pontoon bridge. It's a wooden café
from where you can sit and watch the
world go by.

Transport

Ha Tien can be reached by road from
Chau Doc, Rach Gia and also by ferry
from Phu Quoc Island.

Bicycle
Ha Tien Tourism Coop Ltd rents bikes
and motorbikes.

Boat
The ferry wharf is opposite the Ha Tien
hotel. Ferries to **Phu Quoc** leave at 0800-
0830 and at 1000.

Bus
The bus station is on the way to the
Cambodia border on Highyway 80
north of town. There are buses to
HCMC, at 0700, 0800 and 0900, 10-
12 hrs; and connections with **Rach Gia**,
4 hrs; **Chau Doc**; **Can Tho**; as well as
other delta towns. Reliable **Mai Linh**
runs to **Rach Gia**.

Phu Quoc
Island

well worth visiting for a few days' relaxation

★Phu Quoc is Vietnam's largest island with beautiful sandy beaches and crystal-clear waters along much of its coastline and forested hills and pepper plantations inland. The arrival of numerous new resorts and the opening of the new international airport has seen some of its virgin land disappear under concrete, but, for the moment, it remains a wonderful place and still extremely under-developed in comparison to the major Thai islands.

Sights

Duong Dong is the main town on the island and many of the hotels and resorts are near here on **Truong Beach**. Millions of fish can be seen laid out to dry on land and on tables – all destined for the pot. Before being bottled they are fermented. At the **Khai Hoan fish sauce factory** ① *free*, huge barrels act as vats, each containing fish and salt. If the sauce is made in concrete vats, the taste is lost and so the sauce is cheaper.

Coi Nguon Museum ① *149 Tran Hung Dao St, T77-398 0206, www.coinguon phuquoc.com, daily 0700-1700, 1 English-speaking guide*, displays a huge amount of island creatures, fishing paraphernalia, old currency and Chinese ceramics from shipwrecked boats.

The island is also a centre for South Sea pearls, with 10,000 collected offshore each year. At the gloriously kitch **Phu Quoc Pearl Gallery** ① *10 km south of Duong Dong, www.treasuresfromthedeep.com, daily 0800-1800*, a video demonstrates the farming operation, the tasting of pearl meat and pearl-making is illustrated in the gallery. Some 100 m south of the pearl farm on the coastal road there are two whale dedication temples, **Lang Ca Ong**. In front of one is a crude whale/dolphin statue.

Ganh Dau, at the northwest tip, is 35 km from Duong Dong. The townsfolk speak Khmer because refugees escaping the Khmer Rouge came here and settled with the locals. The Cambodian coast is 4-5 km away and can be seen, as can the last island of Vietnam. (The Cambodians actually claim Phu Quoc as their own.)

Essential Phu Quoc Island

Getting around

While some of the island's roads are surfaced many are still dirt tracks and so the best way to get around the entire island is by motorbike. There are plenty of motorbike taxis and motorbikes are easily available and cheap to hire. The only problem that visitors are likely to encounter is the very limited signposting, which can make some places pretty hard to find without some form of local assistance. Cars with drivers at fairly reasonable costs are available. Ask at hotels.

When to go

The best time to visit is December to May; during the monsoon seas on the east coast can be very rough.

Time required

Popular weekend destination, but take a few more days to fully explore the interior and take boat trips to outlying islands.

Best beaches

Ganh Dau, page 83
Bai Dai, page 84
Sao, page 84

Where to stay

During peak periods, such as Christmas and Tet, it is advisable to book accommodation well in advance. Most of the resorts lie along the west coast to the south of Duong Dong and are within a few kilometres of the airport. Others are on On Lang Beach.

The beach has a few palms and rocks to clamber on and there is a restaurant.

Bai Dai Beach, south of Ganh Danh, is a strip of white sand backed by casuarinas overlooking Turtle Island. Inland from here the area is heavily forested but the wood is protected by law. In this part of the island fish are laid out to dry on large trestle-tables or on the ground for use as fertilizer. South of Dai Beach is **Ong Lang Beach** where there are a couple of resorts, see Where to stay.

The dazzling white sands of **Sao Beach** on the southeast coast are stunning and worth visiting by motorbike. There are a couple of restaurants at the back of the beach.

The inland streams and waterfalls (Da Ban and Chanh streams) are not very dramatic in the dry season but still provide a relaxing place to swim and walk in the forests.

One of the biggest draws are the boat trips around the **An Thoi islands**, scattered islands, like chips off a block, off the southern coast, which offer opportunities for swimming, snorkelling, diving and fishing. It is also possible to stop off to visit an interesting fishing village at Thom Island.

Listings Phu Quoc Island *map p85*

$$$$ Chen Sea Resort & Spa
Ong Lang Beach, T077-399 5895,
www.centarahotelsresorts.com/cpv.
A very inviting resort with lovely villas set back from the yellow sand beach with sunken bathtubs on generous verandas and outdoor rain showers. The narrow strip of golden sand is dotted with paprika-coloured umbrellas, and there's an infinity pool, spa, water sports and

atmospheric restaurant. Excellent buffet breakfast – don't miss the addictive smoothies. Highly recommended.

$$$$ La Veranda
Tran Hung Dao St, Long Beach, T077-398 2988, www.laverandaresort.com.
A beautiful luxury resort with rooms and villas set in luscious gardens leading on to the main beach on the island. All rooms are beautifully furnished and come with TV, DVD player and Wi-Fi. De luxe rooms and villas come with gorgeous 4-poster beds and drapes. There's a spa, pool and the delicious food of the Pepper Tree Restaurant. The welcome and service is exceptional.

Phu Quoc Island

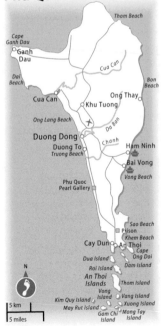

$$$$-$$$ Mai House Resort
Long Beach, T077-384 7003, maihouseresort@yahoo.com.
This is a beautiful resort run by the lovely Tuyet Mai and her husband. The architecture and design is all Mai's work – tasteful with plenty of attention to detail. Set in large flourishing gardens in front of a delicious slice of beach dotted with palms. The 20 a/c bungalows feature 4-poster beds, beamed roofs, pretty tiled bathrooms and balconies with carved balustrades. Sea-view rooms are bigger. Adjoining bungalows available for families. The open fronted small restaurant (with Wi-Fi access and places to lounge) overlooks the beach. One of the best places to eat on the island.

$$$$-$$$ Mango Bay Resort
Ong Lang Beach, T077-3981693 or T9-6968 1820 (mob), www. mangobayphuquoc.com.
A small and environmentally friendly resort located on the beach close to pepper farms. Some bungalows are made from rammed earth and are kitted out with bamboo furniture and tiled floors. There's information on birds and fish, and the restaurant provides a mixture of Vietnamese and Western food at very reasonable prices.

$$$ Bo Resort
Ong Lang Beach, T077-986142/3, www.boresort.com.
This feels like a great escape with 18 stilted bungalows set on a hillside amid flourishing gardens. Rooms come with large rustic bathrooms and alfresco showers. There's no road access to the wild stretch of beach where there are pines, hammocks, kayaks and a beach bar. There's Wi-Fi in the restaurant/bar

and candlelight at night. The owners are warm and friendly.

$$$-$$ Freedomland
Ong Lang Beach, 10-12 mins' walk from beach, T01-226 586802, www.freedomlandphuquoc.com.
This laid-back resort creates a community vibe as all guests eat together at the large dinner table and around campfires. The food is excellent. Wooden stilt bungalows with thatched roofs are scattered around the grounds. Very friendly and highly recommended.

$$ Beach Club
Long Beach, T077-398 0998, www.beachclubvietnam.com.
Luscious golden sands and thatched beach umbrellas at this fantastic, highly rated small resort. The ochre-coloured rooms and 4 bungalows are all close to the sea. It's good value and so always booked up. Reserve well in advance.

$$ Lang Toi
Sao Beach, T09-82337477, langtoi_ restaurant@yahoo.com.vn.
With just 4 beautiful rooms complete with deep bathtubs, large balconies and tasteful wooden furnishings, this house is the best of the 2 options on the stunning Sao Beach. Beachfront restaurant serves all manner of seafood and simpler rice and noodle dishes. Recommended.

Restaurants

The food on Phu Quoc is generally very good, especially the fish and seafood. On the street in Duong Dong try the delicious *gio cuong* (fresh spring rolls). Along the river road a few restaurants also serve good Vietnamese dishes and seafood and are very popular with locals and Vietnamese tourists –

Truong Duong at 30/4 Thanh Tu (T09-146 1419) is one of the best.

Most of the resorts mentioned have beachfront restaurants. The night market is a fantastic place to try lots of different local food in a buzzing atmosphere.

$$$-$$ Itaca Lounge
125 Tran Hung Dao, T0773-992022, www.itacalounge.com.
Chilled out open air place with heavy Greek influences on the menu. Spanish chef Mateu Batista has 25 years of experience and creates a range of creative dished that make this one of the island's must-visit options.

$$$-$$ The Pepper Tree
La Veranda Resort (see Where to stay).
Fine dining in a refined seafront setting with perfect service. The ideal place for a special romantic meal. The pork with local pepper sauce is a treat.

$$$-$$ The Spice House, Cassia Cottage
Ba Keo Beach, T0773-848395, www.cassiacottage.com.
In a lovely garden setting, this fine restaurant has gained a solid reputation for its excellent barbecued seafood and good curries.

$ Buddy's
26 Nguyen Trai St, T77-399 4181.
This is a traveller crowd favourite serving Kiwi ice creams, great shakes and big burgers. Also brews good *Lavazza*.

$ La Cafe
11 Tran Hung Dao St, T90-820 1102.
A tiny streetside cafe serving yoghurts, shakes and breakfasts on cute black-lacquered furniture under beige umbrellas.

Bars and clubs

The Dog Bar
88 Tran Hung Dao St, near the Thien Hai Son Resort, T90-381 4688.
Well-located beer den with cold drinks, pool and sports TV.

Rory's (formerly Amigos)
Next to Veranda, 118/10 Tran Hung Dao, T091-707 0456.
Run by an affable Aussie couple, this beachfront bar and restaurant has a huge deck for great sun set views. Pizzas and burgers, grilled seafood and a large range of cocktails. Good promos and dancing later till the small hours.

Shopping

If you have Vietnamese friends or family and return home without a bottle of the fish sauce you will be in trouble. However, you cannot take the sauce on a **Vietnam Airlines** flight. The Duong Dong market and also the night market are the best places to head for gifts.

Coi Nguon, *149 Tran Hung Dao, T0773-980206, www.coinguonphuquoc.com.* A well-stocked shop selling a wide variety of wares using pearls, conch shells and driftwood, **Coi Nguon** is also home to a good museum.
Treasures from the Deep, *www.treasuresfromthedeep.com.* New Zealand jeweller, which is the best place to buy the pearls the island is famed for.

What to do

Most of the resorts are very happy to arrange tours and they are a good source of up-to-date information. Water sports, cycling tours, boat tours and walking can all be arranged.

Diving
Rainbow Divers, *Tran Hung Dao St, close to the market, T91-723 9433 (mob), www.divevietnam.com.* Long-standing operation with a very good reputation.

Tour operators
John's Tours, *New Star Café, 143 Tran Hung Dao St, T091-910 7086, www.johnsislandtours.com.* Run by the super helpful and friendly John Tran out of the **New Star Caféa** office (next to the alley to La Veranda) and various kiosks on the beach as well as hotel desks. John can organize anything for any budget and knows the island like the back of his hand. Snorkelling, squid fishing, island tours and car hire can all be arranged. Car hire and motorbikes with drivers also arranged.
Tony Travel, *100 Tran Hung Dao St or based at the Rainbow Divers office on Tran Hung Dao St opposite the market, T0913-197334, phuquoctonytourravelpq@yahoo.com.vn.* Kiosks on the beach too. Tony knows Phu Quoc extremely well and speaks fluent English. He would be able to organize almost anything. In his stable are island tours, snorkelling to the south and north islands, deep-sea fishing excursions, car and motorbike rental and hotel and transport reservations. He also runs **Rainbow Divers**.

Transport

You can get to Phu Quoc by boat from Rach Gia or Ha Tien or by plane from Rach Gia and Ho Chi Minh City. Most hotels will provide a free pick-up service from the airport if accommodation is booked in advance. *Xe om* drivers and taxis meet the ferries.

Air

There are daily flights to **HCMC** and **Rach Gia**.

Airline offices Vietnam Airlines, 122 Nguyen Trung Truc St, Duong Dong, T77-399667.

Boat

Most ferries leave from Vong and Nam Ninh ports near the beaches of the same names. John of **John's Tours** (see page 87) can sell all tickets and can advise on schedules. An Thoi port in the south.

Hong Tam, at **John's Tours**, ferries to **Ha Tien** daily at 0830, 1½ hrs. **Superdong**, 1 Tran Hung Dao St, Duong Dong, T077-348 6180. Ferries to **Rach Gia** from Vong Beach at 0800 and 1300, 2½ hrs 1300 arriving 1535. Ferries for **Ha Tien** leave a 0800, 1½ hrs. **Savana**, 21 Nguyen Trai St, Duong Dong, T0773-992999, 1 ferry per day to **Rach Gia**, 1240, 2½ hrs.

Duong Dong Express leaves for **Rach Gia** at 1245 arriving 1515, www.duongdongexpress.com.vn.

Vinashin, 21 Nguyen Trai St, T077-260 0155, leaves 0810.

Cawaco from Ham Ninh to **Ha Tien** at 0830 arriving 1000. Also departs Bai Vong 1400 arriving 1520.

Car, bicycle and motorbike

Cars, motorbikes and bicycles can be rented from resorts.

Taxi

Mai Linh, No 10 30 Thang 4 St, Duong Dong, T77-397 9797. **Sasco**, 379 Nguyen Trung Truc St, T77-399 5599.

Con Dao

a true island paradise

★Con Dao is an archipelago of 14 islands and one of Vietnam's last relatively untouched wilderness areas with great possibilities for wildlife viewing and the country's best diving. The biggest and only permanently settled island is Con Son with a population of approximately 6000 people.

Sights

The combination of mountains and islands, as well as its biodiversity, make Con Dao extremely special. It is also one of Vietnam's last relatively pristine areas. There are just a few main roads around Con Son and an unbelievable lack of traffic. The main hotels face out onto Con Son Bay behind the coastal road. The colourful fishing boats that used to bob and work the sea here have largely been moved to Ben Dam port although a few remain.

The prison system
The prison system operated between 1862 and 1975, first by the French and then by the Americans. **Prison Phu Hai**, which backs on to parts of the Saigon Con Dao Resort, was built in 1862 and is the largest prison on the islands with 10 detention rooms and 20 punishment cells. Inside, the chapel was built by the Americans in 1963. Next door is **Phu Son Prison** built in 1916. The third prison, **Phu Tho**, plus **Camp Phu Tuong** and **Camp Phu Phong** (built in 1962) contained the infamous 'tiger cages' where prisoners were chained and tortured; the enclosures still stand. Metal bars were placed across the roofs of the cells and guards would throw excrement and lime onto the prisoners. In addition, many prisoners were outside in areas known as 'sun-bathing compartments'. Not content on limiting torture methods, a cow manure enclosure was used to dunk prisoners in sewage up to 3 m deep. American-style tiger enclosures were built in 1971 at **Camp Phu Binh**. In total there were 504 tiger cages. Beyond the prisons, inland, is the **Hang Duong cemetery** where many of the victims of the prison are buried. The grave of Le Hong Phong, the very first General Secretary of the Communist Party in Vietnam (1935-1936) and Vo Thi Sau (1933-1952) can be seen among them.

A tour of the prisons and cemetery costs can be arranged through the museum, see below. There is an excellent and well-curated museum just outside the main

Essential Con Dao

Getting around

The main hotels offer a shuttle to the airport, but the best way to get around the island is by hiring a motorbike or a bicycle for shorter trips.

When to go

Between June and September is sea turtle nesting season (records show that the 1st and 15th of the month are best) although good weather is not guaranteed. February to April can be incredibly windy. The wet season lasts from May to November.

Time required

It's possible to see a lot of the island in two days, but three or four will allow you to truly enjoy it.

town, which offers a fascinating if disturbing insight into the island's past. A visit here is highly recommended.

There is a small museum and explanatory displays at the **National Park office headquarters** ⓘ *see below, Mon-Fri 0700-1130, 1330-1700, Sat 0730-1100, 1400-1630.*

Con Dao National Park

29 Vo Thi Sau St, T64-383 0650, www. condaopark.com.vn.

There are a number of activities that can be organized in the national park, from snorkelling and swimming, to forest walks and birdwatching. Diving is available to see some of Con Dao's underwater features, such as its caves, as well as the coral reefs. In 1984 the forests on all 14 islands of the Con Dao archipelago were given official protection, and in 1993, 80% of the land area was designated a national park. In 1998 the park boundaries were expanded to include the surrounding sea.

In 1995, with support from the World Wildlife Fund, the park began a sea-turtle conservation project. Con Dao is the most important sea-turtle nesting site in Vietnam, with several hundred female green turtles (*Chelonia mydas*) coming ashore to lay their eggs every year. Occasionally the hawksbill turtle visits too. Park staff attach a tag to every turtle in order to identify returning turtles, and move the turtles' eggs if they are in danger of being flooded at high tide. The rest of the year the turtles migrate long distances. Recently, a turtle tagged in Con Dao was found in a fishing village in Cambodia – unfortunately the tag was insufficient protection to prevent it being eaten. Also in 1995, park staff identified the presence of dugongs (sea cows), which are mammals that feed on seagrass and can live to more than 70 years. Unfortunately, before the park was established dugongs were caught for meat so now the population in Con Dao is small and endangered.

The coral reefs surrounding the islands are among the most diverse in the country. Scientists have identified more than 200 species of coral and coral fish. In November 1997, typhoon Linda struck the islands and many of Con Dao's coral reefs were damaged.

In the forests scientists have identified more than 1000 plant species, of which several are unique to Con Dao and include many valuable medicinal and timber species. Bird life is also significant with rare species such as the pied imperial pigeon (*Ducula bicolor*) – Con Dao is the only place in Vietnam where you can see this bird –

BACKGROUND
Prisons to paradise

The Portuguese arrived on Con Dao in 1516 but it wasn't until 1702 that a trading post was set up here by the East India Trading Company. Because of the millions of sea birds that inhabited it, it was then called Bird Island. In 1773, it became the home of Nguyen Anh and many mandarin families who fled there after being defeated by the armies of the Tay Son. In 1832, the Con Dao archipelago was handed over to the French by Emperor Tu Duc. Prisons were built in 1862 by Admiral Bonard in which the French incarcerated their more obstinate political prisoners. Up to 12,000 people could be held in the completed prisons. The Con Dao prisons were later used by the government of South Vietnam to hold political prisoners. In 113 years of prison existence 200,000 people were incarcerated here and one tenth of those people died in prison. Remarkably, 153 prisoners volunteered to stay on in Con Son to live after 1975.

Despite grand plans to develop the island, it remains mercifully free of large-scale resorts. Six Senses Con Dao has taken up one of the very best stretches of sand while a Russian hotel is being built on the lighthouse road, but other than that the island has changed little over the last few years.

the red-billed tropicbird (*Phaethon aethereus*) – found on only a few islands in the world – and the brown booby (*Sula leucogaster*) – a rare sea bird that inhabits the park's most remote island, Hon Trung (Egg Island). Egg Island, a speedboat ride northeast of Con Son, is a rugged outcrop hosting thousands of seabirds including sooty and crested terns, white-bellied sea eagles, and the rare, in Vietnam, masked booby. Most of the threats to the islands' natural resources come from development in the form of new roads, houses and the new fishing port built in Ben Dam Bay – an area of once-beautiful coral reef and mangrove forest.

Beaches and bays

Ong Dung Beach can be reached by walking across Con Son Island downhill on a track through the jungle. Plenty of birds can be seen if you trek at the right time of day. You can snorkel around 300 m offshore. There is a forest protection centre at the bay where you can buy food and drink and hire snorkelling gear and a boat. See also Where to stay, below.

Bai Nhat Beach, just before Ben Dam Bay, is a beautiful wild stretch of sand where good swimming is possible.

North of Con Son is **Tre Lon Island**, said to be one of the best places in the archipelago to see coral reefs and reef fish; this was also used as an isolated French prison. Le Duan, former General Secretary of the Communist Party, was imprisoned here from 1931-1936.

Close to the airport is one of the island's best and most wild beaches at **Dam Trau**. Golden sands in a tight curved bay backed by casuarinas can be found here

Vo Thi Sau was born Ba Ria in 1933 and was executed in Con Dao in 1952. At the age of 14 this Vietnamese revolutionary heroine developed an interest in politics and a passionate hatred for the French.

In 1949 she obtained three hand-grenades and, with one, killed a French soldier and injured 20 others. She became a messenger and supplied food and ammunition to the Viet Minh.

In 1950 she tried to assassinate a village headman working for the French but the hand-grenade failed to go off. She was caught, tortured and sentenced to death. She was executed on 23 January 1952 at the age of 18.

but there are no island views. Signposted 'Mieu Cau' on the left just before the airport, it is a 15-minute walk, passing a pagoda flanked by two white horses.

Bay Canh Island is a major sea turtle nesting site; there is also a functioning French-built lighthouse dating from 1883. If you are interested in seeing the turtles arrange to stay overnight through the national park.

Cau Island, east of Bay Canh Island is the only other island in the archipelago with fresh water. It harbours the swifts that make the nests and turtles that come to lay their eggs. It was also an isolated French prison at one time. Pham Van Dong, a former prime minster of both North Vietnam and the reunited Vietnam (1955-1987), was incarcerated here for seven years, from 1929 to 1936.

For swimming, **Lo Voi Beach**, east of the hotels, is good for swimming as is **An Hai Beach** at the other end of the bay. Birdwatching is also possible around the freshwater lake – **Quang Trung** – swamps and tree-covered sand dunes near the park headquarters. Spotters could see the Brahminy kite (*Haliastur Indus*), white-bellied sea eagle, Javan pond heron and cinnamon bittern. On the way to Ong Dung you can see the white-rumped shama, greater racket-tailed drongo, the rare pied imperial pigeon and the even rarer red-billed tropicbird.

At **Dat Doc**, east of Con Son, is a very attractive and pristine bay backed by a sheer cliff face. The **Evason Hideaway & Six Senses Spa** company has built here.

Where to stay

$$$$ Six Senses Con Dao
Dat Doc Beach, www.sixsenses.com.
One of the most fabulous resort in all of
Southeast Asia, this is pure unadulterated
luxury. The duplex villas stretch along
a gorgeous stretch of sand which
is bookended by a grand green hill.
Each villa has its own private pool and
personal butler service. The restaurant
is absolutely first rate serving superb
international and local flavours. The
breakfast takes the 5-star experience to
another level with delicious a la carte
options (the Turkish poached eggs are
amazing) as well as a buffet complete
with a walk-in cold room. Highly
expensive but highly recommended.

$$$ Con Dao Resort
*8 Nguyen Duc Thuan St, T64-383 0939,
www.condaoresort.com.vn.*
Until **Six Senses** arrived on the scene,
this was the best resort on the island.
There are 41 rooms including some in
villas on the beach. The rooms feature
a/c bathtubs, TV and balconies. There's
a pool and a tennis court. There's also a
restaurant which is rather average. Staff
can arrange walking and motorbike tours
of the area.

$$$ Saigon Con Dao
*18 Ton Duc Thang St, T64-383 0336,
www.saigoncondao.com.*
These buildings on the seafront may
remind you of a Cornish seaside hotel
from the 1980s, but they are clean
and comfortable. The restaurant is
not particularly good and the buffet
breakfast caters to Vietnamese tastes.

$$-$ Con Dao Camping
Nguyen Duc Thuan St.
By the old pier, these simple A-frame
huts offer beachfront digs for those
on a budget. Rather dated, they are
nonetheless clean and offer sea views
at very cheap prices.

Restaurants

Until recently there was very little to
choose from on Con Dao, but there are
now a handful of good places in the
main town. There are also plenty of
places to grab a cheap bowl of noodles
around the market and the night food
street nearby features some noodle
stands as well as some seafood. On the
road to Con Dao Camping there are a
number of Vietnamese seafood places
catering to large groups.

$ Bar 200
Pham Van Dong, T064-363 0334.
This new addition to the town also
houses **Senses Diving** school. It's run by
2 Brits and a South African who opened
it up in part to satisfy their own food
cravings. You can therefore find great
Western options including salads and
pizzas as well as good espresso. A great
source of local information and very,
very friendly. A good spot to meet fellow
divers and travellers.

$ Infiniti
Pham Van Dong, T64-383 0083.
This is a very funky cafe which seems
rather out of place in Con Dao's main
town. Run by two friendly brothers, it
serves pizza, excellent chicken burgers,
sublime shakes, beers and cocktails. Also
does a barbecue party on weekends
and regular specials. A great find.

$ Six Senses Con Dao
See Where to stay.
The restaurant here is first-rate, with superb grilled seafood and wide range of local and international flavours. Also has an exceptional wine list. Highly recommended for a treat.

What to do

Boat tours
The National Park organizes boat tours depending on the number of people and the weather. These include trips to Hon Tre Lon, Hon Tre No, Hon Bay Canh and Hon Cau as well as points around Con Son Island.

Diving
This is the premier place to dive in Vietnam. Courses are offered by **Senses Diving** based at **Bar 200**

> **Tip...**
> To see the turtles hatching on Con Dao's beaches, visit May-October.

(see Restaurants). This is a very professional outfit run by highly experienced diver masters.

Transport

Air
Con Dao Airport, T64-383 1973. There are regular flights to and from **Ho Chi Minh City**. Weekly schedules vary throughout the year.

Boat
It is possible to reach Con Dao by boat, but the journey is a nightmare by all accounts and not recommended at all.

Phan Thiet
& Mui Ne

Sahara-like dunes, kitesurfing beaches and fishing villages

Phan Thiet is a fishing town at the mouth of the Ca Ty River. For the traveller the real attraction lies east of town in the form of the 20-km sweep of golden sand of Mui Ne. Here some of Vietnam's finest coastal resorts can be found with some excellent water sports and two of the country's most attractive golf courses. The town has become hugely popular with both kitesurfers and Russians, with plenty of businesses catering to both markets.

Phan Thiet

Despite its modest appearance, Phan Thiet is the administrative capital of Binh Thuan Province. Its main attraction is the 18-hole golf course, designed by Nick Faldo. It is regarded as one of the best in Vietnam, and golfers come from all around the region to play it.

The most distinctive landmark in town is the municipal **water tower** completed in 1934. It is an elegant structure with a pagoda-like roof; built by the infamous 'Red Prince' and first president of Laos. The tower icon features in the logos of many local businesses and agencies. There are a few Ho Chi Minh relics, including a museum on Nguyen Truong To Street and the Duc Thanh school next door, where Ho Chi Minh taught in 1911, but otherwise nothing of interest at the museum.

Van Thuy Thu Temple ① *20A Ngu Ong St, 0730-1130 and 1400-1700,* is the oldest whale temple (built in 1762) in Vietnam. The temple houses more than 100 whale skeletons, including one specimen more than 22 m in length. Like all whale temples, it was originally built by the sea but, as sea levels have receded, this temple is now stranded in the middle of the neighbourhood.

★Mui Ne

Mui Ne is the name of the famous sandy cape and the small fishing village that lies at its end. Mui Ne's claims to fame are its *nuoc mam* (fish sauce) and its beaches where it is possible to do a host of water sports including kiteboarding, for which it is justly famous. Body boarding and surfing are better December to January when there are more waves. The wind dies down at the end of April, and May has virtually no wind. The cape is dominated by some impressive sand dunes; some are golden but in other parts quite red, a reflection of the underlying geology.

Around the village visitors may notice a strong smell of rotting fish. This is the unfortunate but inevitable by-product of fish sauce fermenting in wooden barrels. The *nuoc mam* of Phan Thiet is made from anchovies, as *ca com* on the label testifies. The process takes a year but to Vietnamese palates it is worth every day. *Nuoc mam* from Phan Thiet is regarded highly but not as reverentially as that from the southern island of Phu Quoc.

There are still significant numbers of Cham (50,000) and Ra-glai (30,000) minorities who, until a century ago, were the dominant groups in the region. There are many relics of the Champa kingdom here in Binh Thuan Province, the best and easiest to find being **Po Shanu**, two Cham towers dating from the late eighth century on a hill on the Mui Ne road. They are now somewhat broken down but the road leading up to them makes a nice evening ride; you can watch the sun set and from this vantage point you'll see the physical make-up of the coastal plain and estuaries to the south and the central highlands to the north. Driving up the long climb towards Mui Ne the towers are on the right-hand side of the road and quite

Essential Phan Thiet and Mui Ne

Getting around

Both motorbike taxis and Mai Linh car taxis abound in the town and along the Mui Ne strip.

When to go

The weather in Phan Thiet always seems nice. It is, of course, better in the dry season, December through April. Phan Thiet is most popular with overseas visitors (and the growing number of package tour operators) in the Christmas to Easter period when prices at the some of the better hotels rise by 20% or more. From December to March, Mui Ne loses portions of its beach to the sea.

Time required

Kitesurfers can linger for weeks here, but for the rest two to four days will be ample.

Best excursions from Mui Ne
The red dunes, page 99
The white dunes, page 99
Fairy Stream, page 99

unmissable. Like Cham towers elsewhere in this part of the country they were constructed of brick bound together with resin of the day tree. Once the tower was completed timber was piled around it and ignited; the heat from the flames melted the resin, which solidified on cooling.

Hon Rom and around
Hon Rom, about 15 km by motorbike or bicycle from Mui Ne, is the name of the undeveloped bay north of Mui Ne and is accessible only from Mui Ne. North of Hon Rom are **Suoi Nuoc**, **Binh Thien Village** and **Turtle Island**. The Full Moon Beach Resort runs the Full Moon Villas and Jibe's II at Suoi Nuoc.

Tourist information

Binh Thuan Tourist
82 Trung Trac St, T62-381 6821,
www.binhthuan-tourist.com.
Arranges tours and car rentals.

Where to stay

Phan Thiet

$$$$ DuParc Phan Thiet Ocean Dunes & Golf Resort
1 Ton Duc Thang St, T62-382 2393,
www.vietnamgolfresorts.com.
On the beach just outside Phan Thiet, this is set behind lovely gardens. 123 comfortable rooms (although some of these are showing their age) in a bland building and new well-appointed villas with beach views. Good facilities, 2 pools, 2 restaurants with tasty food, bar, tennis courts and gym. Guests enjoy a 30% discount on green fees at the adjacent 18-hole champion golf course, the **Ocean Dunes Golf Club**.

Mui Ne
Weekends tend to be busier as Mui Ne is a popular escape for expats from HCMC. There has been a great construction boom and there are now many places to stay at a range of prices. Fortunately supply has kept up with demand so Mui Ne offers good value. Advisable to book ahead as the popular places fill up fast particularly around Christmas and Tet and Vietnamese public holidays.

$$$$ Anantara Mui Ne Resort and Spa
Nguyen Dinh Chieu, T062-374 1888,
www.anantara.com.
A fantastic 5-star resort with impeccable service, good restaurant, sea-view rooms and a great slice of beach. The wine cellar is very well stocked and there is also an excellent gym.

$$$$ Mia Mui Ne
T62-384 7440, www.miamuine.com.
This is a gorgeous resort. Designed in the most charming style its bungalows and rooms are simple and cool and surrounded by dense and glorious vegetation. For inspiration and good taste it ranks among the best in Vietnam. Its pool has been extended and the bathrooms for the superior rooms enlarged. It has an excellent restaurant and bar. A good buffet breakfast is included.

$$$$ Victoria Phan Thiet Beach Resort & Spa
T62-381 3000, www.victoriahotels-asia.com.
Part of the **Victoria Group**, the resort has 59 upgraded thatched bungalows with outdoor rain showers and 3 villas, built in country-house style in an attractive landscaped setting. It is well equipped with restaurants, bar, 2 pools, sports facilities, a children's club and a spa. A great place to bring kids who love the donkey that's available for rides in the grounds. Very friendly staff and a good buffet breakfast.

$$$$-$$$ Coco Beach (Hai Duong)
T62-384 7111-3, www.cocobeach.net.
The European owners live here and the place is well run. Not luxurious but friendly and impeccably kept. 28 wooden bungalows and 3 wooden, 2-bedroom 'villas' facing the beach. Beautiful setting, lovely pool and relaxing. Excellent restaurant and a beachclub. **Coco Beach** was the first

resort on Mui Ne and it is pleasing how it remains easily among the best.

$$$ Full Moon Beach
T62-384 7008, www.windsurf-vietnam.com.

Visitors are assured of a friendly reception by the French and Vietnamese couple who own and run the place. Accommodation is in a variety of types: some rooms are spacious, others a little cramped, some brick, some bamboo. The most attractive rooms have a sea view and constant breeze. There is a good restaurant. They also run the **Full Moon Village** along the coast in Suoi Nuoc which is a very tranquil spot away from all the other resorts.

$$$-$$ Saigon Mui Ne
T62-384 7303, www.saigonmuine resort.com.

This is a Saigon tourist resort, perfectly professional but lacking flair and imagination. Bungalows, pool, jacuzzi, restaurant, spa, fitness centre and kiteboarding classes.

$$-$ Hiep Hoa
T62-384 7262, T090-812 4149 (mob), hiephoatourism@yahoo.com.

This is an attractive place. Now with 15 a/c rooms. It's quiet, clean and with its own stretch of beach. Popular and should be booked in advance. Its rates are excellent value for Mui Ne; they go down in the low season.

$$-$ Mui Ne Backpackers Resort
88 Nguyen Dinh Chieu, T062-384 7047, www.muinebackpackers.com.

One of the best options for those on a budget and one of the longest standing in the area. There is a small swimming pool and a variety of different room options to choose from. Located right on the beach, the sea view.

Restaurants

Mui Ne
Of the hotel restaurants the **Mia** and **Victoria** stand out. Many hotels do good barbecues at the weekend. There are many local seafood joints along the main road either side of the resort strip where the catch of the day is grilled – it's best to wander along and pick the busiest place.

$$ El Latino
Nguyen Dinh Chieu, T62-3743 5950.

A very welcoming little spot serving up some quality Mexican fare including great tacos and burritos, although the servings are on the small side. Has some coaches for laid-back dining in a funky open-air space.

$$ Forest Restaurant
7 Nguyen Dinh Chieu St, T62-384 7589.

Local dishes and lots of seafood, this garden-jungle setting puts on live music throughout the evening. Popular with the town's expats recommend this place for the good food, despite the touristy vibe.

$$-$ Jibe's Beach Club
T62-384 7405. Open 0700-late.

Popular chill-out bar serving burgers, salads and food with a French bent thanks to theowner, Pascal. In the daytime there is a kitesurf school cafe vibe, but in the evenings white linens come out and there is a more sophisticated ambiance. Recommended.

$$-$ Shree Ganesh
57 Nguyen Dinh Chieu, T62-374 1330.

This popular Omar's franchise serves North Indian and Tandoori cuisine. One of the best in Mui Ne with consistently high reviews for many years.

Bars and cafés

Mui Ne

Jibe's Beach Club
See Restaurants.
A laid back bar with quieter tunes, some good wine and a beachfront setting.

Joe's Cafe
139 Nguyen Dinh Chieu St, T62-374 3447, joescafemuine.com.
Ever popular and always busy spot with live music every night in a garden setting.

Pogo
www.thepogobar.com.
Just down from **Sinh Tourist** with cocktails, and local and international food. Keeps going later than most thanks to the roaring bonfires.

Wax
68 Nguyen Dinh Chieu St, T62-384 7001.
Located beside the beach at Windchamp Resort, **Wax** is dance-part central, especially during holidays.

Shopping

Mui Ne
There is now a large selection of shops in Mui Ne spanning the west end of the beach. Almost anything can be found, from beachwear, water sports equipment, pearls and jewellery to lacquerware and crocodile leather.

What to do

Phan Thiet
Golf
Ocean Dunes Golf Club, *1 Ton Duc Thang St, T62-382 3366, www. oceandunesgolf.vn.* This Nick Faldo-designed 18-hole, 6147-m course is highly regarded. It has a fully equipped

club house with bar and restaurant, pro-shop and locker rooms.

Tennis
Du Parc Ocean Dunes & Golf Resort, *see Where to stay.*

Mui Ne
The dunes and Fairy Stream
Tours to the red and white sand dunes and the Fairy Stream are top of most people's list when they visit Mui Ne and with very good reason. It's possible to hire a motorbike and venture out solo. The red dunes are very close to town and the white dunes are about an hour further on. Every motorbike hire place will be able to provide a map. The dunes are spectacular and best visited in the late afternoon. Kids hiring out plastic boards for sliding down the steep sand banks can be rather persistent. If you travel to the white dunes in the heat of the day, be sure to take enough fuel for the return leg and plenty of water for the dunes themselves. All tour operators offer trips to these dunes, some including jeep transport and rides on quad bikes.

Golf
Sea Links Golf & Country Club, *T62-374 1666, www.sealinksvietnam.com.* This 18-hole course has breathtaking 270-degree views of Mui Ne's coast. The property has been expanded to include a luxury hotel, villas, and has plans to develop a private beach, luxury hotel and shopping centre.

Therapies
The Village, *Victoria Phan Thiet Beach Resort & Spa, see Where to stay, above.* The hotel's own on-site centre offers the best massage in town by the most experienced therapists.

Water sports

Mui Ne is the water sports capital of Vietnam. The waters can be crowded with windsurfers and kiteboarders. The combination of powerful wind and waves attract huge numbers of kitesurfers. Equipment and training is offered by numerous centres. **Jibe's Beach Club**, T62-384 7405, T091-316 2005 (mob), www.windsurf-vietnam. com. There are plenty of places offering lessons in town, but this is the original centre, which is part of and close to Full Moon Beach Resort. **Jibe's** is the importer of sea kayaks, windsurfers, surfboards, sailboats, SUP (stand-up paddle) and kitesurf equipment. Equipment is available for purchase or for hire by the hour, day or week. Hourly windsurf lessons, multi-day kite-surf lessons and boogie board and kayak hire.

Tour operators

Sinh Tourist, 144 Nguyen Dinh Chieu St, T62-384 7542, muine@thesinhtourist.vn. A branch of the tour operator good for **Open Tour Bus** tickets and local tours to the sand dunes, fishing village and Phan Thiet city tour. Transport rented. **Victor Tours & Coco Cafe**, 121A Nguyen Dinh Chieu, across from Full Moon Resort, T98-959 1599. **Victor Tours** offers a full range of tour to all the local sites and books bus transport throughout Vietnam. Customs tours and unique outings are also available.

Transport

Bicycles and motorbikes

Xe oms are abundant in Phan Thiet town, as are reputable taxis. Bikes and motorbikes can be rented from hotels or tour operators, see **Victor Tours**, tour operators, above, and are the best way to explore the vicinity.

Bus and Open Tour Bus

The bus station is on the east side of town. Connections with all neighbouring towns. A local bus plies the nearby **Phan Thiet Coop** supermarket to Mui Ne route, as do taxis. Phuong Trang and Sinh Tourist Open Tour Buses drop off and pick up from all resorts on Mui Ne. The **Sinh Tourist** bus departs from its resort and Phuong Trang from its central office. To **Nha Trang** and **HCMC** twice a day at 1300 and 2345 (also 0800 to HCMC) 5½ hrs, both journeys. To **Dalat**, 7 hrs.

   Phuong Trang, 97 Nguyen Dinh Chieu St, T62-374 3113, www.phuongtrang dalat.com. This Dalat-based company has emerged as the leader in Vietnam, with the most reliable, trustworthy and comfortable services anywhere south of Hué.

Car

Victor Tours can arrange car hire, as can most hotels.

Taxi

Taxis are plentiful and run on meters.

Train

The Phan Thiet train station connects with the old station at Muong Man, 12 km to the west, on its way to HCMC. Trains leave Phan Thiet daily at in the early afternoon. From Muong Man there are also slow trains north to **Hanoi**. The trip from Phan Thiet to **HCMC** is a comfortable and scenic route.

Background
Vietnam

History 105
Modern Vietnam 125
Culture 128

History

The earliest record of humans in Vietnam is from an archaeological site on Do Mountain, in the northern Thanh Hoa Province. The remains discovered here have been dated to the Lower Palaeolithic (early Stone Age). So far, all early human remains have been unearthed in North Vietnam, invariably in association with limestone cliff dwellings. Unusually, tools are made of basalt rather than flint, the more common material found at similar sites in other parts of the world.

Archaeological excavations have shown that between 5000 BC and 3000 BC, two important Mesolithic cultures occupied North Vietnam: these are referred to as the **Hoa Binh** and **Bac Son** cultures after the principal excavation sites in Tonkin. Refined stone implements and distinctive hand axes with polished edges (known as Bacsonian axes) are characteristic of the two cultures. These early inhabitants of Vietnam were probably small, dark-skinned and of Melanesian or Austronesian stock.

There are 2000 years of recorded Vietnamese history and another 2000 years of legend. The Vietnamese people trace their origins back to 15 tribal groups known as the **Lac Viet** who settled in what is now North Vietnam at the beginning of the Bronze Age. Here they established an agrarian kingdom known as Van-lang that seems to have vanished during the third century BC.

Pre-colonial history

The beginning of Vietnamese recorded history coincides with the start of **Chinese cultural hegemony** over the north, in the second century BC. The Chinese dominated Vietnam for more than 1000 years until the 10th century AD and the cultural legacy is still very much in evidence, making Vietnam distinctive in Southeast Asia. Even after the 10th century, and despite breaking away from Chinese political domination, Vietnam was still overshadowed and greatly influenced by its illustrious neighbour to the north. Nonetheless, the fact that Vietnam could shrug off 1000 years of Chinese subjugation and emerge with a distinct cultural heritage and language says a lot for Vietnam's strength of national identity.

Ly Dynasty
The Ly Dynasty (1009-1225) was the first independent Vietnamese dynasty. Its capital, Thang Long, was at the site of present day Hanoi and the dynasty based its system of government and social relations closely upon the Chinese Confucianist model.

The first Ly emperor, and one of Vietnam's great kings, was Ly Cong Uan who was born in AD 974. He is usually known by his posthumous title, **Ly Thai To**, and reigned for 19 years from 1009-1028. Ly Cong Uan was raised and educated by monks and acceded to the throne when, as the commander of the palace guard in

Hoa Lu (the capital of Vietnam before Thang Long or Hanoi) and with the support of his great patron, the monk Van Hanh, he managed to gain the support of the Buddhist establishment and many local lords. During his reign, he enjoyed a reputation not just as a great soldier, but also as a devout man who paid attention to the interests and wellbeing of his people. He tried to re-establish the harmony between ruler and ruled which had suffered during the previous years and he even sent his son to live outside the walls of the palace so that he could gain a taste of ordinary life and an understanding of ordinary people.

Ly Cong Uan was succeeded by his son, Ly Phat Ma, who is better known as **Ly Thai Tong** (reigned 1028-1054). Ly Phat Ma had been prepared for kingship since birth and he proved to be an excellent ruler during his long reign. It is hard to generalize about this period in Vietnamese history because Ly Phat Ma adapted his pattern of rule no less than six times during his reign. Early on he challenged the establishment, contending for example that good governance was not merely a consequence of following best practice but depended upon good kingship. Later he was more of an establishment figure. Perhaps his greatest military success was the mounting of a campaign to defeat the Cham in 1044 from which he returned with shiploads of plunder. His greatest artistic legacy was the construction of the One Pillar Pagoda or Chua Mot Cot in Hanoi.

Ly Phat Ma was succeeded by his son, Ly Nhat Ton, posthumously known as **Ly Thanh Tong** (reigned 1054-1072). History is not as kind about Ly Thanh Tong as it is about his two forebears. Nonetheless he did challenge the might of the Chinese along Vietnam's northern borders – largely successfully – and like his father also mounted a campaign against Champa (see page 107) in 1069. Records indicate that he spent a great deal of time trying to father a son and worked his way through numerous concubines and at last, a son was born to a concubine of common blood in 1066 and named Ly Can Duc.

Ly Can Duc was proclaimed emperor in 1072 when he was only six years old and, surprisingly, remained king until he died in 1127. His death marks the end of the Ly Dynasty for he left no heir and the crown passed to the maternal clan of his nephew. There followed a period of instability and it was not until 1225 that a new dynasty – the Tran Dynasty – managed to subdue the various competing cliques and bring a semblance of order to the country.

Tran Dynasty

Scholars do not know a great deal about the four generations of kings of the Tran Dynasty. It seems that they established the habit of marrying within the clan, and each king took queens who were either their cousins or, in one case, a half-sister. Such a long period of intermarriage, one imagines, would have had some far-reaching genetic consequences, although ironically the collapse of the dynasty seems to have been brought about after one foolish king decided to marry outside the Tran clan. The great achievement of the Tran Dynasty was to resist the expansionist tendencies of the Mongol forces, who conquered China in the 1250s and then set their sights on Vietnam. In 1284 a huge Mongol-Yuan force, consisting of no fewer than four armies, massed on the border to crush the Vietnamese.

Fortunately the Tran were blessed with a group of brave and resourceful princes (the most notable of whom was Tran Quoc Tuan, better known – and now immortalized in street names in just about every Vietnamese town – as Tran Hung Dao), and in the end the forces of the Tran Dynasty were victorious.

Le Dynasty and the emergence of Vietnam

Le Loi

Despite 1000 years of Chinese domination and centuries of internal dynastic squabbles the Viet retained a strong sense of national identity and were quick to respond to charismatic leadership. As so often in Vietnam's history one man was able to harness nationalistic sentiment and mould the country's discontent into a powerful fighting force: in 1426 it was Le Loi. Together with the brilliant tactician **Nguyen Trai**, Le Loi led a campaign to remove the Chinese from Vietnamese soil. Combining surprise, guerrilla tactics and Nguyen Trai's innovative and famous propaganda, designed to convince defending Ming of the futility of their position, the Viet won a resounding victory which led to the enlightened and artistically distinguished Le period. Le Loi's legendary victory lives on in popular form and is celebrated in the tale of the restored sword in water puppet performances across the country. Following his victory against the Ming he claimed the throne in 1428 and reigned until his death five years later.

Le Thanh Ton

With Le Loi's death the Le Dynasty worked its way through a succession of young kings who seemed to hold the throne barely long enough to warm the cushions before they were murdered. It was not until 1460 that a king of substance was to accede: Le Thanh Ton (reigned 1460-1497). His reign was a period of great scholarship and artistic accomplishment. He established the system of rule that was to guide successive Vietnamese emperors for 500 years. He also mounted a series of military campaigns, some as far as Laos to the west.

Le expansion

The expansion of the Vietnamese state, under the Le, south from its heartland in the Tonkin Delta, followed the decline of the Cham Kingdom at the end of the 15th century. By the early 18th century the Cham were extinct as an identifiable political and military force and the Vietnamese advanced still further south into the Khmer-controlled territories of the Mekong Delta. This geographical over-extension and the sheer logistical impracticability of ruling from distant Hanoi, disseminating edicts and collecting taxes, led to the disintegration of the – ever tenuous – imperial rule. Noble families, locally dominant, challenged the emperor's authority and the Le Dynasty gradually dissolved into internecine strife and regional fiefdoms, namely Trinh in the north and Nguyen in the south, a pattern that was to reassert itself some 300 years later. But although on paper the Vietnamese – now consisting of two dynastic houses, Trinh and Nguyen – appeared powerful, the people were mired in poverty.

There were numerous peasant rebellions in this period, of which the most serious was the **Tay Son rebellion** of 1771. One of the three Tay Son brothers, Nguyen Hue, proclaimed himself **Emperor Quang Trung** in 1788, only to die four years later. His death paved the way for the establishment of the **Nguyen Dynasty** – the last Vietnamese dynasty – in 1802. Despite the fact that this period heralded the arrival of the French – leading to their eventual domination of Vietnam – it is regarded as a golden period in Vietnamese history. During the Nguyen Dynasty, Vietnam was unified as a single state and Hué emerged as the heart of the kingdom.

History of the non-Viet civilizations

Any history of Vietnam must include the non-Vietnamese peoples and civilizations. The central and southern parts of Vietnam have only relatively recently been dominated by the Viets. Before that, these lands were in the hands of people of Indian or Khmer origins.

Funan (AD 100-600)

According to Chinese sources, Funan was a Hindu kingdom founded in the first century AD with its capital, Vyadhapura, close to the Mekong River near the border with Cambodia. A local legend records that Kaundinya, a great Indian Brahmin, acting on a dream, sailed to the coast of Vietnam carrying with him a bow and arrow. When he arrived, Kaundinya shot the arrow and where it landed he established the capital of Funan. Following this act, Kaundinya married the princess Soma, daughter of the local King of the Nagas (giant water serpents). The legend symbolizes the union between Indian and local cultural traditions – the naga representing indigenous fertility rites and customs, and the arrow, the potency of the Hindu religion.

Oc-Eo

Funan built its wealth and power on its strategic location on the sea route between China and the islands to the south. Maritime technology at the time forced seafarers travelling between China and island Southeast Asia and India to stop and wait for the winds to change before they could continue on their way. This sometimes meant a stay of up to five months. The large port city of Oc-Eo offered a safe harbour for merchant vessels and the revenues generated enabled the kings of the empire to expand rice cultivation, dominate a host of surrounding vassal states as far away as the Malay coast and South Burma, and build a series of impressive temples, cities and irrigation works.

Funan reached the peak of its powers in the fourth century and went into decline during the fifth century AD when improving maritime technology made Oc-Eo redundant as a haven for sailing vessels. By the mid-sixth century, Funan, having suffered from a drawn-out leadership crisis, was severely weakened. The Cham ultimately conquered. What is interesting about Funan is the degree to which it provided a model for future states in Southeast Asia. Funan's wealth was built on its links with the sea, and with its ability to exploit maritime trade.

The later rulers of Champa, Langkasuka (Malaya), Srivijaya (Sumatra), and Malacca (Malaya) repeated this formula.

Champa (AD 200–1720)

In South Vietnam, where the dynastic lords achieved hegemony only in the 18th century, the kingdom of Champa – or Lin-yi as the Chinese called it – was the most significant power. The kingdom evolved in the second century AD and was focused on the narrow ribbon of lowland that runs north–south down the Annamite coast with its various capitals near the present-day city of Danang. Chinese sources record that in AD 192 a local official, Kiu-lien, rejected Chinese authority and established an independent kingdom. From then on, Champa's history was one of conflict with its neighbour; when Imperial China was powerful, Champa was subservient and sent ambassadors and tributes in homage to the Chinese court; when it was weak, the rulers of Champa extended their own influence and ignored the Chinese.

The difficulty for scholars is to decide whether Champa had a single identity or whether it consisted of numerous mini-powers with no dominant centre. The accepted wisdom at the moment is that Champa was more diffuse than previously thought and that only rarely during its history is it possible to talk of Champa in singular terms. The endless shifting of the capital of Champa is taken to reflect the shifting centres of power that characterized this 'kingdom'.

Like Funan, Champa built its power on its position on the maritime trading route through Southeast Asia. During the fourth century, as Champa expanded into formerly Funan-controlled lands, they came under the influence of the Indian cultural traditions of the Funanese. These were enthusiastically embraced by Champa's rulers who tacked the suffix '-varman' onto their names (for example, Bhadravarman) and adopted the Hindu-Buddhist cosmology. Though a powerful trading kingdom, Champa was geographically poorly endowed. The coastal strip between the Annamite highlands to the west, and the sea to the east, is narrow and the potential for extensive rice cultivation limited. This may explain why the Champa Empire was never more than a moderate power: it was unable to produce the agricultural surplus necessary to support an extensive court and army, and therefore could not compete with either the Khmers to the south nor with the Viets to the north. But the Cham were able to carve out a niche for themselves between the two, and to many art historians, their art and architecture represent the finest that Vietnam has ever produced.

For over 1000 years the Cham resisted the Chinese and the Vietnamese. But by the time Marco Polo wrote of the Cham, in 1285, their power and prestige were much reduced. Champa saw a late flowering under King Binasuos who led numerous successful campaigns against the Viet, culminating in the sack of Hanoi in 1371. Subsequently, the treachery of a low-ranking officer led to Binasuos' death in 1390 and the military eclipse of the Cham by the Vietnamese. The demographic and economic superiority of the Viet coupled with their gradual drift south contributed most to the waning of the Cham Kingdom, but finally, in 1471 the Cham suffered a terrible defeat at the hands of the Vietnamese. Some 60,000 of their soldiers were killed and another 36,000 captured and carried into captivity, including the King and 50 members of the royal family. The kingdom shrank to a small territory in the vicinity of Nha Trang that survived until 1720 when surviving members of the royal family and many subjects fled to Cambodia to escape from the advancing Vietnamese.

The colonial period
One of the key motivating factors that encouraged the **French** to undermine the authority of the Vietnamese emperors was their treatment of Roman Catholics. Emperor Minh Mang issued an imperial edict outlawing the dissemination of Christianity as a heterodox creed in 1825. The first European priest to be executed was François Isidore Gagelin who was strangled by six soldiers as he knelt on a scaffold in Hué in 1833. In 1840 Minh Mang actually read the Old Testament in Chinese translation, declaring it to be 'absurd'.

Yet, Christianity continued to spread as Buddhism declined and there was a continual stream of priests willing to risk their lives proselytizing. In addition, the economy was in disarray and natural disasters common. Poor Vietnamese saw Christianity as a way to break the shackles of their feudal existence. Fearing a peasants' revolt, the Emperor ordered the execution of 25 European priests, 300 Vietnamese priests, and 30,000 Vietnamese Catholics between 1848 and 1860. Provoked by these killings, the French attacked and took Saigon in 1859. In 1862 **Emperor Tu Duc** signed a treaty ceding the three southern provinces to the French, thereby creating the colony of **Cochin China**. This treaty of 1862 effectively paved the way for the eventual seizure by the French of the whole kingdom.

In 1883 and 1884, the French forced the Emperor to sign treaties making Vietnam a French protectorate. The Emperor called on China for assistance and demanded that provinces resist French rule; but the imperial bidding proved ineffective, and in 1885 the **Treaty of Tientsin** recognized the French protectorates of Tonkin (North Vietnam) and Annam (Central Vietnam), to add to that of Cochin China (South Vietnam).

Resistance to the French: the prelude to revolution
Like other European powers in Southeast Asia, the French managed to achieve military victory with ease, but they failed to stifle Vietnamese nationalism. After 1900, as Chinese translations of the works of Rousseau, Voltaire and social Darwinists such as Herbert Spence began to find their way into the hands of the Vietnamese intelligentsia, so resistance grew. Foremost among these early nationalists were Phan Boi Chau (1867-1940) and Phan Chau Trinh (1871-1926) who wrote tracts calling for the expulsion of the French. But these men and others such as Prince Cuong De (1882-1951) were traditional nationalists, their beliefs rooted in Confucianism rather than revolutionary Marxism. Their efforts and perspectives were essentially in the tradition of the nationalists who had resisted Chinese domination over previous centuries.

Quoc Dan Dang (VNQDD), founded at the end of 1927, was the first nationalist party, while the first significant communist group was the **Indochina Communist**

Party (ICP) established by **Ho Chi Minh** in 1930. Both the VNQDD and the ICP organized resistance to the French and there were numerous strikes and uprisings, particularly during the harsh years of the Great Depression. The Japanese 'occupation' from August 1940 (Vichy France permitted the Japanese full access to military facilities in exchange for allowing continued French administrative control) saw the creation of the **Viet Minh** to fight for the liberation of Vietnam from Japanese and French control.

The Vietnam wars

The First Indochina War (1945-1954)
The war started in September 1945 in the south of the country and in 1946 in the north. These years marked the onset of fighting **between the Viet Minh and the French** and the period is usually referred to as the First Indochina War. The communists, who had organized against the Japanese, proclaimed the creation of the **Democratic Republic of Vietnam (DRV)** on 2 September 1945 when Ho Chi Minh read out the Vietnamese **Declaration of Independence** in Hanoi's Ba Dinh Square. Ironically, this document was modelled closely on the American Declaration of Independence. Indeed, the US was favourably disposed towards the Viet Minh and Ho Chi Minh. Operatives of the OSS (the wartime precursor to the CIA) met Ho Chi Minh and supported his efforts during the war and afterwards Roosevelt's inclination was to prevent France claiming their colony back. Only Winston Churchill's persuasion changed his mind.

The French, although they had always insisted that Vietnam be returned to French rule, were in no position to force the issue. Instead, in the south, it was British troops (mainly Gurkhas) who helped the small force of French against the Viet Minh. Incredibly, the British also ordered the Japanese, who had only just capitulated, to help fight the Vietnamese. When 35,000 French reinforcements arrived, the issue in the south – at least superficially – was all but settled, with Ca Mau at the southern extremity of the country falling on 21 October. From that point, the war in the south became an underground battle of attrition, with the north providing support to their southern comrades.

In the north, the Viet Minh had to deal with 180,000 rampaging Nationalist Chinese troops, while preparing for the imminent arrival of a French force. Unable to confront both at the same time, and deciding that the French were probably the lesser of two evils, Ho Chi Minh decided to negotiate. To make the DRV government more acceptable to the French, Ho Chi Minh proceeded cautiously, only nationalizing a few strategic industries, bringing moderates into the government, and actually dissolving the Indochina Communist Party (at least on paper) in November 1945. But in the same month, he also said: "The French colonialists should know that the Vietnamese people do not wish to spill blood, that it loves peace. But if it must sacrifice millions of combatants, lead a resistance for long years to defend the independence of the country, and preserve its children from slavery, it will do so. It is certain the resistance will win."

ON THE ROAD

Ho Chi Minh: 'He who enlightens'

Ho Chi Minh, one of a number of pseudonyms Ho adopted during his life, was born Nguyen Sinh Cung, or possibly Nguyen Van Thanh (Ho did not keep a diary during much of his life, so parts of his life are still a mystery), in Nghe An Province near Vinh on the 19 May 1890, and came from a poor scholar-gentry family. In the village, the family was aristocratic; beyond it they were little more than peasants. His father, though not a revolutionary, was a dissenter and rather than go to Hué to serve the French, he chose to work as a village school teacher. Ho must have been influenced by his father's implacable animosity towards the French, although Ho's early years are obscure. He went to Quoc Hoc College in Hué and then worked for a while as a teacher in Phan Thiet, a fishing village in South Annam.

In 1911, under the name Nguyen Tat Thanh, he travelled to Saigon and left the country as a messboy on the French ship *Amiral Latouche-Tréville*. He is said to have used the name 'Ba' so that he would not shame his family by accepting such lowly work. This marked the beginning of three years of travel during which he visited France, England, America (where the skyscrapers of Manhattan both amazed and appalled him) and North Africa. Seeing the colonialists on their own turf and reading such revolutionary literature as the French Communist Party newspaper *L'Humanité*, he was converted to communism. In Paris he mixed with leftists, wrote pamphlets and attended meetings of the French Socialist Party. He also took odd jobs: for a while he worked at the **Carlton Hotel** in London and became an assistant pastry chef under the legendary French chef Georges Escoffier.

An even more unlikely story emerges from Gavin Young's *A Wavering Grace* In the book he recounts an interview he conducted with Mae West in 1968 shortly after he had returned from reporting the Tet offensive. On hearing of Vietnam, Mae West innocently said that she "used to know someone *very*, very important there ... His name was Ho ... Ho ... Ho something". At the time she was staying at the Carlton while starring in a London show, *Sex*. She confided to Young: "There was this waiter, cook, I don't know what he was. I know he had the slinkiest eyes though. We met in the corridor. We – well ..." Young writes that "Her voice trailed off in a husky sigh..."

Gradually Ho became an even more committed communist, contributing articles to radical newspapers and working his way into the web of communist

Chinese withdrawal In February 1946, the French and Chinese signed a treaty leading to the withdrawal of Chinese forces and shortly afterwards Ho Chi Minh concluded a treaty with French President de Gaulle's special emissary to Vietnam, Jean Sainteny, in which Vietnam was acknowledged as a 'free' (the Vietnamese word *doc lap* being translated as free, but not yet independent) state that was within the French Union and the Indochinese Federation.

and leftist groups. At the same time he remained, curiously, a French cultural chauvinist, complaining for example about the intrusion of English words like *le manager* and *le challenger* (referring to boxing contests) into the French language. He even urged the French prime minister to ban foreign words from the French press. In 1923 he left France for Moscow and was trained as a communist activist – effectively a spy. From there, Ho travelled to Canton where he was instrumental in forming the Vietnamese communist movement. This culminated in the creation of the Indochina Communist Party in 1930. His movements during these years are scantily documented: he became a Buddhist monk in Siam (Thailand), was arrested in Hong Kong for subversive activities and received a six month sentence, travelled to China several times, and in 1940 even returned to Vietnam for a short period – his first visit for nearly 30 years. Despite his absence from the country, the French had already recognized the threat that he posed and sentenced him to death in absentia in 1930. He did not adopt the pseudonym by which he is now best known – Ho Chi Minh – until the early 1940s.

Ho was a consummate politician and, despite his revolutionary fervour, a great realist. He was also a charming man, and during his stay in France between June and October 1946 he made a great number of friends. Robert Shaplen in his book *The Lost Revolution* (1965) talks of his "wit, his oriental courtesy, his savoir-faire… above all his seeming sincerity and simplicity". He talked with farmers and fishermen and debated with priests; he impressed people wherever he travelled. He died in Hanoi at his house in the former governor's residence in 1969.

Since the demise of communism in the former Soviet Union, the Vietnamese leadership have been concerned that secrets about Ho's life might be gleaned from old comintern files in Moscow by nosy journalists. To thwart such an eventuality, they have, reportedly, sent a senior historian to scour the archives. To date, Ho's image remains largely untarnished – making him an exception amongst the tawdry league of former communist leaders. But a Moscow-based reporter has unearthed evidence implying Ho was married, challenging the official hagiography that paints Ho as a celibate who committed his entire life to the revolution. It takes a brave Vietnamese to challenge established 'fact'. In 1991, when the popular Vietnamese *Youth* or *Tuoi Tre* newspaper dared to suggest that Ho had married Tang Tuyet Minh in China in 1926, the editor was summarily dismissed from her post.

It is interesting to note that in negotiating with the French, Ho Chi Minh was going against most of his supporters who argued for confrontation. But Ho Chi Minh, ever a pragmatist, believed at this stage that the Viet Minh were ill-trained and poorly armed and he appreciated the need for time to consolidate their position. The episode that is usually highlighted as the flashpoint that led to the resumption of hostilities was the French government's decision to open a customs house in Haiphong at the end of 1946. The Viet Minh forces resisted and the rest, as they say, is history. It seems that during the course of 1946 Ho Chi Minh changed his view of the best path to independence. Initially he asked: "Why should we sacrifice 50 or 100,000 men when we can achieve independence within five years through negotiation?" although he later came to the conclusion that it was necessary to fight for independence. The customs house episode might, therefore, be viewed as merely an excuse. The French claimed that 5000 Vietnamese were killed in the ensuing bombardment, versus five Frenchmen; the Vietnamese put the toll at 20,000.

In a pattern that was to become characteristic of the entire 25-year conflict, while the French controlled the cities, the Viet Minh were dominant in the countryside. By the end of 1949, with the success of the Chinese Revolution and the establishment of the Democratic People's Republic of Korea (North Korea) in 1948, the US began to offer support to the French in an attempt to stem the 'Red Tide' that seemed to be sweeping across Asia. At this early stage, the odds appeared stacked against the Viet Minh, but Ho Chi Minh was confident that time was on their side. As he remarked to Sainteny "If we have to fight, we will fight. You can kill 10 of my men for every one I kill of yours but even at those odds, I will win and you will lose". It also became increasingly clear that the French were not committed to negotiating a route to independence.

Dien Bien Phu (1954) and the Geneva Agreement The decisive battle of the First Indochina War was at Dien Bien Phu in the hills of the northwest, close to the border with Laos. At the end of 1953 the French, with American support, parachuted 16,000 men into the area in an attempt to protect Laos from Viet Minh incursions and to tempt them into open battle. The French in fact found themselves trapped, surrounded by Viet Minh and overlooked by artillery. There was some suggestion that the US might become involved, and even use tactical nuclear weapons, but this was not to be. In May 1954 the French surrendered – the most humiliating of French colonial defeats – effectively marking the end of the French presence in Indochina. In July 1954, in Geneva, the French and Vietnamese agreed to divide the country along the 17th parallel, so creating two states – the communists occupying the north and the non-communists occupying the south. The border was kept open for 300 days and over that period about 900,000 – mostly Roman Catholic – Vietnamese travelled south. At the same time nearly 90,000 Viet Minh troops along with 43,000 civilians went north, although many Viet Minh remained in the south to continue the fight there.

The Second Indochina War (1954-1975)
The Vietnam War, but particularly the American part of that war, is probably the most minutely studied, reported, analysed and recorded in history. Yet, as with all wars, there are still large grey areas and continuing disagreement over important episodes.

Ngo Dinh Diem
At the time of the partition of Vietnam along the 17th parallel, the government in the south was chaotic and the communists could be fairly confident that

in a short time their sympathizers would be victorious. This situation was to change with the rise of Ngo Dinh Diem. Born in Hué in 1901 to a Roman Catholic Confucian family, Diem wished to become a priest. He graduated at the top of his class from the French School of Administration and at the age of 32 was appointed to the post of minister of the interior at the court of Emperor Bao Dai. Here, according to the political scientist William Turley, "he worked with uncommon industry and integrity" only to resign in exasperation at court intrigues and French interference. He withdrew from political activity during the First Indochina War and in 1946 Ho Chi Minh offered him a post in the DRV government – an offer he declined.

Turley describes him as a man who was a creature of the past: "For Diem, the mandarin, political leadership meant rule by example, precept and paternalism. His Catholic upbringing reinforced rather than replaced the Confucian tendency to base authority on doctrine, morality and hierarchy. Utterly alien to him were the concepts of power-sharing and popular participation. He was the heir to a dying tradition, member of an elite that had been superbly prepared by birth, training, and experience to lead a Vietnam that no longer existed."

In July 1954 Diem returned from his self-imposed exile at the Maryknoll Seminary in New Jersey to become Premier of South Vietnam. It is usually alleged that the US administration was behind his rise to power, although this has yet to be proved. He held two rigged elections (in October 1955, 450,000 registered voters cast 605,025 votes) that gave some legitimacy to his administration in American eyes. He proceeded to suppress all opposition in the country. His brutal brother, Ngo Dinh Nhu, was appointed to head the security forces and terrorized much of Vietnamese society.

During the period of Diem's premiership, opposition to his rule, particularly in the countryside, increased. This was because the military's campaign against the Viet Minh targeted – both directly and indirectly – many innocent peasants. At the same time, the nepotism and corruption that was endemic within the administration also turned many people into Viet Minh sympathizers. That said, Diem's campaign was successful in undermining the strength of the Communist Party in the south. While there were perhaps 50,000-60,000 party members in 1954, this figure had declined through widespread arrests and intimidation to only 5000 by 1959.

The erosion of the Party in the south gradually led, from 1959, to the north changing its strategy towards one of more overt military confrontation. The same year also saw the establishment of Group 559, which was charged with the task of setting up what was to become the Ho Chi Minh Trail, along which supplies and troops were moved from the north to the south. But, even at this stage, the Party's forces in the south were kept from open confrontation and many of its leaders were hoping for victory without having to resort to open warfare. There was no call for a 'People's War' and armed resistance was left largely to guerrillas belonging to the Cao Dai and Hoa Hao (Buddhist millenarian) sects. The establishment of the National Liberation Front of Vietnam in 1960 was an important political and organizational development towards creating a credible alternative to Diem – although it did not hold its first congress until 1962.

The escalation of the armed conflict (1959-1963)

Viet Cong

The armed conflict began to intensify from the beginning of 1961 when all the armed forces under the communists' control were unified under the banner of the **People's Liberation Armed Forces (PLAF)**. By this time the Americans were already using the term Viet Cong (or VC) to refer to communist troops. They reasoned that the victory at Dien Bien Phu had conferred almost heroic status on the name Viet Minh. American psychological warfare specialists therefore invented the term Viet Cong, an abbreviation of *Viet-nam Cong-san* (or Vietnamese Communists) and persuaded the media in Saigon to begin substituting it for Viet Minh from 1956.

The election of **John F Kennedy** to the White House in January 1961 coincided with the communists' decision to widen the war in the south. In the same year Kennedy dispatched 400 special forces troops and 100 special military advisers to Vietnam, in flagrant contravention of the Geneva Agreement. With the cold war getting colder, and Soviet Premier Nikita Khrushchev confirming his support for wars of 'national liberation', Kennedy could not back down and by the end of 1962 there were 11,000 US personnel in South Vietnam. At the same time the NLF had around 23,000 troops at its disposal. Kennedy was still saying that: "In the final analysis, it's their war and they're the ones who have to win or lose it". But just months after the Bay of Pigs debacle in Cuba, Washington set out on the path that was ultimately to lead to America's first large-scale military defeat.

The bungling and incompetence of the forces of the south, the interference that US advisers and troops had to face, the misreading of the situation by US military commanders, and the skill – both military and political – of the communists, are most vividly recounted in Neil Sheehan's massive book, *A Bright Shining Lie*. The conflict quickly escalated from 1959. The north infiltrated about 44,000 men and women into the south between then and 1964, while the number recruited in the south was between 60,000 and 100,000. In August 1959, the first consignment of arms was carried down the **Ho Chi Minh Trail** into South Vietnam. Meanwhile, Kennedy began supporting, arming and training the Army of the Republic of Vietnam (ARVN). The US however, shied away from any large-scale, direct confrontation between its forces and the Viet Cong.

An important element in Diem's military strategy at this time was the establishment of **strategic hamlets**, better known simply as 'hamleting'. This strategy was modelled on British anti-guerrilla warfare during Malaya's communist insurgency, and aimed to deny the communists any bases of support in the countryside while at the same time making it more difficult for communists to infiltrate the villages and 'propagandize' there. The villages which were ringed by barbed wire were labelled 'concentration camps' by the communists, and the often brutal, forced relocation that peasants had to endure probably turned even more of them into communist sympathizers. Of the 7000-8000 villages sealed in this way, only a fifth could ever have been considered watertight.

In January 1963 at **Ap Bac**, not far from the town of My Tho, the communists scored their first significant victory in the south. Facing 2000 well-armed ARVN troops, a force of just 300-400 PLAF inflicted heavy casualties and downed five helicopters. After this defeat, many American advisers drew the conclusion that if the communists were to be defeated, it could not be left to the ARVN alone – US troops would have to become directly involved. As Lieutenant Colonel John Vann, a US Army officer, remarked after the debacle to the American media (as cited in Neil Sheehan's *A Bright Shining Lie*): "A miserable damn performance. These people won't listen. They make the same goddam mistakes over and over again in the same way."

In mid-1963 a Buddhist monk from Hué committed suicide by dousing his body with petrol and setting it alight. This was the first of a number of self-immolations, suggesting that even in the early days the Diem regime was not only losing the military war but also the 'hearts and minds' war. He responded with characteristic heavy handedness by ransacking suspect pagodas. On 2 December 1963, Diem and his brother Nhu were both assassinated during an army coup.

The American war in Vietnam

The US decision to enter the war has been the subject of considerable disagreement. Until recently, the received wisdom was that the US administration had already taken the decision, and manufactured events to justify their later actions. However, the publication of numerous State Department, Presidential, CIA, Defence Department and National Security Council files – all dating from 1964 – has shed new light on events leading up to American intervention.

In Roger Warner's *Back Fire* (1995), which deals largely with the CIA's secret war in Laos, he recounts a story of a war game commissioned by the Pentagon and played by the Rand Corporation in 1962. They were asked to play a week-long game simulating a 10-year conflict in Vietnam. At the end of the week, having committed 500,000 men, the US forces were bogged down, there was student unrest and the American population had lost confidence in their leaders and in the conduct of the war. When the game was played a year later but, on the insistence of the US Airforce, with much heavier aerial bombing, the conclusions were much the same. If only, if only …

By all accounts, **Lyndon Johnson** was a reluctant warrior. In the 1964 presidential campaign he repeatedly said: "We don't want our American boys to do the fighting for Asian boys". This was not just for public consumption. The files show that LBJ always doubted the wisdom of intervention. But he also believed that John F Kennedy had made a solemn pledge to help the South Vietnamese people, a pledge that he was morally obliged to keep.

It has usually been argued that the executive manufactured the **Gulf of Tonkin Incident** to force Congress and the public to approve an escalation of America's role in the conflict. It was reported that two American destroyers, the *USS Maddox* and *USS C Turner Joy*, were attacked without provocation in international waters on the 2 August 1964 by North Vietnamese patrol craft. The US responded by bombing shore installations while presenting the Gulf of Tonkin Resolution to an outraged Congress for approval. Only two Congressmen voted against the resolution and President Johnson's poll rating jumped from 42% to 72%. In reality, the *USS Maddox* had been involved in electronic intelligence gathering while supporting clandestine raids by South Vietnamese mercenaries – well inside North Vietnamese territorial waters. This deception only became apparent in 1971 when the **Pentagon papers**, documenting the circumstances behind the incident, were leaked to the *New York Times* (the Pentagon papers were commissioned by Defense Secretary McNamara in June 1967 and written by 36 Indochina experts).

But these events are not sufficient to argue that the incident was manufactured to allow LBJ to start an undeclared war against North Vietnam. On 4 August, Secretary of State Dean Rusk told the American representative at the United Nations that: "In no sense is this destroyer a pretext to make a big thing out of a little thing". Even as late as the end of 1964, the President was unconvinced by arguments that the US should become more deeply involved. On 31 August, McGeorge Bundy wrote in a memorandum to Johnson: "A still more drastic possibility which no one is discussing is the use of substantial US armed forces in operation against the Viet Cong. I myself believe that before we let this country go we should have a hard look at this grim alternative, and I do not at all think that it is a repetition of Korea."

But events overtook President Johnson, and by 1965 the US was firmly embarked on the road to defeat. In March 1965, he ordered the beginning of the air war against the north perhaps acting on Air Force General Curtis Le May's observation that "we are swatting flies when we should be going after the manure pile". **Operation Rolling Thunder**, the most intense bombing campaign any country had yet experienced, began in March 1965 and ran through to October 1968. In 3½ years, twice the tonnage of bombs was dropped on Vietnam (and Laos) as during the entire Second World War. During its peak in 1967, 12,000 sorties were being flown each month – a total of 108,000 were flown throughout 1967. North Vietnam claimed that 4000 out of its 5788 villages were hit. Most terrifying were the B-52s that dropped their bombs from such an altitude (17,000 m) that the attack could not even be heard until the bombs hit their targets. Each aircraft carried 20 tonnes of bombs. By the end of the American war in 1973, 14 million tonnes of all types of munitions had been used in Indochina, an explosive force representing 700 times that of the atomic bomb dropped on Hiroshima. As General Curtis Le May explained on 25 November 1965 – "We should bomb them back into the Stone Age". In the same month that Rolling Thunder commenced, marines landed at Danang to defend its airbase, and by June 1965 there were 74,000 US troops in Vietnam. Despite President Johnson's reluctance to commit the US to the conflict, events forced his hand. He realized that the undisciplined South Vietnamese could not prevent a communist victory. Adhering to the domino theory, and with his own and the US's reputation at stake, he had no choice. As Johnson is said to have remarked to his press secretary Bill Moyers: "I feel like a hitchhiker caught in a hail storm on a Texas highway. I can't win. I can't hide. And I can't make it stop."

Dispersal of the north's industry

In order to protect the population in the north, they too were relocated to the countryside. By the end of 1967 Hanoi's population was a mere 250,000 essential citizens – about a quarter of the pre-war figure. The same was true of other urban centres. What the primary US objective was in mounting the air war remains unclear. In part, it was designed to destroy the north's industrial base and its ability to wage war; to dampen the people's will to fight; to sow seeds of discontent; to force the leadership in the north to the negotiating table; and perhaps to punish those in the north for supporting their government.

William Westmoreland, the general appointed to command the American effort, aimed to use the superior firepower and mobility of the US to 'search and destroy' PAVN forces. North Vietnamese bases in the south were to be identified using modern technology, jungle hideouts revealed by dumping chemical defoliants and then attacked with shells, bombs and by helicopter-borne troops. In 'free-fire zones' the army and air force were permitted to use whatever level of firepower they felt necessary to dislodge the enemy. 'Body counts' became the measure of success and collateral damage – or civilian casualties – was a cost that just had to be borne. As one field commander famously explained: "We had to destroy the town to save it." By 1968 the US had more than 500,000 troops in Vietnam, while **South Korean**, **Australian**, **New Zealand**, **Filipino** and **Thai** forces contributed another 90,000. The ARVN officially had 1.5 million men under arms (100,000 or more of these were 'flower' or phantom soldiers, the pay for whom was pocketed by officers in an increasingly corrupt ARVN). Ranged against this vastly superior force were perhaps 400,000 PAVN and National Liberation Front forces.

1964-1968: who was winning?

The leadership in the north tried to allay serious anxieties about their ability to defeat the American-backed south by emphasizing human over physical and material resources. **Desertions** from the ARVN were very high – there were 113,000 from the army in 1965 alone (200,000 in 1975) – and the PAVN did record a number of significant victories. The communists also had to deal with large numbers of desertions – 28,000 men in 1969. By 1967 world opinion, and even American public opinion, appeared to be swinging against the war. Within the US, **anti-war demonstrations** and 'teach-ins' were spreading, officials were losing confidence in the ability of the US to win the war, and the president's approval rating was sinking fast. As the US Secretary of Defense, Robert McNamara is quoted as saying in the *Pentagon Papers*: "... the picture of the world's greatest superpower killing or seriously injuring 1000 non-combatants a week, while trying to pound a tiny, backward nation into submission on an issue whose merits are hotly disputed, is not a pretty one."

But although the communists may have been winning the psychological and public opinion wars, they were increasingly hard-pressed to maintain this advantage on the ground. Continual American strikes against their bases, and the social and economic dislocations in the countryside, were making it more difficult for the communists to recruit supporters. At the same time, the fight against a vastly better equipped enemy was also taking its toll in sheer exhaustion. Despite what is now widely regarded as a generally misguided US military strategy in Vietnam, there were notable US successes (for example, the Phoenix Programme, see page 119). American GIs were always sceptical about the 'pacification' programmes that aimed to win the 'hearts and minds' war. GIs were fond of saying, 'If you've got them by the balls, their hearts and minds will follow.' At times, the US military and politicians appeared to view the average Vietnamese as inferior to the average American. This latent racism was reflected in General Westmoreland's remark that Vietnamese "don't think about death the way we do" and in the use by most US servicemen of the derogatory name 'gook' to refer to Vietnamese.

At the same time as the Americans were trying to win 'hearts and minds', the Vietnamese were also busy indoctrinating their men and women, and the population in the 'occupied' south. In Bao Ninh's moving *The Sorrow of War* (1994), the main character, Kien, who fights with a scout unit describes the indoctrination that accompanied the soldiers from their barracks to the field: "Politics continuously. Politics in the morning, politics in the afternoon, politics again in the evening. 'We won, the enemy lost. The enemy will surely lose. The north had a good harvest, a bumper harvest. The people will rise up and welcome you. Those who don't just lack awareness. The world is divided into three camps.' More politics."

By 1967, the war had entered a period of military (but not political) stalemate. As Robert McNamara writes in his book *In Retrospect: the Tragedy and Lessons of Vietnam*, it was at this stage that he came to believe that Vietnam was "a problem with no solution". In retrospect, he argues that the US should have withdrawn in late 1963, and certainly by late 1967. Massive quantities of US arms and money were preventing the communists from making much headway in urban areas, while American and ARVN forces were ineffective in the countryside – although incessant bombing and ground assaults wreaked massive destruction. A black market of epic proportions developed in Saigon, as millions of dollars of assistance went astray. American journalist Stanley Karnow once remarked to a US official that "we could probably buy off the Vietcong at US$500 a head". The official replied that they had already calculated the costs, but came to "US$2500 a head".

The Tet Offensive, 1968: the beginning of the end

By mid-1967, the communist leadership in the north felt it was time for a further escalation of the war in the south to regain the initiative. They began to lay the groundwork for what was to become known as the Tet (or New Year) Offensive – perhaps the single most important series of battles during the American War in Vietnam. During the early morning of 1 February 1968, shortly after noisy celebrations had welcomed in the New Year, 84,000 communist troops – almost all Viet Cong – simultaneously attacked targets in 105 urban centres. Utterly surprising the US and South Vietnamese, the Tet Offensive had begun.

Preparations for the offensive had been laid over many months. Arms, ammunition and guerrillas were smuggled and infiltrated into urban areas and detailed planning was undertaken. Central to the strategy was a 'sideshow' at Khe Sanh. By mounting an attack on the marine outpost at **Khe Sanh**, the communists successfully convinced the American and Vietnamese commanders that another Dien Bien Phu was underway. General Westmoreland moved 50,000 US troops away from the cities and suburbs to prevent any such humiliating repetition of the French defeat. But Khe Sanh was just a diversion, a feint designed to draw attention away from the cities. In this the communists were successful; for days after the Tet offensive, Westmoreland and the South Vietnamese President Thieu thought Khe Sanh to be the real objective and the attacks in the cities the decoy.

The most interesting aspect of the Tet Offensive was that although it was a strategic victory for the communists, it was also a considerable tactical defeat. They may have occupied the US embassy in Saigon for a few hours but, except in Hué, communist forces were quickly repulsed by US and ARVN troops. The government in the South did not collapse nor did the ARVN. Cripplingly high casualties were inflicted on the communists – cadres at all echelons were killed – morale was undermined and it became clear that the cities would not rise up spontaneously to support the communists. Tet, in effect, put paid to the VC as an effective fighting force. The fight was now increasingly taken up by the North Vietnamese Army (NVA). This was to have profound effects on the government of South Vietnam after reunification in 1975; southern communists and what remained of the political wing of the VC – the government in waiting – were entirely overlooked as northern communists were given all the positions of political power, a process that continues. This caused intense bitterness at the time and also explains the continued mistrust of many southerners for Hanoi. Walt Rostow wrote in 1995 that "Tet was an utter military and political defeat for the communists in Vietnam", but adding "yet a political disaster in the United States". But this was not to matter; Westmoreland's request for more troops was turned down and US public support for the war slumped still further as they heard reported that the US embassy itself had been 'over-run'. Those who for years had been claiming it was only a matter of time before the communists were defeated seemed to be contradicted by the scale and intensity of the offensive. Even President Johnson was stunned by the VC's successes for he too had believed the US propaganda. As it turned out the VC incursion was by a 20-man unit from Sapper Battalion C-10 who were all killed in the action. Their mission was not to take the embassy but to 'make a psychological gesture'. In that regard at least, the mission must have exceeded the leadership's wildest expectations.

The **Phoenix Programme**, established in the wake of the Tet Offensive, aimed to destroy the communists' political infrastructure in the Mekong Delta. Named after the Vietnamese mythical bird the Phung Hoang, which could fly anywhere, the programme sent CIA-recruited and trained Counter Terror Teams – in effect assassination units – into the countryside. The teams were ordered to try and capture communist cadres; invariably they fired first and asked questions later. By 1971, it was estimated that the programme had led to the capture of 28,000 members of the VCI (Viet Cong Infrastructure), the death of 20,000 and the defection of a further 17,000. By the early 1970s the countryside in the Mekong Delta was more peaceful than it had been for years; towns that were previously strongholds of the Viet Cong had reverted to the control of the local authorities. Critics have questioned what proportion of those killed, captured and sometimes tortured were communist cadres, but even communist documents admit that it seriously undermined their support network in the area. In these terms, the Phoenix Programme was a great success.

The costs
The Tet Offensive concentrated American minds. The costs of the war by that time had been vast. The US budget deficit had risen to 3% of Gross National Product by 1968, inflation was accelerating, and thousands of young men had been killed for a cause that, to many, was becoming less clear by the month. Before the end of the year President Johnson had ended the bombing campaign. Negotiations began in Paris in 1969 to try and secure an honourable settlement for the US. Although the last American combat troops were not to leave until March 1973, the Tet Offensive marked the beginning of the end. It was from that date the Johnson administration began to search seriously for a way out of the conflict. The illegal bombing of Cambodia in 1969 and the resumption of the bombing of the north in 1972 (the most intensive of the entire conflict) were only flurries of action on the way to an inevitable US withdrawal.

The Paris Agreement (1972)
US Secretary of State **Henry Kissinger** records the afternoon of 8 October 1972, a Sunday, as the moment when he realized that the communists were willing to agree a peace treaty. There was a great deal to discuss, particularly whether the treaty would offer the prospect of peaceful reunification, or the continued existence of two states: a communist north, and non-communist south. Both sides tried to force the issue: the US mounted further attacks and at the same time strengthened and expanded the ARVN. They also tried to play the 'Madman Nixon' card, arguing that **President Richard Nixon** was such a vehement anti-communist that he might well resort to the ultimate deterrent, the nuclear bomb. It is true that the PAVN was losing men through desertion and had failed to recover its losses in the Tet Offensive. Bao Ninh in his book *The Sorrow of War* about Kinh, a scout with the PAVN, wrote: "The life of the B3 Infantrymen after the Paris Agreement was a series of long suffering days, followed by months of retreating and months of counter-attacking, withdrawal, then counter-attack. The path of war seemed endless, desperate, and leading nowhere."

But the communist leadership knew well that the Americans were committed to withdrawal – the only question was when, so they felt that time was on their side. By 1972, US troops in the south had declined to 95,000, the bulk of whom were support troops. The north gambled on a massive attack to defeat the ARVN and moved 200,000 men towards the demilitarized zone that marked the border between north and south. On 30 March the PAVN crossed into the south and quickly overran large sections of Quang Tri province. Simultaneous attacks were mounted in the west highlands, at Tay Ninh and in the Mekong Delta. For a while it looked as if the south would fall altogether. The US responded by mounting a succession of intense bombing raids that eventually forced the PAVN to retreat. The spring offensive may have failed, but like Tet, it was strategically important, for it demonstrated that without US support the ARVN was unlikely to be able to withstand a communist attack.

Both sides, by late 1972, were ready to compromise. Against the wishes of South Vietnam's President Nguyen Van Thieu, the US signed a treaty on 27 January 1973, the ceasefire going into effect on the same day. Before the signing, Nixon ordered the bombing of the north – the so-called Christmas Campaign. It lasted 11 days from 18 December (Christmas Day was a holiday) and was the most intensive of the war. With the ceasefire and President Thieu, however shaky, both in place, the US was finally able to back out of its nightmare and the last combat troops left in March 1973. As J William Fulbright, a highly influential member of the Senate and a strong critic of the US role in Vietnam, observed: "We [the US] have the power to do any damn fool thing we want, and we always seem to do it."

The Final Phase 1973-1975
The Paris Accord settled nothing; it simply provided a means by which the Americans could withdraw from Vietnam. It was never going to resolve the deep-seated differences between the two regimes and with only a brief lull, the war continued, this time without US troops. Thieu's government was probably in terminal decline even before the peace treaty was signed. Though ARVN forces were at their largest ever and, on paper, considerably stronger than the PAVN, many men were weakly committed to the cause of the south. Corruption was endemic, business was in recession, and political dissent was on the increase. The North's Central Committee formally decided to abandon the Paris Accord in October 1973; by the beginning of 1975 they were ready for the final offensive. It took only until April for the communists to achieve total victory. ARVN troops deserted in their thousands, and the only serious resistance was offered at Xuan Loc, less than 100 km from Saigon. President Thieu resigned on 27 April. ARVN generals, along with their men, were attempting to flee as the PAVN advanced on Saigon. The end was quick: at 1045 on 30 April a T-54 tank (number 843) crashed its way through the gates of the Presidential Palace, symbolizing the end of the Second Indochina War. For the US, the aftermath of the war would lead to years of soul searching; for Vietnam, to stagnation and isolation. A senior State Department figure, George Ball, reflected afterwards that the war was "probably the greatest single error made by America in its history".

Legacy of the Vietnam War

The Vietnam War (or 'American War' to the Vietnamese) is such an enduring feature of the West's experience of the country that many visitors look out for legacies of the conflict. There is no shortage of physically diabled Vietnamese. Many men were badly injured during the war, but large numbers also received their injuries while serving in Cambodia (1979-1989). It is tempting to associate deformed children with the enduring effects of the pesticide **Agent Orange** (1.7 million tonnes had been used by 1973), although this has yet to be proven scientifically.

Bomb damage

Bomb damage is most obvious from the air: well over five million tonnes of bombs were dropped on the country (north and south) and there are said to be 20 million bomb craters – the sort of statistic people like to recount, but no one can legitimately verify. Many craters have yet to be filled in and paddy fields are still pockmarked. Some farmers have used these holes in the ground to farm fish and to use as small reservoirs to irrigate vegetable plots. War scrap was one of the country's most valuable exports. The cities in the north are surprisingly devoid of obvious signs of the bombing campaigns; Hanoi remains remarkably intact. In Hué the Citadel and the Forbidden Palace were extensively damaged during the Tet offensive in 1968 although much has now been rebuilt.

Psychological effect of the war

Even harder to measure is the effect of the war on the Vietnamese psyche. The Vietnamese Communist Party leadership still seem to be preoccupied by the conflict and school children are routinely shown war museums and Ho Chi Minh memorials. But despite the continuing propaganda offensive, people harbour surprisingly little animosity towards America or the West. Indeed, of all Westerners, it is often Americans who are most warmly welcomed, particularly in the south.

But it must be remembered that about 60% of Vietnam's population has been born since the US left in 1973, so have no memory of the American occupation. Probably the least visible but most lasting of all the effects of the war is in the number of elderly widowed women and the number of middle-aged women who never married.

The deeper source of antagonism is the continuing divide between the north and south. It was to be expected that the forces of the north would exact their revenge on their foes in the south and many were relieved that the predicted bloodbath didn't materialize. But few would have thought that this revenge would be so long lasting. The 250,000 southern dead are not mourned or honoured, or even acknowledged. Former soldiers are denied jobs and the government doesn't recognize the need for national reconciliation.

After the war

The Socialist Republic of Vietnam (SRV) was born from the ashes of the Vietnam War on 2 July 1976 when former North and South Vietnam were reunified. Hanoi was proclaimed as the capital of the new country. But few Vietnamese would have guessed that their emergent country would be cast by the US in the mould of a pariah state for almost 18 years. First President George Bush I, and then his successor Bill Clinton, eased the US trade embargo bit by bit in a dance of appeasement and procrastination, as they tried to comfort American business clamouring for a slice of the Vietnamese pie, while also trying to stay on the right side of the vociferous lobby in the US demanding more action on the MIA (missing in action) issue. Appropriately, the embargo, which was first imposed on the former North in May 1964, and then nationwide in 1975, was finally lifted a few days before the celebrations of Tet, Vietnamese New Year, on 4 February 1994.

On the morning of 30 April 1975, just before 1100, a T-54 tank crashed through the gates of the Presidential Palace in Saigon, symbolically marking the end of the Vietnam War. Twenty years later, the same tank – number 843 – became a symbol of the past as parades and celebrations, and a good deal of soul searching, marked the anniversary of the end of the War. To many Vietnamese, in retrospect, 1975 was more a beginning than an end: it was the beginning of a collective struggle to come to terms with the war, to build a nation, to reinvigorate the economy and to excise the ghosts of the past.

Re-education camps
The newly formed Vietnam government ordered thousands of people to report for re-education camps in 1975. Those intended were ARVN members, ex-South Vietnam government members and those that had collaborated with the south regime including priests, artists, teachers and doctors. It was seen as a means of revenge and a way of indoctrinating the 'unbelievers' with communist propaganda. It was reported in the Indochina Newsletter in 1982 that some 80 camps existed with an estimated 100,000 still languishing in them seven years after the war ended. Detainees were initially told that they would be detained for between three days and one month. Those that were sent to the camp were forced to undertake physical labour and survived on very little food and without basic medical facilities.

The boat people
Many Vietnamese also fled, first illegally and then legally through the Orderly Departure Programme.

Invasion of Cambodia
In April 1975, the Khmer Rouge took power in Cambodia. Border clashes with Vietnam erupted just a month after the Phnom Penh regime change but matters came to a head in 1977 when the Khmer Rouge accused Vietnam of seeking to incorporate Kampuchea into an Indochinese Federation. Hanoi's determination to oust Pol Pot only really became apparent on Christmas Day 1978, when 120,000 Vietnamese troops invaded. By 7 January they had installed a puppet government that proclaimed the foundation of the People's Republic of Kampuchea (PRK): Heng Samrin, a former member of the Khmer Rouge, was appointed president. The Vietnamese compared their invasion to the liberation of Uganda from Idi Amin – but for the rest of the world it was an unwelcome Christmas present. The new government was accorded scant recognition abroad, while the toppled government of Democratic Kampuchea retained the country's seat at the United Nations.

But the country's 'liberation' by Vietnam did not end the misery; in 1979 nearly half of Cambodia's population was in transit, either searching for their former homes or fleeing across the Thai border into refugee camps. The country reverted to a state of outright war again, for the Vietnamese were not greatly loved in

Cambodia – especially by the Khmer Rouge. American political scientist Wayne Bert wrote: "The Vietnamese had long seen a special role for themselves in uniting and leading a greater Indochina Communist movement and the Cambodian Communists had seen with clarity that such a role for the Vietnamese could only be at the expense of their independence and prestige."

Under the Lon Nol and Khmer Rouge regimes, Vietnamese living in Cambodia were expelled or exterminated. Resentment had built up over the years Hanoi – exacerbated by the apparent ingratitude of the Khmer Rouge for Vietnamese assistance in fighting Lon Nol's US-supported Khmer Republic in the early 1970s. As relations between the Khmer Rouge and the Vietnamese deteriorated, the communist superpowers, China and the Soviet Union, polarised too – the former siding with Khmer Rouge and the latter with Hanoi.

The Vietnamese invasion had the full backing of Moscow, while the Chinese and Americans began their support for the anti-Vietnamese rebels.

Following the Vietnamese invasion, three main anti-Hanoi factions were formed. In June 1982 they banded together in an unholy alliance of convenience to fight the PRK and called themselves the Coalition Government of Democratic Kampuchea (CGDK), which was immediately recognised by the UN. The three factions of the CGDK were: The Communist Khmer Rouge whose field forces had recovered to at least 18,000 by the late 1980s. Supplied with weapons by China, they were concentrated in the Cardamom Mountains in the southwest and were also in control of some of the refugee camps along the Thai border. The National United Front for an Independent Neutral Peaceful and Co-operative Cambodia (Funcinpec) – known by most people as the Armée National Sihanoukiste (ANS). It was headed by Prince Sihanouk – although he spent most of his time exiled in Beijing; the group had fewer than 15,000 well-equipped troops – most of whom took orders from Khmer Rouge commanders. The anti-Communist Khmer People's National Liberation Front (KPNLF), headed by Son Sann, a former prime minister under Sihanouk. Its 5000 troops were reportedly ill-disciplined in comparison with the Khmer Rouge and the ANS.

The three CGDK factions were ranged against the 70,000 troops loyal to the government of President Heng Samrin and Prime Minister Hun Sen (previously a Khmer Rouge cadre.) they were backed by Vietnamese forces until September 1989.

In the late 1980s the Association of Southeast Asian Nations (ASEAN) – for which the Cambodian conflict had almost become its raison d'être – began steps to bring the warring factions together over the negotiating table. ASEAN countries were united in wanting the Vietnamese out of Cambodia. After Mikhail Gorbachev had come to power in the Soviet Union, Moscow's support for the Vietnamese presence in Cambodia gradually evaporated. Gorbachev began leaning on Vietnam as early as 1987, to withdraw its troops. Despite saying their presence in Cambodia was 'irreversible', Vietnam completed its withdrawal in September 1989, ending nearly 11 years of Hanoi's direct military involvement. The withdrawal led to an immediate upsurge in political and military activity, as forces of the exiled CGDK put increased pressure on the now weakened Phnom Penh regime to begin a round of power sharing negotiations.

Modern Vietnam

The **Vietnamese Communist Party** (**VCP**) was established in Hong Kong in 1930 by Ho Chi Minh and arguably has been more successful than any other such party in Asia in mobilizing and maintaining support. While others have fallen, the VCP has managed to stay firmly in control. To enable them to get their message to a wider audience, the Communist Party of Vietnam have their own website, www.cpv.org.vn.

Vietnam is a one party state. In addition to the Communist Party the posts of president and prime minister were created when the constitution was revised in 1992. The president is head of state and the prime minister is head of the cabinet of ministries (including three deputies and 26 ministries), all nominated by the National Assembly. The current president is Truong Tan Sang and the current prime minister is Nguyen Tan Dung. Although the National Assembly is the highest instrument of state, it can still be directed by the Communist Party. The vast majority of National Assembly members are also party members. Elections for the National Assembly are held every five years. The Communist Party is run by a politburo of 15 members. The head is the general secretary, currently Nguyen Phu Trong. The politburo meets every five years and sets policy directions of the Party and the government. There is a Central Committee made up of 161 members, who are also elected at the Party Congress.

In 1986, at the Sixth Party Congress, the VCP launched its economic reform programme known as *doi moi*, which was a momentous step in ideological terms. However, although the programme has done much to free up the economy, the party has ensured that it retains ultimate political power. Marxism-Leninism and Ho Chi Minh thought are still taught to Vietnamese school children and even so-called 'reformers' in the leadership are not permitted to diverge from the party line. In this sense, while economic reforms have made considerable progress (but see below) – particularly in the south – there is a very definite sense that the limits of political reform have been reached, at least for the time being.

From the late 1990s to the first years of the new millennium there have been a number of arrests and trials of dissidents charged with what might appear to be fairly innocuous crimes and, although the economic reforms enacted since the mid-1980s are still in place, the party resolutely rejects any moves towards greater political pluralism.

Despite the reforms, the leadership is still divided over the road ahead. But the fact that debate is continuing, sometimes openly, suggests that there is disagreement over the necessity for political reform and the degree of economic reform that should be encouraged.

In the country as a whole there is virtually no political debate at all, certainly not in the open. There are two reasons for this apparently curious state of affairs. First there is a genuine fear of discussing something that is absolutely taboo. Second, and more importantly, is the booming economy. Since the 1990s, **economic**

growth in Vietnam has been unprecedented. In 2006 the growth rate was 8.2% but this dropped to 5.3% in 2009. As every politician knows, the one thing that keeps people happy is rising income. Hence with not much to complain about most Vietnamese people are content with their political status quo.

That said, in 2006, Bloc 8406, a pro-democracy group named after its founding date of 8 April 2006, was set up. Catholic priest Father Nguyen Van Ly, editor of the underground online magazine *Free Speech* and a founding member of Bloc 8406, was sentenced to eight years in jail for **anti-government activity**. Four others were also sentenced with him. In March 2007 Nguyen Van Dai and Le Thi Cong Nhan, two human rights lawyers, were arrested on the grounds of distributing material "dangerous to the State" and were sentenced to four and five years in prison respectively. As well as Bloc 8406, other pro-democracy movements include the US-based Viet Tan Party, www.viettan.org, with offices also in Australia, France, Japan, and the People's Democratic Party, among others.

International relations

In terms of international relations, Vietnam's relationship with the countries of the **Association of Southeast Asian Nations (ASEAN)** have warmed markedly since the dark days of the early and mid-1980s and in mid-1995 Vietnam became the association's seventh – and first communist – member. The delicious irony of Vietnam joining ASEAN was that it was becoming part of an organization established to counteract the threat of communist Vietnam itself – although everyone was too polite to point this out. No longer is there a deep schism between the capitalist and communist countries of the region, either in terms of ideology or management. The main potential flashpoint concerns Vietnam's long-term historical enemy – China. The enmity and suspicion that underlies the relationship between the world's last two real communist powers stretches back over 2000 years. Indeed, one of the great attractions to Vietnam of joining ASEAN was the bulwark that it created against a potentially aggressive and actually economically ascendant China.

China and Vietnam, along with Malaysia, Taiwan, Brunei and the Philippines, all claim part (or all) of the East Sea **Hoang Sa** (formerly **Spratly Islands**). These tiny islands, many no more than coral atolls, would have caused scarcely an international relations ripple were it not for the fact that they are thought to sit above huge oil reserves. Whoever can prove rights to the islands lays claim to this undersea wealth. China has been using its developing blue water navy to project its power southwards. This has led to skirmishes between Vietnamese and Chinese forces, and to diplomatic confrontation between China and just about all the other claimants. Although the parties are committed to settling the dispute without resort to force, most experts see the Spratly Islands as the key potential flashpoint in Southeast Asia – and one in which Vietnam is seen to be a central player. **Truong Sa** (formerly **Paracel Islands**) further north are similarly disputed by Vietnam and China.

Rapprochement with the US
One of the keys to a lasting economic recovery was a normalization of relations with the US. From 1975 until early 1994 the US made it largely illegal for any American

or American company to have business relations with Vietnam. The US, with the support of Japan and other Western nations, also blackballed attempts by Vietnam to gain membership to the IMF, World Bank and Asian Development Bank, thus cutting off access to the largest source of cheap credit. In the past, it has been the former Soviet Union and the countries of the Eastern Bloc that have filled the gap, providing billions of dollars of aid (US$6 billion 1986-1990), training and technical expertise. But in 1990 the Soviet Union halved its assistance to Vietnam, making it imperative that the government improve relations with the West and particularly the US.

In April 1991 the US opened an official office in Hanoi to assist in the search for Missing in Action (MIAs), the first such move since the end of the war, and in December 1992 allowed US companies to sign contracts to be implemented after the US trade embargo had been lifted. In 1992, both Australia and Japan lifted their embargoes on aid to Vietnam and the US also eased restrictions on humanitarian assistance. Support for a **full normalization of relations** was provided by French President Mitterand during his visit in February 1993, the first by a Western leader since the end of the war. He said that the US veto on IMF and World Bank assistance had "no reason for being there", and applauded Vietnam's economic reforms. He also pointed out to his hosts that respect for human rights was now a universal obligation, which did not go down quite so well. Nonetheless he saw his visit as marking the end of one chapter and the beginning of another.

This inexorable process towards normalization continued with the full lifting of the trade embargo on 4 February 1994 when President Bill Clinton announced the normalization of trade relations. Finally, on 11 July 1995 Bill Clinton declared the full normalization of relations between the two countries and a month later Secretary of State Warren Christopher opened the new American embassy in Hanoi. On 9 May 1997 Douglas 'Pete' Peterson, the first 'post-war' American ambassador to Vietnam and a former POW who spent six years of the war in the infamous 'Hanoi Hilton', took up his post in the capital.

The progress towards normalization was so slow because many Americans still harbour painful memories of the war. With large numbers of ordinary people continuing to believe that servicemen shot down and captured during the war and listed as MIAs were still languishing in jungle jails, presidents Bush and Clinton had to tread exceedingly carefully.

The normalization of trade relations between the two countries was agreed in a meeting between Vietnamese and US officials in July 1999 and marked the culmination of three years' discussions. But conservatives in the politburo prevented the agreement being signed into law worried, apparently, about the social and economic side effects of such reform. This did not happen until 28 November 2001 when Vietnam's National Assembly finally ratified the treaty. It has led to a substantial increase in bilateral trade.

More good news came for Vietnam when it became the 150th member of the World Trade Organization in January 2007. The immediate effect was the lifting of import quotas from foreign countries thereby favouring Vietnamese exporters. Full benefits are expected to be realised when Vietnam hope to gains full market economy status in 2020.

Culture

People

Vietnam is home to a total of 54 ethnic groups including the Vietnamese (or Kinh) themselves. Life has been hard for many of the minorities who have had to fight not only the French and Vietnamese but often each other in order to retain their territory and cultural identity. Traditions and customs have been eroded by outside influences such as Roman Catholicism and Communism although some of the less alien ideas have been successfully accommodated.

Highland people: the Montagnards of Vietnam

The highland areas of Vietnam are among the most linguistically and culturally diverse in the world. In total, the highland peoples number around seven million. As elsewhere in Southeast Asia, a broad distinction can be drawn in Vietnam between the peoples of the lowlands and valleys and the peoples of the uplands. The former tend to be settled, cultivate wet rice and are fairly closely integrated into the wider Vietnamese state; in most instances they are Viet. The latter are often migratory, cultivate upland crops often using systems of shifting cultivation and are comparatively isolated from the state. The generic term for these diverse peoples of the highlands is Montagnard (from the French, Mountain People), in Vietnamese *nguoi thuong* (highland citizen) or, rather less politely, *moi* (savage or slave). As far as the highland peoples themselves are concerned, they identify with their village and tribal group and not as part of a wider grouping, as highland inhabitants.

Relations between the minorities and the Vietnamese have not always been as good as they are officially portrayed. Recognizing and exploiting this mutual distrust and animosity, both the French and American armies recruited from among the minorities. In 1961 US Special Forces began organizing Montagnards into defence groups to prevent communist infiltration into the Central Highlands from the north. In recent years the government has come to regard the minorities as useful for tourism.

Potentially tourism is a more serious and insidious threat to the minorities' way of life than any they have yet had to face. A great deal has been written about cultural erosion by tourism and any visitor to a minority village should be aware of the extent to which he or she contributes to this process. Traditional means of livelihood are quickly abandoned when a higher living standard for less effort can be obtained from the tourist dollar. Long-standing societal and kinship ties are weakened by the intrusion of outsiders. Young people may question their society's values and traditions that may seem archaic, anachronistic and risible by comparison with those of the modern tourist. And dress and music lose all cultural significance and symbolism if they are allowed to become mere tourist attractions.

Nevertheless, this is an unavoidable consequence of Vietnam's decision to admit tourists to the highland areas. Perhaps fortunately, however, for the time being at least, many of the minorities are pretty inaccessible to the average traveller. Visitors

ON THE ROAD

Visiting minorities: house rules

Etiquette and customs vary between the minorities. However, the following are general rules of good behaviour that should be adhered to whenever possible.

1. Dress modestly without displaying too much flesh.
2. Ask permission before photographing anyone (old people, pregnant women and mothers with babies can object).
3. Only enter a house if invited.
4. Do not touch or photograph village shrines.
5. Do not smoke opium.
6. Avoid sitting or stepping on door sills.
7. Avoid displays of wealth and be sensitive when giving gifts (for children, pens are better than sweets).
8. Avoid introducing Western medicines.
9. Do not sit with the soles of your feet pointing at others (sit cross-legged).
10. If offered a cup of rice wine it is polite to down the first cup in one (what the Vietnamese call *tram phan tram* – 100%).

can minimize their impact by acting in a sensitive way. In addition, you can report to provincial tourism authorities on arrival to check the latest on areas where travel is permitted. But the minority areas of Vietnam are fascinating places and the immense variety of colours and styles of dress add greatly to the visitor's enjoyment.

Bahnar (Ba-na)

This is a Mon-Khmer-speaking minority group concentrated in the central highland provinces of Gia Lai-Kon Tum, numbering about 174,000. Locally powerful from the 15th to 18th centuries, they were virtually annihilated by neighbouring groups during the 19th century. Roman Catholic missionaries influenced the Bahnar greatly and they came to identify closely with the French. Some conversions to Roman Catholicism were made but Christianity, where it remains, is usually just an adjunct to Bahnar animism. Bahnar houses are built on stilts and in each village there is a communal house, or *rông*, which is the focus of social life. When a baby reaches his or her first full month he or she has their ears pierced in a village ceremony equivalent to the Vietnamese *day thang* (see box, page 31); only then is a child considered a full member of the community. Their society gives men and women relatively equal status. Male and female heirs inherit wealth and the families of either husband or wife can arrange marriage. Bahnar practise both settled and shifting cultivation.

Coho (Co-ho, also Kohor, K'Ho, Xre, Chil and Nop)

These are primarily found on the Lam Dong Plateau in Lam Dong Province (Dalat) with a population of about 100,000. Extended family groups live in longhouses or buon, sometimes up to 30 m long. Unusually, society is matrilineal and newly married men live with their wives' families. The children take their mother's name;

if the wife dies young her smaller sister will take her place. Women wear tight-fitting blouses and skirts. Traditional shifting cultivation is giving way to settled agriculture.

Yao (Dao, also Mán)

The Yao live in northern Vietnam in the provinces bordering China, particularly in Lao Cai and Ha Giang. They number 6210,000 and include several sub-groupings, notably the Dao Quan Chet (Tight Trouser Dao), the Dao Tien (Money Dao) and the Dao Ao Dai (Long Dress Dao). As these names suggest, Yao people wear highly distinctive clothing although sometimes only on their wedding day. The **Dao Tien** or Money Dao of Hoa Binh and Son La provinces are unique among the Yao in that the women wear black skirts and leggings rather than trousers. A black jacket with red embroidered collar and cuffs, decorated at the back with coins (hence the name) together with a black red-tasselled turban and silver jewellery are also worn. By contrast men look rather plain in black jacket and trousers. Headgear tends to be elaborate and includes a range of shapes (from square to conical), fabrics (waxed hair to dried pumpkin fibres) and colours.

The women of many branches of Yao shave off their eyebrows and shave back their hair to the top of their head before putting on the turban; a hairless face and high forehead are traditionally regarded as attributes of feminine beauty.

Yao wedding customs are as complex as Yao clothing and vary with each group. Apart from parental consent, intending marriage partners must have compatible birthdays and the groom has to provide the bride's family with gifts worthy of their daughter. If he is unable to do this, a temporary marriage can take place but the outstanding presents must be produced and a permanent wedding celebrated before *their* daughter can marry.

The Yao live chiefly by farming: those in higher altitudes are swidden cultivators growing maize, cassava and rye. In the middle zone, shifting methods are again used to produce rice and maize, and on the valley floors sedentary farmers grow irrigated rice and rear livestock.

Spiritually the Yao have also opted for diversity; they worship *Ban Vuong*, their mythical progenitor, as well as their more immediate and real ancestors. The Yao also find room for elements of Taoism, and in some cases Buddhism and Confucianism, in their elaborate metaphysical lives. Never enter a Yao house unless invited; if tree branches are suspended above the gate to a village, guests are not welcome – reasons might include a post-natal but pre-naming period, sickness, death or special ceremony. Since the Yao worship the kitchen god, guests should not sit or stand immediately in front of the stove.

Ede (Ê-dê, also Rhadê)

Primarily concentrated in the Central Highlands province of Dac Lac and numbering nearly 270,000, they came into early contact with the French and are regarded as one of the more 'progressive' groups, adapting to modern life with relative ease. Traditionally the Ede live in longhouses on stilts; accommodated under one roof is the matrilineal extended family or commune. The commune falls under the authority of an elderly, respected woman known as the *khoa sang* who is responsible for communal property, especially the gongs and jars, which feature in important festivals.

Ede society is matrilocal in that after the girl's family selects a husband, he then comes to live with her. As part of the wedding festivities the two families solemnly agree that if one of the partners should break the wedding vow they will forfeit a minimum of one buffalo, a maximum of a set of gongs. Wealth and property are inherited solely by daughters.

Shifting cultivation is the traditional subsistence system, although this has given way in most areas to settled wet rice agriculture. Spiritually the Ede are polytheist: they number animism (recognizing the spirits of rice, soil, fire and water especially) and Christianity among their beliefs.

Giarai (Gia-rai, also Chó Ray)

Primarily found in Gia Lai and Kon Tum provinces (especially near Play Ku) and numbering 317,557, these are the largest group in the Central Highlands. They are settled cultivators and live in houses on stilts in villages called *ploi* or *bon*. The Giarai are animist and recognize the spiritual dimension of nature; ever since the seventh century they have had a flesh and blood King of Fire and King of Water whose spirit is invoked in rain ceremonies.

Hmong (Hmông, also Mèo and Mi(u)

These are widely spread across the highland areas of the country, but particularly near the Chinese border down to the 18th parallel. The Hmong number about 787,600 (over 1% of Vietnam's population) and live at higher altitudes, above 1500 m, than all other hill people. Comparatively recent migrants to Vietnam, the Hmong began to settle in the country during the 19th century after moving south from China. The Hmong language in its various dialects remained oral until the 1930s when a French priest attempted to Romanize it with a view to translating the Bible. A more successful attempt to create a written Hmong language was made in 1961 but has since fallen into disuse. Nevertheless – or perhaps because of this failure – the Hmong still preserve an extraordinarily rich oral tradition of legends, stories and histories. Hmong people are renowned for their beautiful folk songs. Each branch of the Hmong people preserves its own corpus of songs about love, work and festivals that are sung unaccompanied or with the accompaniment of the *khène*, a small bamboo pipe organ, a two-stringed violin, flutes, drums, gongs and jew's harps. Numerous Hmong dances also exist to celebrate various dates in the social calendar and to propitiate animist spirits.

They have played an important role in resisting both the French and the Vietnamese. Living at such high altitudes they tend to be one of the most isolated of all the hill people. Their way of life does not normally bring them into contact with the outside world that suits them well – the Hmong traders at Sapa are an exception.

High in the hills, flooding is not a problem so their houses are built on the ground, not raised up on stilts. Hmong villages are now increasingly found along the river valleys and roads as the government resettlement schemes aim to introduce them to a more sedentary form of agriculture. The Hmong practice slash-and-burn cultivation growing maize and dry rice. Traditionally opium has been a valuable cash crop. Although fields are often cleared on very steep and rocky slopes, the land is not terraced.

There are a number of different groups among the Hmong including the White, Black, Red and Flower Hmong that are distinguishable by the colour of the women's clothes. Black Hmong wear almost entirely black clothing with remarkable pointed black turbans. White Hmong women wear white skirts and the Red Hmong tie their heads in a red scarf while the Flower Hmong wrap their hair (with hair extensions) around their head like a broad-brimmed hat. However, such numerous regional variations occur that even experts on ethnic minority cultures sometimes have problems trying to identify which branch of Hmong they have encountered.

Serious social problems have occurred among the Hmong owing to opium addiction; with over 30% of the male population of some Hmong villages addicted, the drug has rendered many incapable of work, causing misery and malnutrition for their families and with the drug finding its way on to the streets of Vietnam's cities, the authorities have resolved to clamp down hard on opium production. This has had tragic consequences when the Hmong have tried to protect their livelihoods.

Muong (Mường)

Numbering more than one million the Muong are the fourth largest ethnic minority in Vietnam. They live in the area between northern Thanh Hoa Province and Yen Bai but mainly in Hoa Binh Province. It is thought that the Muong are descended from the same stock as the Viets: their languages are similar and there are also close similarities in culture and religion. But whereas the Vietnamese came under strong Chinese cultural influence from the early centuries of the Christian era, the Muong did not. The Muong belong to the Viet-Muong language group; their language is closest to Vietnamese of all the ethnic minority languages.

Muong practise wet and dry rice cultivation where possible, supplementing their income with cash crops such as manioc, tobacco and cotton. Weaving is still practised; items produced include pillowcases and blankets. Culturally the Muong are akin to the Thai Vietnamese ethnic minority and they live in stilt houses in small villages called *quel*; groupings of from three to 30 quel form a unit called a *muong*. Muong society is feudal in nature with each *muong* coming under the protection of a noble family (*lang*). The common people are not deemed worthy of family names so are all called Bui. Each year the members of a *muong* are required to labour for one day in fields belonging to the lang.

Marriages are arranged: girls, in particular, have no choice of spouse. Muong cultural life is rich, literature has been translated into Vietnamese and their legends, poems and songs are considered particularly fine.

Mnong (Mnông)

The Mnong number some 92,000 people and predominantly live in Dak Lak, Binh Phuoc and Binh Duong province with a smaller group living in Lam Dong province. The Mnong are hunter-gatherers and grow rice. The Mnong village is characterised by a longhouse on stilts although some groups live in normal sized stilt houses. Families are matrilineal and tradition sees the women bare topped and with distended earlobes. It is the Mnong who are the elephant catchers at Ban Don, see page 132.

Nung (Nùng)
Concentrated in Cao Bang and Lang Son provinces, adjacent to the Chinese border, the Nung number approximately 860,000 people. They are strongly influenced by the Chinese and most are Buddhist, but like both Vietnamese and Chinese the Nung practise ancestor worship too. In Nung houses a Buddhist altar is placed above the ancestor altar and, in deference to Buddhist teaching, they refrain from eating most types of meat. The Nung are settled agriculturalists and, where conditions permit, produce wet rice; all houses have their own garden in which fruit and vegetables are grown.

Tay (Tày, also Tho)
The Tay are the most populous ethnic minority in Vietnam; they number about 1.5 million and are found in the provinces of northwest Vietnam stretching from Quang Ninh east to Lao Cai. Tay society was traditionally feudal with powerful lords able to extract from the free and semi-free serfs' obligations such as droit de seigneur. Today Tay society is male dominated with important decisions being taken by men and eldest sons inheriting the bulk of the family's wealth.

Economically the Tay survive by farming and are highly regarded as wet rice cultivators, they are also noted for the production of fruits (pears, peaches, apricots and tangerines), herbs and spices. Diet is supplemented by animal and fish rearing and cash is raised by the production of handicrafts. The Tay live in houses on stilts, located in the river valleys. Tay architecture is quite similar in design to that of the Black Thai, but important differences may be identified, most notably the larger size of the Tay house, the deeper overhang of the thatched or (among more affluent Tay communities) tiled roof and the extent of the railed balcony that often encircles the entire house.

Like the Thai, Tay ancestors migrated south from southern China along with those of the Thai and they follow the three main religions of Buddhism, Confucianism and Taoism in addition to ancestor worship and animist beliefs. While Tay people have lived in close proximity to the Viet majority over a period of many centuries, their own language continues to be their primary means of communication. They hail from the Austro-Asian language family and specifically the Thai-Kadai language group. Tay literature has a long and distinguished history and much has been translated into Vietnamese. During the French colonial period missionaries Romanized Tay script.

Thai (Thái, also Tày D]m)
Numbering more than one million this is the second largest ethnic minority in Vietnam and ethnically distinct from the Thais of modern-day Thailand. There

are two main sub-groups, the Black (Thai Den), who are settled mainly in Son La, Lai Chan, Lao Cai and Yen Bai provinces and the White Thái, who are found predominantly in Hoa Binh, Son La, Thanh Hoa and Vinh Phu provinces, as well as many others, including the Red Thai (Thai Do). The use of these colour-based classifications has usually been linked to the colour of their clothes, particularly the colour of women's shirts. However, there has been some confusion over the origins of the terms and there is every reason to believe that it has nothing to do with the colour of their attire and is possibly linked to the distribution of the sub-groups near the Red and Black rivers. The confusion of names becomes even more perplexing when the Vietnamese names for the sub-groups of Thai people are translated into Thai. Some scholars have taken Thai Den (Black Thai) to be Thai Daeng – *daeng* being the Thai word for red, thereby muddling up the two groups. With the notable exception of the White Thai communities of Hoa Binh, traditional costume for the women of both the Black and White Thai generally features a coloured blouse with a row of silver buttons down the front, a long black skirt, a coloured waist sash and a black headscarf embroidered with intricate, predominantly red and yellow designs.

The traditional costume of the White Thai women of Hoa Binh comprises a long black skirt with fitted waistband embroidered with either a dragon or chicken motif together with a plain pastel coloured blouse and gold and maroon sash.

The Thai cover a large part of northwest Vietnam, in particular the valleys of the Red River and the Da and the Ma rivers, spilling over into Laos and Thailand. They arrived in Vietnam between the fourth and 11th centuries from southern China and linguistically they are part of the wider Thai-Kadai linguistic grouping. Residents of Lac village in Mai Chau claim to have communicated with visitors from Thailand by means of this shared heritage.

The Thai tend to occupy lowland areas and they compete directly with the Kinh (ethnic Vietnamese) for good quality farmland that can be irrigated. They are masters of wet rice cultivation producing high yields and often two harvests each year. Their irrigation works are ingenious and incorporate numerous labour-saving devices including river-powered water wheels that can raise water several metres. Thai villages (*ban*) consist of 40 to 50 houses on stilts; they are architecturally attractive, shaded by fruit trees and surrounded by verdant paddy fields. Commonly located by rivers, one of the highlights of a Thai village is its suspension footbridge. The Thai are excellent custodians of the land and their landscapes and villages are invariably very scenic.

Owing to their geographical proximity and agricultural similarities with the Kinh it is not surprising to see cultural assimilation – sometimes via marriage – and most Thai speak Vietnamese. It's also interesting to note the extent to which the Thai retain a distinctive cultural identity, most visibly in their dress.

When a Thai woman marries, her parents-in-law give her a hair extension (*can song*) and a silver hair pin (*khat pom*) that she is expected to wear (even in bed) for the duration of the marriage. There are two wedding ceremonies, the first at the bride's house where the couple live for one to three years, followed by a second when they move to the husband's house.

Sedang (Xó-d]ng)

Concentrated in Gia Lai and Kon Tum provinces and numbering about 127,000, the Sedang live in extended family longhouses and society is patriarchal. The Sedang practise both shifting agriculture and the cultivation of wet rice. A highly war-like people, they almost wiped out the Bahnar in the 19th century. Sedang thought nothing of kidnapping neighbouring tribesmen to sacrifice to the spirits; indeed the practice of kidnapping was subsequently put to commercial use and formed the basis of a slave trade with Siam (Thailand). Sedang villages, or *ploi*, are usually well defended (presumably for fear of reprisal) and are surrounded by thorn hedges supplemented with spears and stakes. Complex rules designed to prevent in-breeding limit the number of available marriage partners that sometimes results in late marriages.

Other groups

These are Hre (Hrê), in Quang Ngai and Binh Dinh provinces, numbering 113,000 and Stieng/Xtieng (Xtiêng) in Song Be province, with 66,788.

Viet (Kinh)

The 1999 census revealed that 86.2% of the population were ethnic Vietnamese. But with a well-run family planning campaign beginning to take effect in urban areas and higher fertility rates among the ethnic minorities it is likely that this figure will fall. The history of the Kinh is marked by a steady southwards progression from the Red River basin to the southern plains and Mekong Delta. Today the Kinh are concentrated into the two great river deltas, the coastal plains and the main cities. Only in the central and northern highland regions are they outnumbered by ethnic minorities. Kinh social cohesion and mastery of intensive wet rice cultivation has led to their numerical, and subsequently political and economic, dominance of the country. Ethnic Vietnamese are also in Cambodia where some have been settled for generations; recent Khmer Rouge attacks on Vietnamese villages have, however, caused many to flee to Vietnam.

Cham

With the over-running of Champa in 1471 (see page 107) Cham cultural and ethnic identity was diluted by the more numerous ethnic Vietnamese. The Cham were dispossessed of the more productive lands and found themselves in increasingly marginal territory. Economically eclipsed and strangers in their own land, Cham artistic creativity atrophied, their sculptural and architectural skills, once the glory of Vietnam, faded and decayed like so many Cham temples and towers. It is estimated that there are, today, 132,873 Cham people in Vietnam, chiefly in central and southern Vietnam in the coastal provinces extending south from Quy Nhon. Small communities are to be found in Ho Chi Minh City and in the Mekong Delta around Chau Doc. They are artistically the poor relations of their forebears but skills in weaving and music live on.

The Cham of the south are typically engaged in fishing, weaving and other small scale commercial activities; urban Cham are poor and live in slum neighbourhoods. Further north the Cham are wet or dry rice farmers according to local topography; they are noted for their skill in wet rice farming and small-scale hydraulic engineering.

In southern Vietnam the majority of Cham are Muslim, a comparatively newly acquired religion although familiar from earlier centuries when many became acquainted with Islamic tenets through traders from India and the Indonesian isles. In central Vietnam most Cham are Brahminist and the cult of the linga remains an important feature of spiritual life.

Hoa: ethnic Chinese

There are nearly one million ethnic Chinese or Hoa in Vietnam, 80% living in the south of the country. Before reunification in 1975 there were even more; hundreds of thousands left due to persecution by the authorities and a lack of economic opportunities since the process of socialist transformation was initiated. There are now large Vietnamese communities abroad, particularly in Australia, on the west coast of the US and in France. It has been estimated that the total Viet-kieu population numbers some two million. With the reforms of the 1980s, the authorities' view of the Chinese has changed; they now appreciate the crucial role they played, and could continue to play, in the economy. Before 1975, the Hoa controlled 80% of industry in the south and 50% of banking and finance. Today, ethnic Chinese in Vietnam can own and operate businesses and are once again allowed to join the communist party, the army and to enter university. The dark days of the mid-to late 1970s seem to be over.

Viet Kieu: overseas Vietnamese

The largest community of overseas Vietnamese, about 1.1 million, live in the US. The next largest populations are resident in France (250,000) and Australia (160,000), with much smaller numbers in a host of other countries. In 1990, 40,000 returned to visit; in 2003, 340,000 returned 'home'.

Many Viet Kieu are former boat people, while others left the country as part of the UN-administered Orderly Departure Programme that began in earnest in the late 1980s. A smaller number (and one wonders whether they are strictly classed as Viet Kieu) left Vietnam for one of the former COMECON countries at some point between the 1950s and 1980s either to study or to work. The largest number appear to have gone to East Germany from where many have returned to take up important political positions. Those fortunate enough to find themselves in dour East Germany at the time of reunification suddenly found themselves privileged to be citizens of one of the world's richest countries.

As the Viet Kieu have discovered some measure of prosperity in the West, the Vietnamese government is anxious to welcome them back – or rather, welcome their money. So far, however, flows of investment for productive purposes have been rather disappointing and largely concentrated in the service sector, particularly in hotels and restaurants. Far more is thought to have been invested in land and property as overseas Vietnamese have, since 2000, been able to purchase property in their own name. (This, incidentally, has contributed to property speculation and a dizzy spiral of price increases that have made land prices in Ho Chi Minh City and Hanoi some of the most expensive in Asia.) Part of the problem is that many Viet Kieu were escaping from persecution in Vietnam and of all people continue to harbour doubts about a government that is, in essence, the same as the one they fled. On the government's side, they worry that the Viet Kieu may be a destabilizing influence, perhaps even a Fifth Column intent on undermining the supremacy of the Communist Party. Again the leadership have cause for concern as the most vocal opponents of the US policy of rapprochement have been Viet Kieu.

Art and architecture

Dongson culture

The first flourishing of Vietnamese art occurred with the emergence of the Dongson culture (named after a small town near Thanh Hoa where early excavations were focused) on the coast of Annam and Tonkin between 500 and 200 BC. The inspiration for the magnificent bronzes produced by the artists of Dongson originated from China: the decorative motifs have clear affinities with earlier Chinese bronzes. At the same time, the exceptional skill of production and decoration argues that these pieces represent among the first, and finest, of Southeast Asian works of art. This is most evident in the huge and glorious **bronze drums** that can be seen in museums in both Hanoi and Ho Chi Minh City.

Cham art

If there was ever a golden period in Vietnamese art and architecture, it was that of the former central Vietnamese **kingdom of Champa**, centred on the Annamite coast, which flowered in the 10th and 11th centuries. Tragically, however, many of the 250 sites recorded in historical records have been pillaged or damaged and only 20 have survived the intervening centuries in a reasonable state of repair. Most famous are the sites of My Son and Dong Duong, south of Danang. Many of the finest works have been spirited out of the country to private collections and foreign museums, while others were destroyed by bombing and artillery fire during the Vietnam War. Nonetheless, the world's finest collection – with some breathtakingly beautiful work – is to be found in Danang's **Museum of Champa Sculpture**.

The earliest Cham art belongs to the My Son E1 period (early eighth century). It shows stylistic similarities with Indian Sanchi and Gupta works, although even at this early stage in its development Cham art incorporated distinctive indigenous elements, most clearly seen in the naturalistic interpretation of human form. By the Dong Duong period (late ninth century), the Cham had developed a unique style of their own. Archaeologists recognize six periods of Cham art: My Son E1 (early eighth century), Hoa Lai (early ninth century), Dong Duong (late ninth century), Late Tra Kieu (late 10th century), Thap Mam (12th-13th century) and Po Klong Garai (13th-16th century).

The Cham Kingdom was ethnically and linguistically distinct, but was overrun by the Vietnamese in the 15th century. It might be argued, then, that their monuments and sculptures have little to do with Vietnam per se, but with a preceding dynasty.

Hué architecture

More characteristic of Vietnamese art and architecture are the pagodas and palaces at Hué and in and around Hanoi (see box, page 15). But even this art and architecture is not really 'Vietnamese', as it is highly derivative, drawing heavily on Chinese prototypes. Certainly there are some features that are peculiarly Vietnamese, but unlike the other countries of mainland Southeast Asia, the Vietnamese artistic tradition is far less distinct. Vietnamese artistic endeavour was directed more towards literature than the plastic arts.

Contemporary Vietnamese art

The beginnings of contemporary or modern Vietnamese art can be traced back to the creation of the **École de Beaux Arts Indochine** in Hanoi in 1925. By this time there was an emerging westernized intelligentsia in Vietnam who had been schooled in French ways and taught to identify, at least in part, with French culture. Much of the early painting produced by students taught at the École de Beaux Arts Indochine was romantic, portraying an idyllic picture of Vietnamese life and landscape. It was also weak. However, by the 1930s a Vietnamese nationalist tone began to be expressed both in terms of subject matter and technique. For example, paintings on silk and lacquer became popular around this time.

In 1945, with the Declaration of Independence, the École de Beaux Arts Indochine closed, and art for art's sake came to an end. From this point, artists were strongly encouraged to join in the revolutionary project and, for example, paint posters of heroic workers, stoic peasants and brave soldiers. Painting landscapes or pictures of rural life was no longer on the agenda.

In 1950 a new **School of Fine Art** was established in Viet Bac with the sole remit of training revolutionary artists. Central control of art and artists became even more stringent after 1954 when many artists were sent away to re-education camps. Established artists such as Bui Xuan Phai, for example, were no longer permitted either to exhibit or to teach so lacking were they in revolutionary credentials.

In 1957 a new premier art school was created in the capital: the **Hanoi School of Fine Arts**. Students were schooled in the methods and meanings of socialist-realism and Western art became, by definition, capitalist and decadent. But while the state saw to it that artists kept to the revolutionary line, fine art in North Vietnam never became so harsh and uncompromising as in China or the Soviet Union; there was always a romantic streak. In addition, the first director of the Hanoi School of Fine Arts, Nguyen Do Cung, encouraged his students to search for inspiration in traditional Vietnamese arts and crafts, in simple village designs and in archaeological artefacts. Old woodblock prints, for example, strongly influenced the artists of this period.

With *doi moi* – economic reform – has come a greater degree of artistic freedom. The first exhibition of abstract art in Vietnam was held in 1992. Today there are numerous art galleries in Hanoi and Ho Chi Minh City and while artists still paint within limits set by the Communist Party, these have been considerably relaxed.

Lacquerware (son mai)

The art of making lacquerware is said to have been introduced into Vietnam after Emperor Le Thanh Ton (1443-1459) sent an emissary to the Chinese court to investigate the process. Lacquer is a resin from the son tree (*Rhus succedanea or R vernicifera*) that is then applied in numerous coats (usually 11) to wood (traditionally teak), leather, metal or porcelain. Prior to lacquering, the article must be sanded and coated with a fixative. The final coat is highly polished with coal powder. The piece may then be decorated with an incised design, painted, or inset with mother-of-pearl. If mother-of-pearl is to be used, appropriately shaped pieces of lacquer are chiselled out and the mother-of-pearl inset. This method is similar to that used in China, but different from Thailand and Burma. The designs in the north show Japanese influences, apparently because Japanese artists were employed as teachers at the École des Beaux Arts in Hanoi in the 1930s.

Non Lá conical hat

This cone-shaped hat is one of the most common and evocative sights in Vietnam's countryside. Worn by women (and occasionally men), it is usually woven from latania leaves. The poem hats of Hué are particularly well known. Although all peasants in Southeast Asia wear straw hats only the Vietnamese version is perfectly conical and as such instantly identifies the wearer. As well as providing protection from the weather it serves other functions such as fan and rice holder and can even be used for carrying water. It also makes an original lampshade, often to be seen hanging over a pool table in bars in Saigon. It is probably less versatile than its Cambodian equivalent, the *kramar* (cotton scarf), which acts as a sarong, towel, curtain, sheet and baby sling, among its other uses.

Ao dai

This garment exhibits more conspicuously what it was intended to hide. It is the national women's costume of Vietnam, literally, but prosaically it means 'long dress'. *Ao dai* consists of a long flowing tunic of diaphanous fabric worn over a pair of loose-fitting white pants; the front and rear sections of the tunic are split from the waist down. The modern design was created by a literary group called the *Tu Luc Van Doan* in 1932, based on ancient court costumes and Chinese dresses such as the chong san. In traditional society, decoration and complexity of design indicated the status of the wearer (for example, gold brocade and dragons were for the sole use of the emperor; purple for higher-ranked mandarins). The popularity of the *ao dai* is now worldwide and the annual Miss Ao Dai pageant at Long Beach attracts entrants from all over the US. Today *ao dai* is uniform for hotel receptionists and many office workers, particularly in Ho Chi Minh City but less so in cooler Hanoi.

Montagnard crafts

There are more than 50 ethnic minorities and their crafts are highly diverse. Textiles, jewellery and basketwork are the most widely available. The finely worked clothing of the Muong (with Dongson-derived motifs) and indigo-dyed cloth of the Bahnar are two examples of Montagnard crafts.

Drama and dance

Classical Vietnamese theatre, known as *hat boi* (*hat* = to sing; *boi* = gesture, pose), shows close links with the classical theatre of China. Emperor Tu Duc had a troupe of 150 female artists and employed stars from China via a series of extravagant productions. Since the partition of the country in 1954, there has developed what might be termed 'revolutionary realist' theatre and classical Vietnamese theatre is today almost defunct. However, the most original theatrical art form in Vietnam is *mua roi nuoc* or **water puppet theatre**. This seems to have originated in northern Vietnam during the early years of this millennium when it was associated with the harvest festival (at one time scholars thought water puppet theatre originated in China before being adopted in Vietnam). An inscription in Nam Ha province mentions a show put on in honour of King Ly Nhan Ton in 1121. By the time the French began to colonize Vietnam in the late 19th century it had spread to all of the major towns of the country.

As the name suggests, this form of theatre uses the surface of the water as the stage. Puppeteers, concealed behind a bamboo screen symbolizing an ancient village communal house, manipulate the characters while standing in a metre of water. The puppets – some over half a metre tall – are carved from water resistant *sung* wood that is also very lightweight and then painted in bright colours. Most need one puppeteer to manipulate them, but some require three or four. Plays are based on historical and religious themes: the origins of the Viet nation, legends, village life, and acts of heroism. Some include the use of fireworks – especially during battle scenes – while all performances are accompanied by folk opera singers and traditional instruments. Performances usually begin with the clown, Teu, taking the stage and he acts as a linking character between the various scenes.

The most famous and active troupe is based in Hanoi (see page 41), although in total there are about a dozen groups. Since the 1980s Vietnamese writers have turned their attention from revolutionary heroes to commentary on political and social issues of the day. Consequently, many plays have failed to see the light of day and those that have are often been badly mauled by the censoring committee's scissors; references to corrupt officials and policemen seldom make the transition from page to stage.

Language

The Vietnamese language has a reputation for being fiendishly difficult to master. Its origins are still the subject of dispute; at one time thought to be a Sino-Tibetan language (because it is tonal), it is now believed to be Austro-Asiatic and related to Mon-Khmer. Sometime after the ninth century, when Vietnam was under Chinese domination, Chinese ideograms were adapted for use with the Vietnamese language. This script – *chu nho* (scholar's script) – was used in all official correspondence and in literature right through to the early 20th century. Whether this replaced an earlier writing system is not known. As early Vietnamese nationalists tried to break away from Chinese cultural hegemony in the late 13th century, they devised their own script, based on Chinese ideograms but adapted to meet Vietnamese language needs. This became known as *chu nom* (vulgar script). So, while Chinese words formed the learned vocabulary of the intelligentsia (largely inaccessible to the man on the street or in the paddy field), non-Chinese words made up a parallel popular vocabulary.

Finally, in the 17th century, European missionaries under the tutelage of Father Alexandre-de-Rhodes created a system of Romanized writing: *quoc ngu* (national language). It is said that Rhodes initially thought Vietnamese sounded like the 'twittering of birds' (a view interestingly echoed by Graham Greene in *The Quiet American*: "To take an Annamite to bed with you is like taking a bird: they twitter and sing on your pillow") but had mastered the language in six months. The first *quoc ngu* dictionary (Vietnamese-Portuguese-Latin), *Dictionarium Annamiticum Lusitanum et Latinum*, was published in 1651. *Quoc ngu* uses marks – so-called diacritical marks – to indicate tonal differences. Initially it was ignored by the educated unless they were Roman Catholic and it was not until the early 20th century that its use became a mark of modernity among a broad spectrum of Vietnamese. Even then, engravings in the mausoleums and palaces of the royal family continued to use Chinese characters. It seems that the move from *chu nom* to *quoc ngu*, despite the fact that it was imposed by an occupying country, occurred as people realized how much easier it was to master. The first *quoc ngu* newspaper, *Gia Dinh Bao* (Gia Dinh Gazette), was published in 1865 and *quoc ngu* was adopted as the national script in 1920.

Standard Vietnamese is based on the language spoken by an educated person living in the vicinity of Hanoi. This has become, so to speak, Vietnam's equivalent of BBC English. There are also important regional dialects in the centre and south of the country and these differ from Standard Vietnamese in terms of tone and vocabulary, but use the same system of grammar.

Literature

In ancient Vietnam, texts were reproduced laboriously, by scribes, on paper made from the bark of the mulberry tree (*giay ban*). Examples exist in Ho Chi Minh City, Paris, Hanoi and Hué. Printing technology was introduced in the late 13th century, but due to the hot and humid climate no early examples exist.

Vietnam has a rich folk literature of fables, legends, proverbs and songs, most of which were transmitted by word of mouth. In the 17th and 18th centuries, satirical poems and, importantly, verse novels (*truyen*) appeared. These were memorized and recited by itinerant storytellers as they travelled from village to village.

Like much Vietnamese art, Vietnamese literature also owes a debt to China. Chinese characters and literary styles were duplicated and although a tradition of *nom* literature did evolve (*nom* being a hybrid script developed in the 13th century), Vietnamese efforts remained largely derivative. One exception was the scholarly **Nguyen Trai** who bridged the gap; he excelled in classical Chinese *chu nho* as well as producing some of the earliest surviving, and very fine, poetry and prose in the new *chu nom* script. An important distinction is between the literature of the intelligentsia (essentially Chinese) and that of the people (more individualistic). These latter *nom* works, dating from the 15th century onwards, were simpler and concerned with immediate problems and grievances. They can be viewed as the most Vietnamese of literary works and include *Chinh Phu Ngam* (Lament of a Soldier's Wife), an anti-war poem by Phan Huy Ich (1750-1822). The greatest Vietnamese literature was produced during the social and political upheavals of the 19th century: *Truyen Kieu* (The Tale of Kieu) written by Nguyen Du (1765-1820) is a classic of the period. This 3254-line story is regarded by most Vietnamese as their cultural statement par excellence (see the next section for a taster). Nguyen Du was one of the most skilled and learned mandarins of his time and was posted to China as Vietnam's Ambassador to the Middle Kingdom. On his return, Nguyen Du wrote the *Truyen Kieu* (or *Kim Van Kieu*), a celebration of Vietnamese culture, in the lines of which can be traced the essence of Vietnamese-ness.

French influence, and the spread of the Romanized Vietnamese script, led to the end of the Chinese literary tradition by the 1930s and its replacement by a far starker, freer, Western-derived style. Poetry of this period is known as *Tho Moi* (New Poetry). The communist period has seen restrictions on literary freedom and in recent years there have been numerous cases of authors and poets, together with journalists, being imprisoned owing to the critical nature of their work. Much of Vietnam's literature is allegorical (which people readily understand); this reflects a centuries-old intolerance of criticism by the mandarin and royal family. Although the Communist Party might be expected to approve of anti-royal sentiment in literature it seldom does, fearing that the Party itself is the true object of the writer's scorn.

Kieu: oriental Juliet or prototype Miss Saigon?

The tale of Kieu is a true story of pure love corrupted by greed and power. It also offers a fascinating glimpse into the Vietnamese mind and Vietnamese sexual mores. Kieu is in love with the young scholar Kim and early on in the story she displays her physical and moral qualities:

"A fragrant rose, she sparkled in full bloom, bemused his eyes, and kindled his desire. When waves of lust had seemed to sweep him off, his wooing turned to wanton liberties. She said: 'Treat not our love as just a game – please stay away from me and let me speak. What is a mere peach blossom that one should fence off the garden, thwart the bluebird's quest? But you've named me your bride – to serve her man, she must place chastity above all else.'"

But the overriding theme of the story is the ill-treatment of an innocent girl by a duplicitous and wicked world unopposed by Heaven. Unmoved by Kieu's sale into prostitution the fates actively oppose her wishes by keeping her alive when she attempts to kill herself.

Any respite in her tale of woe proves short-lived and joy turns quickly to pain. The story illustrates the hopelessness of women in a Confucianist, male-dominated world; Kieu likens herself to a raindrop with no control over where she will land. Early on in the story when Kim is away attending to family matters Kieu has to choose between Kim, to whom she has pledged herself, and her family. Such is the strength of family ties that she offers herself to be sold in marriage to raise money for her kith and kin:

"By what means could she save her flesh and blood? When evil strikes you bow to circumstance. As you must weigh and choose between your love and filial duty, which will turn the scale? She put aside all vows of love and troth – a child first pays the debts of birth and care."

Kieu gets married off to an elderly 'scholar' called Ma who is in fact a brothel keeper; but before removing her from her family he deflowers her. Kieu is now commercially less valuable but Ma believes he can remedy this:

"One smile of hers is worth pure gold – it's true. When she gets there, to pluck the maiden bud, princes and gentlefolk will push and shove. She'll bring at least three hundred liang, about what I have paid – net profit after that. A morsel dangles at my mouth – what God serves up I crave, yet money hate to lose. A heavenly peach within a mortal's grasp: I'll bend the branch, pick it, and quench my thirst. How many flower-fanciers on Earth can really tell one flower from the next? Juice from pomegranite skin and cockscomb blood will heal it up and lend the virgin look. In dim half-light some yokel will be fooled: she'll fetch that much, and not one penny less."

Kieu's sorrows deepen; she becomes a concubine of a married brothel patron, Thuc. After a year of happiness together with Thuc his spurned wife, Hoan, decides to spoil the fun. Kieu ends up as a slave serving Thuc and Hoan. She laments her fate knowing full well the reason for it:

"I've had an ample share of life's foul dust, and now this swamp of mud proves twice as vile. Will fortune never let its victims go but in its snares and toils hold fast a rose? I sinned in some past life and have to pay: I'll pay as flowers must fade and jade must break."

She later commits her only earthly crime stealing a golden bell and silver gong from the shrine she is charged with keeping, and flees to seek sanctuary in a Buddhist temple. But when her crime comes to light she is sent to live with the Bac family that, again on the pretext of marriage, sells her to another brothel. This time she meets a free-spirited warlord Tu Hai:

"A towering hero, he outfought all foes with club or fist and knew all arts of war. Between the earth and heaven he lived free...."

who rescues her from the brothel. They become soul- and bed-mates until, after six months, Tu Hai's wanderlust and urge to fight take him away from her. He returns a year later victorious in battle. At this stage the story reaches a happy (and false) ending; Tu Hai sends his Captains out to round up all those who have crossed Kieu's path.

"Awesome is Heaven's law of recompense – one haul and all were caught, brought back to camp. Under a tent erected in the midst, Lord Tu and his fair lady took their seats. No sooner had the drumroll died away than guards checked names, led captives to the gate. 'Whether they have used you well or ill,' he said, 'pronounce yourself upon their just deserts.' "

Those who have shown Kieu kindness are rewarded while those who have harmed her are tortured. The exception is Hoan who, cruel though she was, Kieu releases (after torture) in a show of mercy following Hoan's plea "I have a woman's mind, a petty soul, and jealousy's a trait all humans share" – Kieu had been living with Hoan's husband for a year.

All is well for five years until another warlord, Lord Ho, flatters Kieu encouraging her to persuade Tu to put down his sword and make peace with the emperor. Guileless Kieu does so and "Lord Tu lets flags hang loose, watch-drums go dead. He slackened all defence – imperial spies/observed his camp and learned of its true state." All is lost: Tu is killed, Kieu has betrayed her hero and she is married off to a tribal chief. She throws herself into a river but yet again fails to die. Eventually Kieu, is reunited with Kim and her family:

"She glanced and saw her folks – they all were here: Father looked quite strong, and Mother spry; both sister Van and brother Quan grown up; and over there was Kim her love of yore."

Kieu and Kim hold a wedding feast and share a house but not a bed; Kim has sons by Van, Kieu's sister, and they all settle down to an untroubled life overseen by a more benevolent Heaven.

Huynh Sang Thong's translation is considered the finest and is accompanied by excellent notes which explain the Vietnamese phrasing of the original and which set the story in context. Translation and commentary will bring Truyen Kieu to a wider and, one hopes, appreciative audience and help shed some light on what many Vietnamese regard as their most important cultural statement.

A Vietnamese account of the 'American' War

Most visitors to Vietnam, if they were not involved in the war themselves, gain their views from literature and films made by Westerners, for Westerners. It is rare for people to have access to Vietnamese literary perspectives on the war, partly because most that do exist are not translated and because, in comparison to the torrent of especially American accounts, there have been comparatively few written by Vietnamese. One of these few is Bao Ninh's moving and poetic *The Sorrow of War* that was first published in Vietnamese in 1991 under the title *Thân Phân Cua Tinh Yêu*. In Vietnam it was a huge success, no doubt prompting its translation into English by Frank Palmos. The English edition was published in 1994 and it is available in paperback. This is not a romantic vision of war, a macho account relishing the fight, nor once revelling in victory, but a deeply sad and melancholic book. Perhaps this is because Bao Ninh is recounting his story from the position of one who was there. He served with the Glorious 27th Youth Brigade, joining-up in 1969 at the age of 17. Of the 500 who went to war with the Glorious 27th, he was one of just 10 to survive the conflict. For those who want an alternative perspective, the book is recommended.

Practicalities
Vietnam

Getting there 147
Getting around 148
Local customs and conduct . 159
Essentials A-Z 156
Index...................... 164
Acknowledgements........ 167
Credits 168

Getting there

Flights from Europe
In Western Europe, there are direct flights to Vietnam from London, Paris and Frankfurt with **Vietnam Airlines/Air France**. These code-shared flights last 12 hours. There are also direct **Vietnam Airlines** flights from Moscow.

Flights from other European hubs go via Bangkok, Singapore, Kuala Lumpur, Hong Kong or UAE states. Airlines include **Air France, Cathay Pacific, Emirates, Thai Airways, Singapore Airlines, Malaysia Airlines, Lufthansa** and **Qatar**.

Flights from the USA and Canada
By far the best option is to fly via **Bangkok, Taipei, Tokyo** or **Hong Kong** and from there to Vietnam. The approximate flight time from Los Angeles to **Bangkok** is 21 hours. **United** flies from LA and Chicago via Tokyo and from San Francisco via Seoul to Vietnam. **Thai Airways, Delta, United** and **Air Canada** fly to Bangkok from a number of US and Canadian cities.

Flights from Australia and New Zealand
There are direct flights from Adelaide, Melbourne, Sydney, Perth, Auckland and Wellington with **Cathay Pacific, Malaysia Airlines, Singapore Airlines** and **Thai Airways. Qantas** flies from Sydney, Adelaide and Melbourne to Ho Chi Minh City. **Air Asia** has cheap flights via KL.

From Sydney the flights to Vietnam are eight hours 45 minutes direct.

Flights from Asia
HCMC is very well connected to cities all over East Asia.

Airport information
The international airport in Ho Chi Minh City is **Tan Son Nhat Airport** (SGN), see page 45.

Getting around

Public bus and train services are notoriously slow, and as hiring a self-drive car is not a possibility in Vietnam, many visitors opt to take a tour, which saves a lot of time. The popular Open Tour Bus service operates down to the Delta and onto Cambodia. The more adventurous might hire a motorbike, and for the islands the domestic air network can be utilized.

Air

Vietnam Airlines is the national carrier and flies to multiple domestic destinations. **VietJetAir** is the low-cost alternative and offers a good service. Remember that during holiday periods flights get extremely busy.

Road

Open Tour Buses, see below, are very useful and cheap for bridging important towns. Many travellers opt to take a tour to reach remote areas because of the lack of self-drive car hire and the dangers and slow speed of public transport.

Bus
Roads in Vietnam are notoriously dangerous. As American humourist PJ O'Rourke wrote: "In Japan people drive on the left. In China people drive on the right. In Vietnam it doesn't matter." Since Highway 1 is so dangerous and public transport buses are poor and slow, most travellers opt for the cheap and regular **Open Tour Bus** (private minibus or coach) that covers the length of the country. See www.thesinhtourist.vn/openbus/vcvx/open-bus/all for schedules.

If you do opt for **public buses** note that most bus stations are on the outskirts of town; in bigger centres there may be several stations. Long-distance buses invariably leave very early in the morning (0400-0500). Buses are the cheapest form of transport, although sometimes foreigners find they are being asked for two to three times the correct price. Prices are normally prominently displayed at bus stations. Less comfortable but quicker are the minibus services, which ply the more popular routes.

Car hire
Self-drive car hire is not available in Vietnam. It is, however, possible to hire cars with drivers and this is a good way of getting to more remote areas with a group of people. Car hire prices increase by 50% or more during Tet.

Motorbike and bicycle hire
Most towns are small enough to get around by bicycle, and this can also be a pleasant way to explore the surrounding countryside. However, if covering large areas then a motorbike will mean you can see more and get further off the beaten track.

Motorbikes and bicycles can be hired by the day in the cities, often from hotels and travellers' cafés. You do not need a driver's licence or proof of motorbike training to hire a motorbike in Vietnam, however, it is compulsory to wear a helmet. Also, lack of a license will no doubt invalidate your travel insurance.

Motorbike taxi and cyclo

Motorcycle taxis, known as *xe om* (*ôm* means to cuddle) are ubiquitous and cheap. You will find them on most street corners, outside hotels or in the street. If they see you before you see them, they will whistle to get your attention.

Cyclos are bicycle trishaws. Cyclo drivers charge double or more that of a *xe om*. A number of streets in the centres of Ho Chi Minh City are one-way or out of bounds to cyclos, necessitating lengthy detours which add to the time and cost.

Taxi

Taxis ply the streets of Ho Chi Minh City and other large towns and cities. They are cheap, around 12,000d per kilometre. Always use the better-known taxi companies to avoid any issues. Mai Linh is one of the most widely found reliable firms.

River

The **Victoria** hotel chain (www.victoriahotels-asia.com) runs a Mekong Delta service for its guests. Ferries operate between Rach Gia and Phu Quoc; Ha Tien and Phu Quoc. The ferry to Con Dao is not recommended.

Train

The only train service in the region is the HCMC line to and from Phan Thiet, which is a comfortable and scenic route. Most ticket offices have some staff who speak English. Queues can be long and some offices keep unusual hours. If you are short of time and short on patience it may well pay to get a tour operator to book your ticket for a small commission or visit the Ho Chi Minh City railway office in Pham Ngu Lao.

Where to stay

Accommodation ranges from luxury suites in international five-star hotels and spa resorts to small, family hotels and homestays with local people in the Mekong Delta. During peak seasons – especially December to March and particularly during busy holidays such as Tet, Christmas, New Year's Eve and around Easter – booking is essential. Expect staff to speak English in all top hotels. Do not expect it in cheaper hotels or in more remote places, although most places employ someone with a smattering of a foreign language.

Private, mini hotels are worth seeking out as, being family-run, guests can expect good service. Mid-range and tourist hotels may provide a decent breakfast that is often included in the price. Many luxury and first-class hotels and some three-star hotels charge extra for breakfast and, on top of this, also charge 10% VAT and 5% service charge. When quoted a hotel price you should ask whether that includes these two taxes; it is marked as ++ (plus plus) on the bill.

There are some world-class beach resorts in Phu Quoc, Mui Ne and Con Dao. To stay in a homestay, you must book through a tour operator or through the local tourist office; you cannot just turn up. Homestays are possible on farms and in orchards in the Mekong Delta.

National parks offer everything from air-conditioned bungalows to shared dormitory rooms to campsites where, sometimes, it is possible to hire tents. Visitors may spend a romantic night on a boat on the Mekong Delta. Boats range from the fairly luxurious to the basic. Most people book through tour operators.

You will often have to leave your passport at hotel reception desks for the duration of your hotel stay. It will be released to you temporarily for bank purposes or buying an air ticket. Credit cards are widely accepted but there is often a 2-4% fee for paying in this manner. Tipping is not expected in hotels in Vietnam.

The age of consent in Vietnam is 18. There are rules relating to a Vietnamese person of the opposite sex being in your hotel room. It depends on the attitude of the hotel. Travellers normally get their laundry done in hotels. In cheap hotels it's inexpensive. Cheaper hotels and laundries in the hotel districts charge by weight. The smarter places charge by the item and the bill can be huge as a result.

Price codes

Where to stay	Restaurants
$$$$ over US$100	$$$ over US$12
$$$ US$46-100	$$ US$6-12
$$ US$20-45	$ under US$6
$ under US$20	

Prices refer to the cost of a double room in high season, including taxes.

Prices refer to the cost of a two-course meal for one person, excluding drinks or service charge.

Food & drink

Food

Food is a major attraction of Vietnam; it is plentiful and almost always delicious. Outstanding Vietnamese, French and international cuisine is served in first-class restaurants and humble foodstalls alike. The quality will be, in the main, exceptional. The accent is on local, seasonal and fresh produce and the rich pickings from the sea, along Vietnam's 2000-km coastline, will always make it far inland too. While most small places will focus on one or two dishes, many larger restaurants offer a variety of cuisine from the regions. Ho Chi Minh City offers a wide range of cuisines besides Vietnamese. Eating out, especially at street restaurants, is very cheap.

Dishes

Pho (pronounced *fer*), a bowl of flat, white, noodle soup served with chicken or beef, is utterly delicious. The soup is made from stock flavoured with star anise, ginger and other spices and herbs but individual recipes often remain a closely guarded secret. Vietnamese usually eat *pho* in the morning, but you will be able to find it throughout the day. On each table of a *pho* restaurant in the south sits a plate of fresh green leaves: mint, cinnamon, basil and the spiky looking *ngo gai*, together with bean sprouts, chopped red chillies, barbecue sauce and sliced lemons, enabling patrons to produce their own variations on a theme.

Another local speciality found mainly further south is *com tam* or broken rice. *Com tam* stalls abound on the streets and do brisk trade at breakfast and lunch. They tend to be low-cost canteens. The steamed broken rice is eaten with fried chicken, fish, pork and vegetables and soup is normally included in the price. You will also find cheap *com bing dan* restaurants everywhere which feature rice and a wide variety of dishes which you can select, buffet style.

There are many types of Vietnamese roll: the most common are deep-fried spring rolls (confusingly, *cha gio* in the south and *nem ranh* in the north) but if these appear on your table too frequently, look for the fresh or do-it-yourself types, such as *bi cuon* or *bo bia*. Essentially, these are salads with prawns or grilled meats wrapped in rice paper.

Vietnamese salads (*goi* in the south and *nom* in the north) are to die for. The best known is the green papaya salad with dried beef (*nom du du bo kho*); others include *goi xoai* (mango salad) and *goi buoi* (pomelo salad). They all involve a wonderful fusion of herbs and vegetables with sweet and spicy tastes rolled in.

Delicious seafood is a staple across the land. It would be invidious to isolate a particular seafood dish when there are so many to chose from. Prawns are prawns – the bigger and the less adulterated the better. But a marvellous dish that does deserve commendation is crab in tamarind sauce. This glorious fusion of flavours, bitter tamarind, garlic, piquant spring onion and fresh crab is quite delicious.

All Vietnamese food is dipped, whether in fish sauce, soy sauce, chilli sauce, peanut sauce or pungent prawn sauce (*mam tom* – avoid if possible) before eating.

ON THE ROAD

Bird's nest soup

The tiny nests of the brown-rumped swift (*Collocalia esculenta*), also known as the edible-nest swiftlet or sea swallow, are collected for bird's nest soup, a Chinese delicacy, throughout Southeast Asia.

The semi-oval nests are made of silk-like strands of saliva secreted by the birds which, when cooked in broth, softens and becomes a little like noodles. Like so many Chinese delicacies, the nests are believed to have aphrodisiac qualities and the soup has even been suggested as a cure for HIV. The red nests are the most highly valued, and the Vietnamese Emperor Minh Mang (1820-1840) is said to have owed his extraordinary vitality to his inordinate consumption of bird's nest soup. This may explain why restaurants serving it are sometimes associated with massage parlours.

Collecting the nests is a precarious but profitable business and in some areas mafias of concessionaires vigorously guard and protect their assets. The men who collect the nests on a piecework basis risk serious injury climbing rickety ladders to cave roofs in sometimes almost total darkness, save for a candle strapped to their heads.

As each course is served so a new set of dips will accompany. Follow the guidance of your waiter or Vietnamese friends to get the right dip with the right dish.

Eating out

When it comes to food, Vietnamese do not stand on ceremony and (perhaps rather like the French) regard peripherals such as furniture, service and ambience as mere distractions to the task of ploughing through plates, crocks, casseroles and tureens charged with meats, vegetables and soups. Do not expect good service, courses to arrive in the right order, or to eat at the same time as your companions, but do expect the freshest and tastiest food you will find anywhere.

While it is possible to eat very cheaply in Vietnam (especially outside Ho Chi Minh City) the higher class of restaurant, particularly those serving foreign cuisine, can prove quite expensive, especially with wine. But with judicious shopping around it is not hard to find excellent value for money, particularly in the small, **family restaurants**. Some restaurants (mostly expensive ones) add 5% service charge and the government tax of 10% to the bill. See page 150 on restaurant classification.

For day trips, an early morning visit to the **markets** will produce a picnic fit for a king: hard-boiled quails' eggs, thinly sliced garlic sausage, pickled vegetables, beef tomatoes, cucumber, pâté, cheese, warm baguettes and fresh fruit.

The thing that separates India from China is that in the former there are prohibitions governing the consumption of just about everything. In the latter anything and everything can be – and is – eaten. Vietnam of course falls under Chinese sway. Therefore anyone who self imposes restrictions on his eating habits is regarded as a bit of a crank. There are **vegetarian restaurants** in Vietnam but these usually sell different types of tofu dressed to look like meat. The vegetable section of most 'normal' restaurants has vegetables – but cooked with pork, with beef or with prawns, rarely pure vegetables. Nevertheless there are a few Vietnamese vegetarians and twice a month a great many people eat vegetarian so restaurants are aware of the concept and the number of veggie specific places is on the up.

Given the large proportion of the population aged 16 and under no Vietnamese restaurant is put out by **children**. Indeed any restaurant frequented by Vietnamese families will have kids running around everywhere. So parents need have no fears about their children's behaviour upsetting anyone.

Note that Vietnamese get up early and so lunchtime starts at 1100 and some more local places will be shutting up shop for lunch by 1300.

Drink

Locally produced fresh beer is called *bia hoi*. It is cold and refreshing, and weak and cheap enough to drink in quite large volumes. It is usually consumed in small pavement cafés where patrons sit on small plastic stools. Most *bia hoi* places serve simple and inexpensive food. As the beer is fresh it has to be consumed within a short period of brewing hence most towns, even quite small ones, have their own brewery. Bars and restaurants do not sell *bia hoi*, hence customers usually have a choice of the regional bottled brew or Tiger, Heineken or Carlsberg. 'Beer clubs' haver become very popular in HCMC in the last year or two, most of which sell Czech or German beers plus a range of Belgian options by the bottle.

Rice and **fruit wines** are produced and consumed in large quantities in upland areas, particularly in the north of Vietnam. Rice wines are fairly easily found, however. There are two types of rice wine, *ruou nep* and *ruou de*. *Ruou nep* is a viscous wine made from sticky rice. *Ruou de* is a rice spirit and very strong.

The Chinese believe that **snake wines** increase their virility and are normally found in areas with a large Chinese population. It is called a wine despite being a spirit. Other wines include the body and parts of seahorses, gecko, silkworms and bees.

There is a fantastic range of different **fruit wines** but unless you make a real effort it can be quite hard to find them. Wines are made from just about all upland fruits: plum, strawberry, apple and, of course, grapes, although grape wine in Vietnam is generally disappointing. The others are fiery and warm, strong and, bought by the bottle, cheap.

What to do

Many operators offer organized trips to Vietnam, ranging from a whistle-stop tour of the highlights to specialist trips that focus on a specific destination or activity. The advantage of travelling with a reputable operator is that your accommodation, transport and activities are all arranged for you in advance – particularly valuable if you only have limited time in the region. Specialist tour operators can be found on page 161.

Safety is always an issue when participating in adventurous sports: make sure you are fully covered by your travel insurance; check the credentials of operators offering adventure activities; and make sure that vehicles and safety equipment are in a good condition.

Birdwatching

Vietnam may not seem like the first choice for a birdwatching holiday (indeed, many visitors comment that there are few birds around) but for those in the know it has become one of the top birding destinations of the region in recent years. Tram Chim National Park is the place to go to in this region.

Contact
Vietnam Birding, Vietnam Birding, www.vietnambirding.com. Contact Richard Craik for more information or advice on birding, or to organize birding tours throughout Vietnam.

Cookery classes

There are increasingly more of these available with hotels and restaurants in major cities and resorts offer courses. Some operators offer tours that include half a day or one day of cooking for those who would like to see more than just the inside of a hotel kitchen. The variety is already quite broad. Check hotel flyers, the web or adverts in local magazines.

Cycling and mountain biking

Being flat over great distances, cycling is a popular activity in Vietnam. The main problem is the traffic. It's recommended that any tour is planned off-road or on minor roads, not Highway 1. Many cyclists prefer to bring their own all-terrain or racing bikes but it's also possible to rent from tour organizers.

Contact
Spice Roads, 14/1-B Soi Promsi 2, Sukhumvit 39, Klongtan Nua, Wattana, Bangkok, T66 2-712 5305, www.spice roads.com. A recommended biking company that operates throughout Asia.

Diving and snorkelling

Snorkelling in the seas of Vietnam is a limited activity. Much of the coast has very poor visibility. Away from the deltas the water is still quite turbid. In those places where snorkelling and diving is said to be good (such **Phu Quoc**) the best time of year to dive varies with location – contact the diving operators in the relevant section for full details.

Ecotourism

Since the early 1990s there has been a significant growth in ecotourism, which promotes and supports the conservation of natural environments and is also fair and equitable to local communities. While the authenticity of some ecotourism operators needs to be interpreted with some care, there is both a huge demand for this type of activity and also significant opportunities to support worthwhile conservation and social development initiatives.

Contact
International Eco-Tourism Society (www.ecotourism.org) and **Tourism Concern** (www.tourismconcern.org.uk) develop and promote ecotourism projects in destinations all over the world and their websites provide details for initiatives throughout Southeast Asia. A number of Vietnam-based operators are also now members of the **Responsible Travel Club**, www.rtcvietnam.org, which works with both WWF and SNV.

Golf

Golf in Vietnam can be traced back to the 1930s when the emperor Bao Dai laid a course in Dalat. After a period of dormancy, golf in Vietnam has mushroomed over the past few years. There are now many international standard courses all over the country and green fees are reasonable. There are very good courses around HCMC and Mui Ne.

Motorbiking and Vespa tours

Touring northern Ha Giang province on a motorbike is one of the most exciting things you can do here. Other cross-country and cross-border tours are possible. Companies use a range of bikes from the temperamental Minsk to the Honda Baja. Vespa tours are available from **Ho Chi Minh City** to **Mui Ne**.

Windsurfing and kitesurfing

Kite and windsurfing are found largely in Mui Ne. Here **Jibe's Beach Club** is leading the way organizing international tournaments. Mui Ne offers near-perfect conditions in season; equipment can be rented or bought at many places.

Essentials A-Z

Accident and emergency

Contact the relevant emergency service and your embassy. Make sure you obtain police/medical records in order to file insurance claims. If you need to report a crime, visit your local police station and take a local with you who speaks English. If you have a medical emergency, ask your hotel which nearby hospital is recommended. **Ambulance** T115, **Fire** T114, **Police** T113.

Customs and duty free

Duty-free allowance is 400 cigarettes, 50 cigars or 100 g of tobacco, 1.5 litres of spirits, plus items for personal use. Export of wood products or antiques is banned. You cannot import pornography, anti-government literature, photos or movies nor culturally unsuitable children's toys.

Disabled travellers

Considering the proportion of the country's population that is seriously disabled, foreigners might expect better facilities and allowances for the immobile. But there are very few. However, some of the more upmarket hotels do have a few designated rooms for the disabled. For those with walking difficulties many of the better hotels do have lifts. Wheelchair access is improving with more shopping centres, hotels and restaurants providing ramps for easy access. People sensitive to noise will find Vietnam, at times, almost intolerable.

Drugs

In the south you may be offered weed, but rarely anything else, although ecstasy is becoming more popular among the younger generation. Attitudes to traffickers are harsh, although the death penalty (now by lethal injection and not firing squad) is usually reserved for Vietnamese and other Asians whose governments are less likely to kick up a fuss.

Electricity

Voltage 110-240. Sockets are round 2-pin. Sometimes they are 2 flat pin. A number of top hotels now use UK 3 square-pin sockets.

Embassies and consulates

For a list of Vietnamese embassies abroad, see http://embassy.goabroad.com.

Festivals and public holidays

Vietnamese festivals are timed according to the Vietnamese lunar calendar.
Late Jan-Mar (movable, 1st-7th day of the new lunar year) **Tet**.
Mar (movable, 6th day of 2nd lunar month) **Hai Ba Trung Day**. Celebrates the famous Trung sisters who led a revolt against the Chinese in AD 41 (see box, page 55).
Apr (5th or 6th, 3rd lunar month) **Thanh Minh** (New Year of the Dead or Feast of the Pure Light). People are supposed to walk outdoors to evoke the spirit of the dead and family shrines and tombs are traditionally cleaned and decorated.

May (15th day of the 4th lunar month) Celebration of the birth, death and enlightenment of the Buddha.
Aug (movable, 15th day of the 7th lunar month) **Trung Nguyen** (Wandering Souls Day). One of the most important festivals. During this time, prayers can absolve the sins of the dead who leave hell and return, hungry and naked, to their relatives. The Wandering Souls are those with no homes to go to. There are celebrations in Buddhist temples and homes, food is placed out on tables and money is burned.
Sep (movable, 15th day of the 8th month) **Tet Trung Thu** (Mid-Autumn Festival) This festival is particularly celebrated by children. It is based on legend and there are various stories as to its history. One of the legends is about a Chinese king who went to the moon. When he returned, the king wished to share what he had seen with the people on earth.

In the evening families prepare food including sticky rice, fruit and chicken to be placed on the ancestral altars. Moon cakes (egg, green bean and lotus seed) are baked (with some variations on these ingredients offered by some of the smarter hotels such as chocolate), lanterns made and painted, and children parade through towns with music and lanterns. It is particularly popular in Hanoi and toy shops in the Old Quarter decorate stores with lanterns and masks.
Nov (movable, 28th day of the 9th month) **Confucius' Birthday**.

Public holidays
1 Jan New Year's Day.
Late Jan-Mar (movable, 1st-7th day of the new lunar year) **Tet**.
3 Feb Founding anniversary of the Communist Party of Vietnam.
30 Apr **Liberation Day** of South Vietnam and HCMC.
1 May **International Labour Day**.
19 May **Anniversary of the Birth of Ho Chi Minh** (government holiday) The majority of state institutions will be shut on this day but businesses in the private sector remain open.
2 Sep **National Day**.
3 Sep **President Ho Chi Minh's Anniversary**.

Health

See your doctor or travel clinic at least 6 weeks before your departure for general advice on travel risks, malaria and vaccinations (see also below). Make sure you have travel insurance, get a dental check-up (especially if you are going to be away for more than a month), know your own blood group and if you suffer a long-term condition such as diabetes or epilepsy make sure someone knows or that you have a **Medic Alert** bracelet/necklace with this information on it (www.medicalert.co.uk).

Vaccinations
The following vaccinations are advised: BCG, Hepatitis A, Japanese Encephalitis, Polio, Rabies, Tetanus, Typhoid and Yellow Fever.

Health risks
Malaria exists in rural areas in Vietnam. The choice of malaria prophylaxis will need to be something other than chloroquine for most people, since there is such a high level of resistance to it. Always check with your doctor or travel clinic for the most up-to-date advice.

Malaria can cause death within 24 hrs. It can start as something just resembling an attack of flu. You may feel tired, lethargic, headachy, feverish; or more seriously, develop fits, followed by coma and then death. Have a low index of suspicion because it is very easy to write off vague symptoms, which may actually be malaria. If you have a temperature, go to a doctor as soon as you can and ask for a malaria test. On your return home if you suffer any of these symptoms, get tested as soon as possible, even if any previous test proved negative; the test could save your life.

The most serious viral disease is **dengue fever**, which is hard to protect against as the mosquitos bite throughout the day as well as at night. Bacterial diseases include **tuberculosis** (TB) and some causes of the more common traveller's **diarrhoea**. Lung fluke (**para-gonimiasis**) occurs in Vietnam. A fluke is a sort of flattened worm. In the Sin Ho district the locals like to eat undercooked or raw crabs, but our advice is to leave them to it. The crabs contain a fluke which, when eaten, travels to the lungs. The lung fluke may cause a cough, coughing 'blood', fever, chest pain and changes on your X-ray which will puzzle a British radiologist. The cure is the same drug that cures schistosomiasis (another fluke which can be acquired in some parts of the Mekong Delta).

Consult the WHO website, www. who.int, for further information and heed local advice on the ground. There are high rates of **HIV** in the region, especially among sex workers.

Medical services
Western hospitals staffed by foreign and Vietnamese medics exist and HCMC. If you need to access medical services, ask your hotel which hospital in the area is recommended.

Useful websites
www.btha.org British Travel Health Association (UK). This is the official website of an organization of travel health professionals.
www.cdc.gov US government site that gives excellent advice on travel health and details of disease outbreaks.
www.fitfortravel.scot.nhs.uk A-Z of vaccine/health advice for each country.
www.who.int The WHO Blue Book lists the diseases of the world.

Insurance

Always take out travel insurance before you set off and read the small print carefully. Check that the policy covers the activities you intend or may end up doing. Also check exactly what your medical cover includes, such as ambulance, helicopter rescue or emergency flights back home. Also check the payment protocol. You may have to pay up first before the insurance company reimburses you. Keep receipts for expensive personal effects, such as jewellery or cameras. Take photos of these items and note down all serial numbers. You are advised to shop around.

Internet

Although emailing is easy and Wi-Fi is widespread, access to the web is slightly restricted, for example BBC and Facebook are periodically blocked.

Language

You are likely to find some English spoken wherever there are tourist services but outside tourist centres communication can be a problem for those who have no knowledge of Vietnamese. Furthermore, the Vietnamese language is not easy to learn. For example, pronunciation presents enormous difficulties as it is tonal. On the plus side, Vietnamese is written in a Roman alphabet making life much easier; place and street names are instantly recognizable. French is still spoken and often very well by the more elderly and educated Vietnamese and older German speakers are common in the north too.

Local customs and conduct

Vietnam is remarkably relaxed and easy going with regard to conventions. The people, especially in small towns and rural areas, can be pretty old-fashioned, but it is difficult to cause offence unwittingly.

Appearance
The main complaint Vietnamese have of foreigners is their fondness for dirty and torn clothing. Backpackers come in for particularly severe criticism and the term *tay ba lo* (literally 'Western backpacker') is a contemptuous one reflecting the low priority many budget travellers seem to allocate to personal hygiene and the antiquity and inadequacy of their shorts and vests.

Shoes should be removed before entering temples and before going into people's houses. Modesty should be preserved and excessive displays of bare flesh are not considered good form, particularly in temples and private houses. (Not that the Vietnamese are unduly prudish, they just like things to be kept in their proper place.) Shorts are fine for the beach and travellers' cafés but not for smart restaurants.

Conduct
Kissing and canoodling in public are likely to draw attention, not much of it favourable. But walking hand in hand is now accepted as a Western habit. Hand shaking among men is a standard greeting and although Vietnamese women will consent to the process, it is often clear that they would prefer not to.

Terms of address
Vietnamese names are written with the surname first, followed by the first name. Thus Nguyen Minh is not called Nguyen as we would presume in the West but Minh. The conventions around how to address people according to age are quite complicated and visitors will not be expected to master them.

Religion
The Vietnamese are open to religious experiences of all kinds. Vietnam is predominantly a Buddhist country. Following Chinese tradition, ancestor worship is widely practiced and animism (the belief in and worship of spirits of inanimate objects such as venerable trees, the land, mountains and so on) is widespread. The government is hostile to proselytizing, particularly by Christians. However, foreigners are perfectly free to attend services. In Ho Chi Minh City one or two services in the Notre Dame Cathedral are in French and in English. Protestant churches are found throughout the country to a lesser degree then the Roman Catholic Church but all services are in Vietnamese.

Money

→ *US$1 = 21,500d, €1 = 23,000d, £1 = 32,000d. Mar 2015.*

The unit of currency is the Vietnam Dong. Under law, shops should only accept dong but in practice this is not enforced and dollars are accepted in some places. ATMs are plentiful in HCMC and are now pretty ubiquitous in all but the smallest of town, but it is a good idea to travel with US dollars cash as a back up. Try to avoid tatty notes.

Banks in the main centres will change other major currencies including UK sterling, Hong Kong dollars, Thai baht, Swiss francs, euros, Australian dollars, Singapore dollars and Canadian dollars. **Credit cards** are increasingly accepted, particularly Visa, MasterCard, Amex and JCB. Large hotels, expensive restaurants and medical centres invariably take them but beware a surcharge of between 2.5% and 4.5%. Most hotels will not add a surcharge onto your bill if paying by credit card. Prepaid currency cards allow you to preload money from your bank account, fixed at the day's exchange rate, and are accepted anywhere that you can use debit or credit cards. They are issued by specialist money changing companies, such as Travelex, Caxton FX and the post office. You can top up and check your balance by phone, online and sometimes by text.

Cost of travelling

On a budget expect to pay around US$6-15 per night for accommodation and about US$6-12 for food. A good mid-range hotel will cost US$15-35. There are comfort and cost levels anywhere from here up to more than US$200 per night. For travelling, many use the Open Tour Buses as they are inexpensive and, by Vietnamese standards, 'safe'. Slightly more expensive are trains followed by planes.

Opening hours

Banks Mon-Fri 0800-1600. Many close 1100-1300 or 1130-1330.
Offices Mon-Fri 0730-1130, 1330-1630.
Restaurants, **cafés**, **bars** Daily from 0700 or 0800 although some open earlier. Bars are generally closed by midnight, but some stay open much later, particularly in HCMC.
Shops Daily 0800-2000. Some stay open longer, especially in tourist centres.

Police and the law

If you are robbed in Vietnam, report the incident to the police (for your insurance claim). If you are arrested, ask for consular assistance and English-speaking staff.

Involvement in politics, possession of political material, business activities that have not been licensed by appropriate authorities, or non-sanctioned religious activities (including proselytizing) can result in detention. Sponsors of small, informal religious gatherings such as bible-study groups in hotel rooms, as well as distributors of religious materials, have been detained, fined and expelled (source: US State Department). The army are extremely sensitive about all their military buildings and become exceptionally irate if you take a photo. Indeed there are signs to this effect outside all military installations.

Safety

Travel advisories

The US State Department's travel advisory: **Travel Warnings & Consular**

Information Sheets, www.travel.state.gov, and the UK Foreign and Commonwealth Office's travel warning section, www.fco.gov.uk, are useful.

Do not take any valuables on to the streets of HCMC as bag and jewellery snatching is a problem. The situation in other cities is not so bad but take care as you would in any city. Always use major taxi firms and avoid those with blacked-out windows.

Lone women travellers generally have fewer problems than in many other Asian countries. The most common form of harassment usually consists of comic and harmless displays of macho behaviour.

In HCMC around Pham Ngu Lau Western men may be targeted by prostitutes on street corners, in tourist bars and those cruising on motorbikes.

Student travellers

Discount travel is provided to those under 22 and over 60. Anyone in full-time education is entitled to an International Student Identity Card (www.isic.org). These offer special rates on all forms of transport. They sometimes permit free or discounted admission to museums and sights.

Telephone

Vietnam's IDD is 0084; directory enquiries: 1080; operator-assisted domestic long-distance calls 103; international directory enquiries 143; yellow pages 1081.

To make a domestic call dial 0 + area code + phone number. Note that all numbers in this guide include the area code. All post offices provide international telephone services. Pay-as-you-go SIM cards are available from a number of operators including

Mobiphone and Vinaphone. These are cheap and so are calls and data.

Time

Vietnam is 7 hrs ahead of GMT.

Tipping

Vietnamese do not normally tip if eating in small restaurants but may tip in expensive bars. Big hotels and restaurants add 5-10% service charge and the government tax of 10% to the bill.

Tourist information

The national tourist office is Vietnam National Administration of Tourism (www.vietnamtourism.com), whose role is to promote Vietnam as a tourist destination rather than to provide tourist information. Visitors to its offices can get some information and maps but they are more likely to be offered tours. Good tourist information is available from tour operators in the main tourist centres.

Tour operators

For countrywide tour operators, see the What to do sections throughout the guide. For details of specialist tours and activities, see pages 154.

In the UK
Audley Travel, New Mill, New Mill Lane, Witney, Oxfordshire OX29 9SX, T01993-838000, www.audleytravel.com.
Buffalo Tours UK, The Old Church, 89B Quicks Rd, Wimbledon, London SW19 1EX, T020-8545 2830, www.buffalotours.com.
See Asia Differently, T020-8150 5150, SeeAsiaDifferently.com. A UK/Asian-based tour company

specializing in customized Southeast Asian tours.

In North America

Adventure Center, 1311 63rd St, Suite 200, Emeryville, CA, T+1-800 228 8747, www.adventurecenter.com.

Global Spectrum, 3907 Laro Court, Fairfax, VA 22031, T+1-800 419 4446, www.globalspectrumtravel.com.

Hidden Treasure Tours, 509 Lincoln Boulevard, Long Beach, NY 11561, T877-761 7276 (USA toll free), www.hiddentreasuretours.com.

Journeys, 107 April Drive, Suite 3, Ann Arbor, MI 48103-1903, T734-665 4407, www.journeys.travel/.

Myths & Mountains, 976 Tree Court, Incline Village, Nevada 89451, T+1-800 670-MYTH, www.mythsandmountains.com.

In Australia and New Zealand

Buffalo Tours, L9/69 Reservoir St, Surry Hills, Sydney, Australia 2010, T61-2-8218 2198, www.buffalotours.com.

Intrepid Travel, 360 Bourke St, Melbourne, Victoria 3000, T+61-03-8602 0500, www.intrepidtravel.com.au.

Travel Indochina, Level 10, HCF House, 403 George St, Sydney, NSW 2000, T1300-138755 (toll free), www.travelindochina.com.au.

In Vietnam

Asia Pacific Travel, 87 Hoang Quoc Viet St, Cau Giay District, Hanoi, T4-3756 8868/3836 4212, www.asiapacifictravel.vn. Arranges tours throughout Vietnam.

Buffalo Tours, 70 Ba Trieu, Hanoi, T+84 4 3828 0702. www.buffalotours.com.

David W. Lloyd
Photography
Tours & Workshops

Capture Vietnam with resident photographer, David W. Lloyd.

Lloyd's work is published in the New York Times, Travel + Leisure, Wanderlust and more. He is also author of the Footprint Vietnam guidebook.

Develop your skills in destinations such as Hanoi, Sapa, Ha Giang and Hoi An.

www.davidwlloydphotography.com
+ 0084 (0) 1228 403 308

Exotissimo, 80-82 Phan Xich Long St, Phu Nhuan District, Ho Chi Minh City, T+84 8-3995 9898, www.exotissimo.com.
Indochina Travelland, 10 Hang Mam, T+84 984 999 386, www.indochinatravelland.com.

Visas and immigration

UK visitors have 2 options for visas. The first is to apply for a visa in the UK from the Vietnam embassy. The price for this changes regularly so it is best to contact the embassy direct. You must send the application form, fee and photos together with your passport. The 2nd option avoids this hassle – instead apply for an invitation letter (for example from Indochina Travelland – see above) and then pay for your visa on arrival at the airport. Those travelling in the region can obtain visas at Vietnamese consulates.

Immigration offices

Ho Chi Minh City
Immigration office, 254 Nguyen Trai St, T08-3832 2300. Changes visa to specify overland exit via Moc Bai if travelling to Cambodia, or for overland travel to Laos or China. Also for visa extensions.

Index

A

accidents 156
accommodation 150
　price codes 150
air travel 147, 148
ambulance 156
architecture 137
Army of the Republic of
　Vietnam (ARVN) 114
art 137
avian flu 158

B

Bac Lieu 69
Bahnar 129
banks 160
beer 153
Ben Tre 52
Betel nut 37
bicycle hire 148
Binh Tay Market 25
birdwatching 154
Black Lady Mountain (Nui
　Ba Den) 31
boat travel 149
books 141
bus travel 148

C

Can Tho 64, **66**
Cao Dai Great Temple 30
Cao Lanh 62
Cao Mau 71
Car hire 148
Cham 135
Cham art 137
Champa 107
Cham villages 77

Chau Doc 73
Cholon (Chinatown) 23
Cochin China 108
Con Dao National Park 90
conical hat 139
consulates
　Vietnamese 156
cookery classes 154
crafts 139
Cu Chi Tunnels 28
cuisine 151
customs 156
cycling 154
cyclos 149

D

Democratic Republic of
　Vietnam (DRV) 109
dengue fever 158
de Rhodes, Father
　Alexandre 141
diarrhoea 158
Diem 115
Dien Bien Phu 112
disabled travellers 156
diving 154
dong 160
Dongson culture 137
Dragon Island 52
drama 140
drinking 151
drugs 156
duty free 156
dynasties
　Le 105
　Ly 103
　Nguyen 106
　Tran 104

E

ecotourism 155
Ede 130
electricity 156
embassies
　Vietnamese 156
emergency telephone
　numbers 156
Emperor Tu Duc 108
ethnic Chinese 136

F

festivals 156
First Indochina War
　(1945-1954) 109
food 151
Funan 106

G

Giac Lam Pagoda 26
Giac Vien Pagoda 26
Giarai 131
Golf 155
Gulf of Tonkin Incident
　115

H

hamleting 114
Ha Tien 80
health 157
Highland people 128
hill tribes 128
history 103
HIV 158
Hmong 131
Hoa 136
Ho Chi Minh 109, 110, 125

Ho Chi Minh City 9, **12**, **15**, **17**
  Archbishop's Palace 16
  Ben Thanh Market 20
  Botanical Gardens and Zoo 18
  Continental Hotel 11
  Fine Arts Museum 21
  General Post Office 13
  Ho Chi Minh City Museum 20
  Hotel Caravelle 11
  Independence Palace 14
  Lam Son Square 9
  Le Duan Street 18
  listings 32
  Mariamman Hindu Temple 20
  Museum of Vietnamese History 19
  Nguyen Hue Boulevard 11
  Notre Dame Cathedral 12
  Opera House 9
  Phung Son Tu Pagoda 22
  War Remnants Museum 16
  Xa Loi Pagoda 18
honda ôm 149
Hon Rom 96
hospitals 158
hostels 150
hotels 150
  price codes 150
Hre 135
Hué architecture 138

I

immigration 163
Indochina Communist Party (ICP) 108
Indochina Wars 109, 112
insurance 158
internet 158
Invasion of Cambodia 123

J

Japanese 'occupation' 109
Johnson, Lyndon 115

K

Kennedy, John F 114
Khe Sanh 118
Kinh 135
Kissinger, Henry 120
kitesurfing 155

L

lacquerware 139
language 140, 158
laundries 150
law 160
Le Dynasty 105
Le Loi 105
Le Thanh Ton 105
Le Van Duyet 28
literature 141
Ly Dynasty 103

M

malaria 157
Marco Polo 107
markets 152
medical services 158
Mekong Delta Hydrology 55
Ming Dynasty Assembly Hall 24

minibuses 148
Mnong 132
Money 160
Montagnards 128
motorbike hire 148
motorbike taxi 149
mountain biking 154
Mui Ca Mau National Park 71
Mui Ne 95
Muong 132
Museum of Vietnamese Traditional Medicine 28
My Tho 49, **50**

N

National Liberation Front of Vietnam 113
Nghia An Assembly Hall 23
Ngo Dinh Diem 112
Nguyen Dynasty 106
Nixon, President Richard 120
Non Lá 139
Nui Sam (Sam Mountain) 76
Nung 133

O

Oc-Eo 80, 106
opening hours 160
Open Tour Bus 148

P

Paracel Islands 126
Paris Agreement (1972) 120
People 128
People's Liberation Armed Forces (PLAF) 114
Pham Ngu Lao 22
Phan Thiet 95

pho 151
Phoenix Island 52
Phoenix Programme 119
Phung Son Pagoda 26
Phuoc Hai Tu (Emperor of Jade Pagoda) 27
Phu Quoc Island 83, **85**
police 156, 160
politics 125
price codes 150
public holidays 157

Q

Quan Am Pagoda 25
Quoc Dan Dang (VNQDD) 108

R

Rach Gia 78
rail travel
  getting around 149
religion 159
restaurants 151
  price codes 150
Rhodes, Father Alexandre 141
rice wine 153
river travel 149

S

Sa Dec 59
safety 160
SARS 158
Second Indochina War (1954-1975) 112
Sedang 135
snake wines 153
snorkelling 154
Socialist Republic of Vietnam (SRV) 122
sport 154
Spratly Islands 126
Stieng 135
strategic hamlets 114
student travellers 161

T

Tam Son Assembly Hall 23
taxi 149
Tay 133
Tay Son Rebellion 106
telephone 161
Tet Offensive 118
Thai 133
theatre 140
Thien Hau Temples 24
time 161
tipping 161
tourist information 161
tour operators 161
train travel 149
Tran Dynasty 104
Tran Hung Dao Temple 27
transport
  bicycle 148
  buses 148
  cyclo 149
  honda ôm 149
  motorbike 148
  motorcycle taxi 149
  river boat services 149
  taxis 149
  train 149
traveller's cheques 160
Tra Vinh 57
Treaty of Tientsin 108
Trung Nguyen 157
tuberculosis 158

U

U Minh Forest 71
Unicorn Island 52

V

VC, *see Viet Cong*
Viet Cong 114
Viet Kieu 136
Viet Minh, creation of 109
Vietnamese Communist Party (VCP) 125
Vietnam Wars 109
Vinh Long 53
Vinh Nghiem Pagoda 27
visas 163

W

water puppet theatre 140
weather 10
Westmoreland, General William 117, 119
windsurfing 155
wine 153

X

xe ôm 149
Xtieng 135

FOOTPRINT

Features

A gift for Phuc Khoat 75
Betel nut 37
Bird's nest soup 152
Buddhist martyrs: self-immolation as
    protest 21
History of the city 19
Ho Chi Minh: 'He who enlightens' 110
Hydrology of the Mekong Delta 55

Mekong homestays 54
Military might 81
Prisons to paradise 91
Rice research 68
The changing face 14
Visiting minorities: house rules 129
Vo Thi Sau 92

Acknowledgements

For help on the road my thanks go to: Ashley Carruthers, Allan Goodman, Ben Mitchell, Caroline Mills, Cyril Boucher, Deb and Howard Limbert, Etienne Bossot, Kon Sa Nay Luet, Khiem Vu, Linh Phan, Luke H Ford, Nguyen Tuan Dung, Nguyen Thanh Truc, Binh, Bamboo and all the other guides at Oxalis, Ryan Deboodt, Sophie Hughes, Soeren Pinstrup, Tran Nhat Quang and Van Phan Trang. I am also indebted to Claire Boobbyer, previous author of this book. Lastly, huge thanks to my wife and best friend, Beck.

Credits

Footprint credits

Editor: Stephanie Rebello
Production and layout: Emma Bryers
Maps: Kevin Feeney
Colour section: Angus Dawson

Publisher: Patrick Dawson
Managing Editor: Felicity Laughton
Administration: Elizabeth Taylor
Advertising sales and marketing:
John Sadler, Kirsty Holmes

Photography credits
Front cover: jethuynh/Shutterstock.com
Back cover: Tonkin image/Shutterstock.
com. Bottom: Tonkin image/
Shutterstock.com

Colour section
Inside front cover: David Lloyd: David
Lloyd; shutterstock: Duc Den Thui/
Shutterstock.com, Saigon Photography.
Page 1: shutterstock: jethuynh/
Shutterstock.com. **Page 2**: shutterstock:
antb. **Page 4**: shutterstock: LehaKoK,
ducvien/Shutterstock.com. **Page 5**:
shutterstock: Tonkin image, Quang Tran/
Shutterstock.com, Duy Do – VietNam
Images, ThangCao. **Page 6**: shutterstock:
Vietnam Art/Shutterstock.com. **Page 7**:
shutterstock: ThangCao, Tonkin
image, Patrik Dietrich/Shutterstock.
com. **Page 8**: shutterstock: jethuynh/
Shutterstock.com.

All rights reserved. No part of this
publication may be reproduced, stored
in a retrieval system, or transmitted, in
any form or by any means, electronic,
mechanical, photocopying, recording,
or otherwise without the prior
permission of Footprint Handbooks Ltd.

Publishing information
Footprint Ho Chi Minh City & South
Vietnam
2nd edition
© Footprint Handbooks Ltd
May 2015

ISBN: 978 1 910120 28 6
CIP DATA: A catalogue record for this
book is available from the British Library

® Footprint Handbooks and the
Footprint mark are a registered
trademark of Footprint Handbooks Ltd

Published by Footprint
6 Riverside Court
Lower Bristol Road
Bath BA2 3DZ, UK
T +44 (0)1225 469141
F +44 (0)1225 469461
footprinttravelguides.com

Distributed in the USA by
National Book Network, Inc.

Every effort has been made to ensure
that the facts in this guidebook are
accurate. However, travellers should still
obtain advice from consulates, airlines,
etc about travel and visa requirements
before travelling. The authors and
publishers cannot accept responsibility
for any loss, injury or inconvenience
however caused.

Printed in Spain by GraphyCems